DEVELOPING CHINESE FLUENCY
An Introductory Course

Nǐ   Wǒ   Tā

VOLUME 1

TRADITIONAL CHINESE EDITION

張霓 Phyllis Zhang

with *Learn About Culture* by
Li Wei and Robert Moore

CENGAGE
Learning

Australia • Brazil • Mexico • Singapore • United Kingdom • United States

**Ni Wo Ta / Developing Chinese Fluency:
An Introductory Course
Traditional Chinese, Volume 1**
Phyllis Zhang

Product Director:
Beth Kramer

Senior Product Managers:
Nicole Morinon, Martine Edwards

Managing Developer:
Katie Wade

Content Coordinator:
Gregory Madan

Product Assistant:
Kimberley Hunt

Associate Media Developer:
Patrick Brand

Executive Market Development Manager:
Ben Rivera

Senior Content Project Manager:
Aileen Mason

Manufacturing Planner:
Betsy Donaghey

Rights Acquisition Specialist:
Jessica Elias

Asia:

Publishing Director:
Roy Lee

Editorial Manager:
Lan Zhao

Associate Development Editor:
Titus Teo

Product Manager:
Mei-Yun Loh

Senior Product Manager:
Joyce Tan

Regional Manager, Production and Rights:
Pauline Lim

Senior Production Executive:
Cindy Chai

Creative Manager:
Melvin Chong

Designer:
Redbean De Pte Ltd

Compositor:
Puey Yan Goh

Illustrators:
Zheng Yan, Andrew Ng

Cover Images:
Cengage Learning

For product information and technology assistance, contact us at
Cengage Learning Customer & Sales Support, 1-800-354-9706

For permission to use material from this text or product,
submit all requests online at **www.cengage.com/permissions**.
Further permissions questions can be emailed to
permissionrequest@cengage.com.

Library of Congress Control Number: 2013951707

ISBN-13: 978-1-285-45680-5
ISBN-10: 1-285-45680-7

Cengage Learning
200 First Stamford Place, 4th Floor
Stamford, CT 06902
USA

Cengage Learning is a leading provider of customized learning solutions with office locations around the globe, including Singapore, the United Kingdom, Australia, Mexico, Brazil and Japan. Locate your local office at **international.cengage.com/region**.

Cengage Learning products are represented in Canada by Nelson Education, Ltd.

For your course and learning solutions, visit **www.cengage.com**.

Purchase any of our products at your local college store or at our preferred online store **www.cengagebrain.com**.

Instructors: Please visit **login.cengage.com** and log in to access instructor-specific resources.

Printed in the United States of America
1 2 3 4 5 6 7 17 16 15 14 13

To the Student

Welcome to Ni Wo Ta!

Ni Wo Ta is an innovative introductory program that uses a functional approach, an engaging video program, and robust multimedia integration to help you explore the richness of Chinese language and culture.

Filmed on location in Beijing, China, the video program features realistic conversations between native speakers using all the words and structures you will learn in the course, while immersing you in the cultural context and experiences of the everyday person. *Ni Wo Ta* will help you acquire a thorough grounding in vocabulary and grammar that as a beginning student you need in order to express yourself well at this level and to prepare you for the next level of Chinese learning. You will get plenty of practice in the skills of listening, speaking, reading, and writing. The activities have been carefully designed so that you first develop confidence with the new vocabulary and grammar before you are required to produce it. You will also have the opportunity to get to know your classmates and your instructor better while you engage in the language practice activities in every unit.

The *Ni Wo Ta* text is paired with iLrn™: Heinle Learning Center, an all-in-one online course management system that offers a dynamic audio- and video-enhanced language learning environment. With iLrn™, you will have access to an interactive online version of this textbook. All media, tutorials, and activities are embedded in the eBook at point of use. You will receive instant feedback when you complete an exercise and will have access to a wealth of data about your performance, allowing you to learn more effectively.

Ni Wo Ta: *The Video Program*

Set in Beijing, China, the video tells the story of a Chinese family, as their son, Xiaodong, begins his first year of college. Xiaodong and other characters in the video will show you how Chinese is used in real-life situations. You will see, hear, and practice interesting conversations.

Student Textbook

The Student Textbook contains the information and activities that you need for in-class use and self-study. The textbook contains four preliminary units, fourteen core units, and a concluding unit. The textbook, intended for a year-long course at the college level, is split into two volumes.

The preliminary units prepare you for the core units with an introduction to the Chinese language and an overview of the Chinese writing and phonetic systems. Each core unit contains two lessons – *Part A* and *Part B*. Each lesson has vocabulary and grammar sections with presentations and explanations, two pages related to the video story to help you understand and work with the video segment, and activities for grammar, listening, and speaking practice. Each core unit ends with a reading on Chinese culture and a Review and Integration section that summarizes key vocabulary and grammar points while further reinforcing your interpersonal, interpretive, and presentational skills.

At the end of the textbook, you will find a comprehensive reference section with Chinese-English and English-Chinese glossaries, a grammar quick study reference chart, and the complete transcript of the video program.

Literacy Workbook

The purpose of the Literacy Workbook is to give you a step-by-step guide to producing the Chinese script, both by hand and by using a computer keyboard. It also includes extra reading and writing practice to reinforce what has been learned in class.

Each lesson includes tracing exercises to help you produce core vocabulary words in the correct stroke order. Besides handwriting, the program also develops your keyboard skills, since the computer has become the main medium for written communication. The typing exercises will help you to type Chinese using the pinyin system.

A reading program, consisting of 10 episodes of a narrative story enhanced with exercises, is provided in Volume 2 for students to review and consolidate their vocabulary and grammar during their summer vacation. For advanced beginners, this narrative series can also serve as enrichment exercises during the semester for accelerated literacy development.

iLrn™

Everything you need to master the skills and concepts of the course is built into this online system, including an audio- and video-enhanced eBook, integrated textbook activities with immediate feedback, companion videos, voice-recorded activities, a VoiceBoard, *ShareIt!* to allow you to collaborate on documents, and a diagnostic study tool to help you prepare for exams.

Ni Wo Ta Chinese Character Trainer App

The *Ni Wo Ta* Chinese Character Trainer app is a wonderful study aid you can use to practice characters on the go! It includes all the key characters presented in the course. You can review word definitions, watch an animation of each character's stroke order, and trace or write characters using your finger. The app checks every stroke you draw, helping you recognize and correct mistakes as you go along.

Acknowledgements

Ni Wo Ta is the outcome of many years of research and piloting, and endless hours of writing, rewriting, and fine tuning. This project would not have seen the light of day if not for the dedicated efforts of many individuals, and I want to acknowledge and thank them properly.

For the past few years, I have had the greatest pleasure of working with and learning from many talented individuals who have inspired me enormously throughout the course of this project. I am deeply thankful to Jianhua Bai, Chuanren Ke, and Ted Tao-chung Yao, who provided valuable feedback and guidance on the initial design of this program. I benefited greatly from talks by Honggang Jin on task-based language instruction and research, and Tim Tianwei Xie and Debao Xu on virtual learning. I also want to give special thanks to the people who have expressed appreciation for my previous work, which gave me immense encouragement while working on this project, including George Chao, Jianfei Ma, Madeline Spring, Chengzhi Chu, and Zhengsheng Zhang, among others.

I also want to thank the executive team at Cengage Learning for believing in my vision and for supporting this project. In particular, I want to thank P.J. Boardman, Beth Kramer, Tat-Chu Tan, Seok-Hoon Lee, and Roy Lee for their sustained support in seeing this project through. Special thanks to senior product manager Martine Edwards and former acquisition editor Nicole Morinon for their guidance and direction, and product manager Mei-Yun Loh for bringing together the best people for this project. I am deeply indebted to the editorial manager, Lan Zhao, whom I worked with on a day-to-day basis for these past few years, for her confidence in and enthusiasm for this project, her insightful comments, her meticulous editing and her amazing attention to the smallest details in all stages of the development. Her outstanding work has made a significant difference to the final product.

I'd like to thank other members of the team, especially Titus Teo for his dedicated editorial work; designers Ruby Lim and Puey Yan Goh and illustrators Andrew Ng and Zheng Yan for making the pages look stunning; Aileen Mason, Lauren MacLachlan, and Betsy Donaghey for their production and manufacturing work; and Morgen Gallo, Patrick Brand, and Mei-Yun Loh for realizing the technological vision of this program.

I also want to thank Peter Schott for his guidance on the production of the video program, Yan Cui, the director and producer, for taking our story to another level, and co-producer Ge Bin for bringing together a beautiful cast who has made the characters in the story come to life.

Contributors and Reviewers

I'd like to express my deep appreciation to Li Wei and Robert Moore (Rollins College) for writing excellent notes for the culture sections, and Yong Ho (United Nations) for providing an overview of the Chinese language for this book. Their contributions have greatly enriched the contents of this book. I also want to thank my former colleague and friend Yuanyuan Meng (Columbia University) for contributing a series of reading stories and exercises to enhance the *Ni Wo Ta* Workbook (Volume II), in addition to her valuable suggestions for the improvement of the final version of the Textbook.

Special thanks also go to the following individuals for creating communicative tasks for the *Review and Integration* section of this program:

Jin Zhang (MIT) for activities in **6.19** (#2, 3, and 5), **8.19** (#4 and 5), and **9.19** (#3 and 4)
Nan Meng (Ph.D from Ohio State University) for activities in **2.19** (#1-4)
Qin Xu (Thomas Jefferson High School for Science and Technology) for activities in **7.19** (#4 and 5)

I'd like to thank Yajuan Liu (student at Nanjing University) and Ting Gong (student at George Washington University) for providing detailed information on Chinese college students in China and assisting in the language check of my scripts. I want to express my thanks to Xuefei Hao and Nan Meng (formerly Ph.D candidates at Ohio State University) for their detailed comments on my initial scripts. My thanks also go to my Chinese colleagues of George Washington University for providing resources or feedback whenever I sought their help.

During the development stages of this book, numerous Chinese language professors have served as reviewers and provided thoughtful commentary on the manuscript. Their effort and critiques have greatly contributed to the quality of this book. I'd like to thank them all:

Advisory Board Members

Haiyong Liu	Wayne State University, MI
Xianmin Liu	Vanderbilt University, TN
Weihsun Mao	Ohlone College, CA
Liuxi Meng	Kennesaw State University, GA
Lo Sun "Lotus" Perry	University of Puget Sound, WA
Jasmine Tang	State University of New York at Geneseo
Xiaojun Wang	Western Michigan University
Xiaohong Wen	University of Houston, TX

Reviewers

Mark Alves	Montgomery College at Rockville, MD
Alan Berkowitz	Swarthmore College, PA
Gloria Bien	Colgate University, NY
Wesley Borton	Elizabeth City State University, NC
Shelley Chan	Wittenberg University, OH
John Chang	University of Southern California, CA
Liana Chen	(formerly) Pennsylvania State University, PA
Shu-chen Chen	University of Virginia, VA
Sophia Chen	California Polytechnic State University, San Luis Obispo, CA
Xi Chen	George Mason University, VA
Chyi Chung	Northwestern University, IL
Ruby Costea	Montgomery College at Rockville, MD

Wen-Hua Du	Pennsylvania State University, PA
Hongchu Fu	Washington and Lee University, VA
Yan Gao	North Georgia College and State University, GA
Lin Gu	The University of Iowa Graduate College, IA
Li Han	Rhodes College, TN
Donghui He	Whitman College, WA
Tianshu He	Duke University, NC
Yong Ho	United Nations
Ching-hui Hsiao	Texas State University, TX
Guiling Hu	University of Maryland, College Park, MD
Hong Jiang	Northwestern University, IL
Rosalind Kan	University of Alaska Fairbanks, AK
David Keenan	University of California, Santa Cruz, CA
Julia Kessel	New Trier High School, IL
Wei Lai	Queensborough Community College, NY
Chang Soo Lee	New Mexico State University Carlsbad, NM
Jungjung Lee-Heitz	University of Maryland, College Park, MD
Jinhua Li	University of North Carolina at Asheville, NC
Tonglu Li	Iowa State University, IA
Wei Li	Lone Star College–North Harris, TX
Xue Guang Lian	City College of San Francisco, CA
Annie Liu	North Central College, IL
Haiyong Liu	Wayne State University, MI
Shijuan Liu	Indiana University of Pennsylvania, PA
Xianmin Liu	Vanderbilt University, TN
Yu Liu	Brigham Young University, UT
Chan Lu	Loyola Marymount University, CA
Jing Luo	Bloomsburg University of Pennsylvania, PA
Weihsun Mao	Ohlone College, CA
Miao Marone	Mercer University, GA
Duosi Meng	University of Illinois at Chicago, IL
Liuxi Meng	Kennesaw State University, GA
Yuanyuan Meng	Columbia University
Tao Ming	Concordia College, MN
Ling Mu	Yale University, CT
Lo Sun "Lotus" Perry	University of Puget Sound, WA
Yanrong Qi	University of Oklahoma, OK
Xizhen Qin	University of South Florida, FL
Cynthia Shen	University of Florida, FL
Curtis Smith	Grand Valley State University, MI
Madeline Spring	Arizona State University, AZ
Shuhui Su	Grove City College, PA

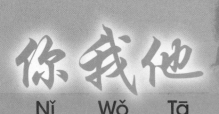

你我他
Nǐ Wǒ Tā

VOLUME 1

DEVELOPING CHINESE FLUENCY
An Introductory Course

Contents

你我他
Nǐ Wǒ Tā

VOLUME 2

DEVELOPING CHINESE FLUENCY
An Introductory Course

Contents

 Video

Scope & Sequence

Functions & Global Tasks	Core Vocabulary	Grammar	Culture
Unit 3 My Things 我的東西			
• Describing and commenting on things • Stating a change of situation	• School supplies: 筆，紙，書… • Clothing items: 衣服，褲子，運動服… • Measure words: 本，支，件，元，塊… • Adjectives to describe objects: 漂亮，老，貴…	• Subject + Adj phrases: 東西很多 • Particle 了 for changed status: 我高了 • Adjectives as modifiers: 新書，便宜的書包… • Adj-的 as noun phrases: 大的，新的… • 要 as auxiliary verb and verb	• Expenses in college
Unit 4 Money and Shopping 買東西			
• Making purchases • Expressing preferences • Negotiating prices	• Basic clothing items: 帽子，鞋子，毛衣… • Color words: 紅色，藍色，綠色… • Money measure units: 毛，角，分 • Shopping: 試，穿，講價，打折，付錢…	• Numerical expressions with 多: 三塊多，二十多塊… • Prepositions with action verbs: 跟室友説話 • 來/去 with action verb phrases: 去商店買東西 • Verb duplication: 看看 • The topic-comment structure	• The Chinese currency
Unit 5 Hobbies and Activities 我的愛好			
• Saying what you like to do • Describing how well someone does something • Making suggestions and requests • Telling about when and where an event is taking place	• Hobbies and pastimes: 運動，音樂，籃球，電影… • Adverbs of frequency: 經常，有時候，不常… • Action verbs: 看，聽，寫，唱…	• VO-phrases: 看書，打球，唱歌… • Prepositional phrases with 跟: 跟他一起學，跟他學… • V-得 phrases: 看得很多，唱得不好… • Progressive verb forms: 在看書，在打球… • 都/也-V phrases • Negative imperative: 別説話，別去那兒…	• Extracurricular activities
Unit 6 Time and Activity Schedule 時間和活動			
• Telling time • Describing a daily schedule • Talking about activities at school	• Time expressions: 今年，一月，星期二，小時，分鐘… • Daily routine: 起床，上課，吃飯，做作業… • School facilities: 教室，圖書館…	• Sequence of time: Year-month-day • Time-when phrases: 昨天，上個星期… • Time duration: 半個小時的考試 • Conjunctions 除了……還 and 除了……都 • Adverbs: 就，才	• School schedules
Unit 7 Making Travel Plans 旅行計劃			
• Talking about things to do • Making plans for a vacation • Discussing travel itineraries	• Means of transport: 汽車，公交車，火車，地鐵，飛機… • Vacations: 寒假，春假，暑假，新年… • Activities: 旅遊，過年，滑雪…	• Future activities • The 要 V 了 structure • Event sequence • Embedded questions	• New Year's Gala

Scope & Sequence

Functions & Global Tasks	Core Vocabulary	Grammar	Culture
Unit 8　About a Past Event 上個周末做什麼了?			
• Talking about recent activities • Recounting a past event • Describing a series of activities • Making a phone call	• Food: 中餐，西餐，麵包，牛奶… • Measure words: 場，家，頓，碗… • Phone-related phrases: 發短信，接電話，回電話…	• Sentence-final 了: 我去買東西了。 • Verb 了 + detail: 買了很多書… • The 是…V 的 construction • Past progressive: …的時候，我正在… • Paired conjunctions: 一邊…，一邊… • Reported speech: 她問曉雪去哪兒了。	• Campus activities
Unit 9　Background and Experiences 談談經歷			
• Asking for personal information • Giving background information • Setting up a meeting schedule	• School terms: 主修，輔修，數學，物理… • Contact information: 地址，電子信箱，號碼…	• Aspect marker 過 • Paired conjunctions 雖然……可是…… • [Time elapsed] + 沒 V 了: 一個月沒去了… • Order of elements in a postal address	• On- and off-campus jobs
Unit 10　Food and Dining 這家餐館比別家好			
• Making comparisons • Ordering food • Describing food • Talking about dining choices	• Eating and food: 中餐，菜，牛肉，海鮮，色拉… • Taste and flavor: 甜，鹹，酸，辣… • Popular dishes: 宮保雞丁，麻婆豆腐，酸菜魚…	• Comparatives: A 跟 B (不) 一樣 (好) A 比 B 好 A 沒有 B (那麼) 好 A 比 B 更好 A 和 B 有什麼不同 • Superlatives: 最好，最喜歡	• Chinese food and dining
Unit 11　Around the Neighborhood 談談社區			
• Identifying locations • Describing a neighborhood • Giving directions	• Places around town: 小區，公園，銀行，超市，購物中心… • Locative words and phrases: 附近，這邊，旁邊，左邊…	• Existential sentences: 那裡有一個… • Localizers: 旁邊，附近，前面… • Prepositional phrase + verb: 往前走，往右拐…	• Housing in China

Main Cast of Characters

 林小東 **LIN Xiaodong:** Raised in northeastern China, Xiaodong now lives in Beijing with his family. You'll learn more about him and his family in the beginning of the story.

 白曉雪 **BAI Xiaoxue:** A first-year student in the same school as LIU Ying. What is the name of the school they are attending? Can you guess which male character takes an interest in Xiaoxue?

 陳一龍 **CHEN Yilong:** Xiaodong's roommate and better known as "Ah Long"(阿龍). His father is a successful southern businessman and his mother is a native of Beijing. Find out what Ah Long loves to do most.

 劉英 **LIU Ying:** A college student who seems to have a busy schedule every day. What are her usual activities?

 林小南 **LIN Xiaonan:** Xiaodong's younger sister. Is she a high school or college student? What are her aspirations for her future? Why is her family allowed to have two children under China's one-child policy? You'll learn more about this in the section on Chinese culture.

 Katie: An American high school student who previously lived in China as a child and now revisits China as a participant of a Mandarin immersion program for one semester. She is living with the Lin family.

 Jack: An American college student who has come to China for the first time. What does he hope to accomplish on this trip?

 林子新 **LIN Zixin:** Xiaodong's father.

 于華 **YU Hua:** Xiaodong's mother, a returned overseas Chinese.

OVERVIEW:
THE CHINESE LANGUAGE

Of all the major ancient civilizations in the world, the Chinese civilization is the only one whose existence has never been interrupted. Many causative factors have been attributed to this continuity, but the unbroken use of a common language, particularly a learned written language, has generally been recognized as a major contributing factor to this enduring culture. With a little education, people in China today can read classical literature written 3,000 years ago, while few English speakers can read the works of Chaucer, written in the fourteenth century, much less Beowulf, written between the eighth and eleventh centuries.

Chinese is spoken by over one billion people in mainland China, a vast land of 3.7 million square miles. It is also spoken in Singapore and in Chinese overseas communities all over the world. Chinese ranks as the most spoken language on the planet. With the political and economic rise of China in the international arena, an increasing number of people are learning Chinese in various parts of the world. As of 2013, the total number of the students learning Chinese at the present time worldwide is estimated at 40 million. You are to be congratulated on your wise decision to learn Chinese and be one of these 40 million forward-thinking individuals. Knowledge of Chinese will stand you in good stead, as it will certainly open many doors for you in your career, your travels, and your understanding of the soul of a great civilization.

Mandarin Chinese

Chinese comprises a variety of dialects (regional languages) distributed over the whole of China. Dialects of Chinese can be so drastically different from each other that they are often not mutually intelligible. The most widely used form of Chinese is Mandarin, spoken by 900 million people, that is, three-quarters of the population. A large number of these Mandarin speakers live in northern China.

Standard Mandarin, called Guoyu (國語) or Putonghua (普通話), is based on, but not identical to, the Beijing dialect. The term Guoyu, which means "national language," is used in Taiwan, and in some overseas Chinese communities. The term Putonghua, which means "common speech," is used in mainland China. This standard form of Chinese has become the administrative and official medium of communication. It is used on television, in radio broadcasts, and in movies. More importantly, it has been made the language of instruction in primary and secondary schools. As such, Guoyu/Putonghua is the "prestige" form of speech that most people in China learn. With a multitude of mutually unintelligible dialects, a lingua franca that speakers of all languages and dialects can use to communicate is essential, and Mandarin has been the natural choice for the role. In addition to China, Mandarin is spoken by more than one million people in such Asian countries as Singapore, Malaysia, Indonesia, Brunei, Mongolia, Thailand, and the Philippines.

Hanyu, Zhongwen, and Huayu

Like the word "Mandarin," the term "Chinese" has two equivalents in the Chinese language. These two equivalents are Hanyu (漢語) and Zhongwen (中文). Unlike Putonghua and Guoyu, Hanyu and Zhongwen carry different connotations. The term Hanyu, which is widely used in China to refer to the Chinese language and is adopted as the title for most Chinese language

textbooks, literally means "the language of the Han." If you have some familiarity with Chinese history, you will know that Han was the second imperial dynasty of China (206 b.c.e.–220 c.e.). Due to its importance in history, the name Han came to be used to refer to the ethnic Chinese. It is not difficult to see that Hanyu is not a politically correct term to use, because Chinese is also spoken by most of the minority groups in China as the second language and by some of them as their first language. For this reason, Zhongwen is considered a better term. It simply means the language of the Chinese people. In Singapore and parts of the Southeast Asia, the term Huayu (華語) is sometimes used to refer to the Chinese language, as Hua is another word for China.

Chinese is a member of the Sino-Tibetan language family and as such differs markedly from the Indo-European languages in terms of its system of sounds, its grammar, and its writing system.

The Pinyin System

Chinese is not a phonetic language and its characters do not bear any resemblance to their actual pronunciation. A system of transcribing Chinese phonetically was thus needed to assist people in learning to read words in Chinese. The *pinyin* (which literally means "putting sounds together") system is the predominant phonetic system in mainland China. It was developed in 1958 using the Roman alphabet, and has been in use worldwide since the late 1970s.

The *pinyin* system is characterized by its syllabic structure. A syllable always consists of a final (F), or an initial + a final (IF), with the latter being the most common sound combination. There are 6 simple finals (vowels) and 21 initials in Mandarin Chinese. With F and IF as the predominant syllabic patterns, there is naturally a poverty of possible sound combinations in Chinese (only a few hundred). The result of this poverty is the proliferation of homophones: words that are pronounced the same but have different meanings. This is not convenient or effective for communication. To alleviate this problem, Chinese resorts to a variety of means, chief among them is the use of four tones. By introducing four tones in Mandarin, the total number of possible sound combinations is quickly boosted to around 1600. This is still not enough for effective communication, but it is a step in the right direction.

Although the severely restricted number of possible sound combinations poses a hindrance to effective communication, there is at least a bright side for students

Preface to the Orchid Pavillion Poems, by Wang Xizhi (303-361), Jin Dynasty

of Chinese in that they are not obliged to learn too many sound combinations, and they know from the outset of their studies exactly how many sound combinations they will have to learn. When they have learned all the possible sound combinations together with the four tones, there is not a single additional sound combination that they will ever need to learn.

Chinese Grammar

Chinese grammar is actually very simple. Words are invariable; they do not change no matter how they are used. In Chinese, the equivalent of "I" does not become "me," "is" does not become "was," and "ox" does not become "oxen." In English, distinctions such as person (I, you, we, they), number (man, men), tense (they go, they went), etc., are all very important. In Chinese, none of these distinctions are made. Syntactic and lexical meanings are not indicated through the manipulation of word forms, but through word order, specific particles, and vocabulary items. This lack of inflectional changes is a boon for students of Chinese, as they do not have to memorize a myriad of conjugational forms.

Writing in Chinese

Of all the major writing systems in the world, Chinese is the only one that has no phonetic alphabet. Its writing

system is neither alphabetic nor phonetic, because its characters do not indicate the sound of the word. The Chinese writing system uses a logographic script in the form of characters (visual symbols representing words). It was mentioned earlier that many of the dialects in China are not mutually intelligible, but all dialects use the same written form. People in China who cannot communicate through speech can communicate through the written language. This linkage can even facilitate to some extent communication between people in China and the Japanese, and Korean people, as they all use Chinese characters. This unified writing system has helped keep China from disintegration during the last two millennia. The writing system has definitely been a link for the Chinese to connect to their literary tradition and cultural past. The characters serve another important function. Mention was made earlier to the limited number of possible sound combinations and the abundance of homophones in Chinese. Although the use of tones can help alleviate this problem to some degree, characters are the ultimate solution and the only way to distinguish words. Ten words may be pronounced exactly the same, but they are all written differently.

Chinese Characters

Chinese characters are often thought of as pictures representing objects and concepts. This may be true of the earliest Chinese writing traceable to the fourteenth century b.c.e., when it was largely pictographic in nature (using line drawings to represent concrete and familiar objects). But almost from the very beginning, pictograms were found inadequate to represent everything, especially abstract ideas. This is when ideograms came in. Ideograms are graphic representations of abstract and symbolic ideas. For those pictographic characters, centuries of refining and stylizing resulted in the almost total loss of images and graphic quality.

Students of Chinese often wonder how many characters they need to learn in order to have a reading knowledge of Chinese materials other than classical literature. Various estimates have been given, ranging from 3,000 to 5,000. Statistics show that the average high school graduate

© Chinajiuyutang

in China knows between 3,500 and 4,500 characters. Knowledge of 2,000 to 2,500 characters is probably adequate to read non-academic and non-technical material. This would probably be equivalent to the vocabulary of the average student beginning middle school in China. Note that the majority of words used in contemporary Chinese are disyllabic or polysyllabic, consisting of two or more syllables or characters. The actual words you learn from these 2,000 to 2,500 characters are enormous, because juxtaposing two or more characters results in new words with different meanings.

A cursory look at any older Chinese dictionary will reveal that many of the characters are very complex in structure, consisting of up to 20 or more strokes. They are complicated to write and difficult to remember. This also explains why illiteracy had been widespread in China up to the mid-twentieth century. In response to the pressing need to simplify the writing system, the Chinese government has introduced a total of 2,515 simplified characters since 1956. The most common forms of simplification are the reduction of strokes in certain characters and assignment of a component to stand for the whole. As for what form to learn, make your decision based on your purpose. Study simplified characters if you need to read literature from mainland China, traditional characters if you plan to read materials from Taiwan. There are teachers of Chinese who suggest that students should learn to read both forms, but write in the simplified form only. Many software programs and all Chinese word processing programs can be great aids in moving between traditional and simplified characters. With a click of a button, most of these programs will convert all the simplified characters that you input into traditional characters or the other way round.

Tips for Learning Chinese

Due to its drastic differences from English in pronunciation, grammar, and writing, Chinese is not an easy language for Americans to learn. In fact, it is considered to be a Category IV language by the United States Foreign Service Institute (FSI). Languages in this group are deemed by the FSI as the most difficult languages for English speakers to master. The implication for you is that you need to be prepared for a long haul in order to reach proficiency in Chinese. There are no shortcuts or magic wands you can use to achieve quick results, but the following tips have proven useful and effective, particularly for beginning students of Chinese:

- Avail yourself of mobile technology and download popular apps onto your smart phone (if you have one) to practice pronunciation, vocabulary, and character writing. Many English-Chinese and Chinese-English online dictionaries are also useful.

- Watch Chinese soap operas, particularly those that are set in contemporary Chinese scenes. They can greatly enhance your listening comprehension. Although you may find it difficult to understand them at the beginning, the story and subtitles are useful aids.

- Try to read to a native speaker as often as you can to make your pronunciation accurate.

- Subscribe to a Chinese podcast to receive daily or regular delivery of short audio lessons.

- Ultimately, there is no better way to learn Chinese than spending a year or a semester studying in China. The constant exposure, the total immersion, and the close proximity to speakers of the language will make it very difficult for you not to pick up the language in a relative short period of time with relative ease and lots of confidence and fun. So, if your school has a study abroad program or exchange program with China, take advantage of it!

(By Yong Ho)

A PRONUNCIATION AND THE PHONETIC SYSTEM:
Basic Concepts

PRONUNCIATION BASICS

Experience the Sound

Word groups:	Personal pronouns, family members, relationships
Monosyllabic words:	你(nǐ), 我(wǒ), 他(tā)
Disyllabic words with the neutral tone:	你們(nǐmen), 爸爸(bàba), 我的(wǒ de), 你們的(nǐmen de)
Change of tones:	我爸爸(wǒ bàba), 你姐姐(nǐ jiějie)

Learn About the Phonetic System

Initials, finals, and tones
The four tones, the neutral tone, and tone marks
Change of tone (tone sandhi):

Focus on Fluency and Accuracy

Exercises on pronunciation, listening, and *pinyin*

Initials: **b, p, m, f, w, d, t, n, l, g, k, h**
Finals: **a, o, e, i, u, ai, ei, ao, ou, uo, an, en, ang, eng, ong**

Feel the Speech: Flow of Tones and Syllables

Family and relationships

OBJECTIVES

Pronunciation:	• Understanding the basic concepts of Mandarin sounds and tones;
	• Pronouncing the words taught in this lesson using appropriate tones;
	• Pronouncing short phrases with the third tones adjusted.
Pinyin:	• Identifying initials and finals in the words covered in this lesson;
	• Pronouncing 12 initials and 15 finals.

PRONUNCIATION BASICS

 The following activities are enhanced by an online multimedia program.

Main Features: In this lesson, we will focus on groups of words and phrases that include <u>personal pronouns</u> and <u>words for family members</u> occurring as single syllables or short phrases. While learning basic words, you'll experience simple forms of Chinese sounds, particularly in the form of <u>reduplicated syllables</u>. In addition, you'll be exposed to <u>all the tones in Chinese</u> and see how the neutral tone and the third tone work. Keep in mind, the main goal of these exercises is for you to gain some initial experience and to master basic concepts rather than to memorize words. To achieve optimal results, it is important that the instructions and each step in the exercises are followed closely.

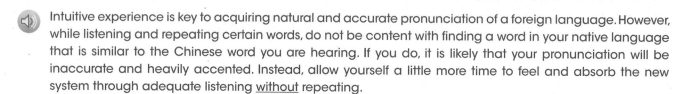

A | 1.1) EXPERIENCE THE SOUND

Intuitive experience is key to acquiring natural and accurate pronunciation of a foreign language. However, while listening and repeating certain words, do not be content with finding a word in your native language that is similar to the Chinese word you are hearing. If you do, it is likely that your pronunciation will be inaccurate and heavily accented. Instead, allow yourself a little more time to feel and absorb the new system through adequate listening <u>without</u> repeating.

Step 1 *View and Listen*	While looking at the pictures or videos, listen to the sounds and words in each group you hear and concentrate on comprehension. Do not repeat yet!
Step 2 *Listen <u>and</u> Listen*	Close your eyes and "feel" the sounds and tones. Try to hear the *differences* as well as the similarities between Chinese and your native language. Just listen!
Step 3 *Listen and Repeat*	With your eyes still closed and your mind relaxed, listen to each sound three times, and then imitate it 2–3 times.
Step 4 *Repeat and Write*	After repeating the sound, look at the screen to see the pinyin spelling of the sound or word, then write it down in the blank space under each word or on a piece of paper as you say the word 2–3 times.

1) Group 1a: Personal Pronouns — Singular　　　The lowest and the highest tones　　(Steps 1-4)

Experience the different tones used with these pronouns. You may want to regard them as level, rising, or falling. Where is each word pitched, low or high? How low or high? Which is level (stays at one point)?

你	我	他	她	The highest one is called the 1st tone (T1).
____	____	____	____	The lowest one is called the 3rd tone (T3).
you	I, me	he, him	she, her	

2) Group 1b: Personal Pronouns — Plural　　　The neutral tone　　(Steps 1-4)

The plural form of the personal pronouns has a suffix (-men) attached to the singular form, which is pronounced with the neutral tone (e). Try to decide how the neutral tone works; is it said at a fixed pitch point or is it adjustable? Also, is T3 in a disyllabic word (nimen, women) the same in tone and length as T3 in a monosyllable (ni, wo)?

你們	我們	他們	她們	
_____	_____	_____	_____	The neutral tone may swing up and down.
you	we, us	they, them	they, them	

3) Group 1c: Personal Pronouns — Possessive　　　Neutral tone: single and double　　(Steps 2-4)

The personal pronouns can be changed into the possessive case by attaching *de*, a particle with a neutral tone. Note the plural form of a possessive pronoun has two neutral tones.

你的	我的	他的	她的	你們的	我們的	他們的
_____	_____	_____	_____	_____	_____	_____
your, yours	my, mine	his	her, hers	your, yours	our, ours	their, theirs

4) Group 2a: Family Members　　　The reduplicated form; the fourth tone　　(Steps 1-4)

Most titles of family members are in the reduplicated form (i.e., AA, BB) with the second syllabus carrying a neutral tone. Note how the neutral tone is adjusted according to the tone before it. Also note a new tone in this group (the first and the last two items), which is called the fourth tone. Is it high, low, or midpoint? Is it level, rising, or falling?

爸爸	媽媽	哥哥	姐姐	弟弟	妹妹
_____	_____	_____	_____	_____	_____
dad	mom	big brother	big sister	little brother	little sister

5) Group 2b: The extended Family The second tone (Steps 1-4)

This group allows you to practice the second tone (items 1, 3, 4, and 7) in addition to all the other tones. To get the feel for the second tone, you need to give yourself a little more time to experience the swings and the ups and downs of all tones.

爺爺	奶奶	婆婆	伯伯	叔叔	姑姑	姨姨
grandpa	grandma	grandma	uncle	uncle	aunt	aunt

6) Group 3:   Relationships Changes of the third tone (tone sandhi) (Steps 1-4)

Unlike other major tones, the third tone changes its length and pitch point if it is followed by another syllable. In this exercise a pronoun (wǒ) is in front of a title. How is the third tone affected by the tone following it? That is, does it become shorter in length, and also higher or lower in pitch?

我媽媽	我爺爺	我姐姐	我弟弟
my mom	my grandpa	my older sister	my younger brother
3 - **1** - 0	3 - **2** - 0	3 - **3** - 0	3 - **4** - 0

A | 1.2) LEARN ABOUT THE PHONETIC SYSTEM

Initials, finals, and tones

See Appendix 1 for the complete chart of *pinyin* initials and finals.

1. A Chinese sound normally consists of an initial, a final, and a tone. Some sounds may have no initial or have a neutral tone.

2. An initial is usually a consonant: m, n, t. For example, in nǐ and tā, n and t are initials. There are 23 initials (including w and y) in *pinyin*.

3. Initials can be unaspirated, i.e., pronounced without a burst of air, such as b, d, g, or aspirated, such as p, t, k.

4. A final can be a simple final, a compound final, or a final with a nasal ending. A simple final contains a single vowel (a, i, o), a compound final contains two or three vowels (ai, ei, ou), and a final with a nasal ending contains one or two vowels with -n or -ng (an, ang, ong, iong). There are 37 finals in *pinyin* (including er and ê).

The four tones, the neutral tone, and tone marks

1. There are four regular tones (1, 2, 3, 4), and a neutral tone (0).
2. The tone mark is placed above the vowel: a, o, e, i, u, ü

The first tone:	High flat ("ceiling")	tā, māma, gēge, shūshu
The second tone:	Rising	yéye, bóbo, yíyi
The third tone:	Low ("floor") or low rising	wǒ, nǐ, jiějie, nǎinai
The fourth tone:	Falling	bàba, dìdi, mèimei
The neutral tone:	Tone sandhi	nǐmen, māma

Change of tone (tone sandhi)

The neutral tone (Tone 0) is normally light and unaccented. However, its pitch varies according to the tone immediately before it. Basically, it takes a lower pitch point when it follows a high-point tone (Tones 1, 2, and 4), and a higher point when it follows a low-point tone (Tone 3).

Tones 1/2/4 + Tone 0	→	Tone 0 drops low	māma, yéye, bàba
Tone 3 (low) + Tone 0	→	Tone 0 slightly rises	jiějie, nǐ de

The third tone sandhi

Tone 3 has three forms: full, half, and tone sandhi. The half third tone is the most common.

When	Form used	Example
Stressed final syllable	full third tone w/rising	hǎo, nǐ
Tone 3 + any other tone	half third tone w/o rising	wǒ māma, nǐ bàba, nǐmen
Tone 3 + Tone 3	Tone 2 + Tone 3	wó jiějie, ní nǎinai

1) Review the sounds and words in this lesson.

Listen to each group of words and write them down in pinyin, then check your answers.

1) (Pronouns) _____ 他，我，你，我們，
你們，他們

2) (Possessive pronouns) _____ 你的，我們的

3) (Family) _____ 哥哥，爸爸，弟弟，
媽媽，姐姐，妹妹

4) (Extended family) _____ 爺爺，姨姨，奶奶，
姑姑，叔叔，伯伯

2) Practice: More initials   b p m f w;   d t n l;   g k h

Here are more initials to practice.

Listen to each group, focusing on the initials. In the second round, repeat after each word.

1) 爸 bà   怕 pà   法 fǎ   馬 mǎ   搭 dā   他 tā

2) 姑 gū   哭 kū   怒 nù   路 lù   讀 dú   圖 tú

3) 哥 gē   科 kē   喝 hē   樂 lè   德 dé   特 tè

4) 弟 dì   替 tì   你 nǐ   裡 lǐ   筆 bǐ   米 mǐ

3) Identify initials   b p m f w;   d t n l;   g k h

Listen to each group of sounds and write down the appropriate initials. The first group is done for you.

1) 窩 w   摸 m   鍋 g

2) 把 ___   爬 ___   大 ___

3) 發 ___   提 ___   卡 ___

4) 隔 ___   可 ___   河 ___

5) 錄 ___   努 ___   度 ___

4) Practice: Compound finals   ai ei ao ou uo/o

Here are more finals to practice. Listen to each group focusing on the finals. In the second round, repeat after each word.

"ou" is pronounced like "o" in English.
"uo" is written as "o" for this group: b, p, m, f, w (i.e., bo instead of buo ...)

1) 來 lái   雷 léi   勞 láo

2) 買 mǎi   美 měi   卯 mǎo

3) 號 hào   後 hòu   或 huò

4) 刀 dāo   都 dōu   多 duō   do   ✗

5) 波 bō   坡 pō   摸 mō   buo, puo, muo   ✗

5) Practice with nasal finals: an en ang eng ong

甘 gān   跟 gēn   剛 gāng   耕 gēng   工 gōng

函 hán   痕 hén   行 háng   恆 héng   紅 hóng

6) Identify finals   ai ei ao ou uo/o an en ang eng ong

Choose the sound you hear.

1)   a. wuo   b. wo   c. wa
2)   a. guo   b. gou   c. gu
3)   a. ke   b. ken   c. ko
4)   a. bo   b. ba   c. bao
5)   a. po   b. pa   c. pu
6)   a. dou   b. duo   c. du
7)   a. mai   b. mei   c. man
8)   a. mou   b. mo   c. muo
9)   a. man   b. mai   c. mi
10) a. gen   b. geng   c. gan
11) a. gen   b. gan   c. gang
12) a. nen   b. nan   c. neng
13) a. fen   b. fan   c. fang
14) a. fen   b. fan   c. fang
15) a. lan   b. leng   c. long
16) a. pen   b. peng   c. pang

Family and relationships

With your eyes closed and your mind relaxed, listen to the phrases without repeating them. Try to enjoy the sounds as music without thinking of the tone marks! In the second round, you may "sing along."

1) Family and relatives

Note when indicating family relationships, possessive adjectives (**wǒ de, nǐ de, tā de**) can be shortened to **wǒ, nǐ, tā,** followed by the title of a relative. This rule, however, does not apply to other nouns (e.g., my dog, his book).

a)
我媽媽	你爸爸	你哥哥	我姐姐	他妹妹	你弟弟
wǒ māma	nǐ bàba	nǐ gēge	wǒ jiějie	tā mèimei	ní dìdi
my mom	your dad	your big brother	my big sister	his little sister	your little brother

b)
媽媽的媽媽	爸爸的爸爸	媽媽的爸爸	爸爸的媽媽
māma de māma	bàba de bàba	māma de bàba	bàba de māma
mom's mom	dad's dad	mom's dad	dad's mom

c)
媽媽的哥哥	媽媽的弟弟	爸爸的姐姐	爸爸的妹妹
māma de gēge	māma de dìdi	bàba de jiějie	bàba de mèimei
mom's older brother	mom's younger brother	dad's older sister	dad's younger sister

2) Tongue twister: Phoenixes   an en eng ong ua uang

Listen to this tongue twister multiple times before trying it yourself. (**ua** and **uang** are finals that will be covered later.)

紅鳳凰	黃鳳凰	粉紅鳳凰花鳳凰
hóng fènghuáng	huáng fènghuáng	fěnhóng fènghuáng huā fènghuáng
red phoenix	yellow phoenix	pink phoenix (and) multicolored phoenix

INTRODUCTION

Getting started with writing Chinese (I): Understanding the strokes

CHINESE WRITING BASICS

Experience the Writing

Basic strokes and simple characters 一 丨 亅 丿 丶 丶 ﹀ ノ 乛 𠃌 乚 𠃌

Practice steps

Focus on Fluency and Accuracy

Exercises on the basic strokes and simple characters

OBJECTIVES
- Understanding the concept of strokes in the Chinese writing system;
- Knowing the names of most common strokes;
- Writing the basic strokes with accuracy;
- Distinguishing similar strokes;
- Writing numbers with Chinese characters.

INTRODUCTION
Getting Started with Writing Chinese (I): Understanding the Strokes

Basic strokes: The basic building blocks of Chinese characters are strokes, which function pretty much like letters in the English alphabet except that there is no predictable regularity with the way they are combined to form a character. There are 8 basic strokes in Chinese, which are illustrated below:

	Name in English	Name in Pinyin	Examples
、	Dot	diǎn	主
一	Horizontal stroke	héng	大
丨	Vertical stroke	shù	十
丿	Left-falling stroke	piě	八
乀	Right-falling stroke	nà	人
乛	Turning or cornering stroke	héng zhé	口
㇀	Tick	tí	地
乛亅乚乁乙	Hook	gōu	你小良我凰

Stroke count: Certain strokes can be combined to form variations. As long as they are written continuously with the tip of the pen staying on the paper, they are considered as one stroke. The count of the strokes in a character is very important, as characters are indexed in a Chinese dictionary according to the number of their strokes.

Stroke order: In writing a character, it is not only important to get the end product right, but also important to follow the proper stroke order. The general rules are as follows:

Top first, then bottom	三，工，土
Left first, then right	川，仁，林
Horizontal first, then vertical	十，干，井
Left-falling first, then right-falling	文，人，八
Outside first, then inside	月，用，同
Center vertical first, then sides	小，水，永
Bottom stroke last	王，里，玉
Frame closed with last stroke	回，四，日

(Introduction by Yong Ho)

CHINESE WRITING BASICS

The following exercises are provided in full in the Workbook: Literacy Development.

B 1.1) EXPERIENCE THE WRITING

Before starting the following hands-on exercises, make sure you understand the basic concepts of **strokes, stroke count, stroke orientation, and stroke order** introduced in the previous section. In this part of the lesson we'll practice common strokes. Follow the steps closely.

1 **Know the stroke**   Take a good look at the stroke and learn the stroke name.
2 **View the animation**   Watch where the pen/brush starts and moves and in what direction.
3 **Finger writing**   Write in the air with your finger, following the animation.
4 **Trace on paper**   Reflect on the writing guide <u>and then</u> trace the stroke/character on paper.

> Note: For each stroke, finish it with <u>one</u> stroke without breaking it down to pieces. <u>Never</u> repair a stroke by patching it up or fixing an imperfect shape. Rewrite it!

Trace and write: 一 丨 亅 丿 乀 丶 ⸯⸯ ⼃ 乛 乛 乚 乛

B 1.2) FOCUS ON FLUENCY AND ACCURACY

1) What strokes do you recognize in these items? What are their names in Chinese?

   a. 八   b. 宀   c. 十   d. 儿

   e. 扌   f. 小   g. 口   h. 又

2) Trace and write:

一 二 三 四 五 六 七 八 九

十 冫 宀 冂 凵 匚 勹 匕 儿

PRE-UNIT

2 基礎訓練

A PRONUNCIATION:
Unique Sounds and Their *Pinyin* Rules

PRONUNCIATION BASICS

Experience the Sound

Word groups: Numbers, measure words, nouns, specifiers

Monosyllabic words: 一(yī), 個(gè), 張(zhāng), 新(xīn)

Disyllabic words with
the neutral tone: 孩子(háizi), 兒子(érzi), 桌子(zhuōzi)

Phrases: 一個孩子(yí gè háizi), 幾張桌子(jǐ zhāng zhuōzi)

Learn About the Phonetic System

Pinyin: The dummy final "i" with zh, ch, sh, z, c, s, r

Pinyin spelling rules: The dummy "y" for the i-group sounds

Focus on Fluency and Accuracy

Exercises on pronunciation, listening, and *pinyin*
Initials: **j, q, x, y, zh, ch, sh, z, c, s**
Finals: **The i-group**

Feel the Speech: Flow of Tones and Syllables

The Number-Measure-Noun form with sample phrases

OBJECTIVES

Pronunciation: • Understanding the basic concept of connecting tones and syllables
(the Nu-M-N form);
• Pronouncing the unique initial sounds containing such initials as
j, q, x, zh, ch, sh, z, c;
• Distinguishing aspirated and unaspirated sounds: g/k, j/q, zh/ch, z/c;
• Saying short phrases with appropriate sounds and tones.

Pinyin: • Identifying initials and finals in the sounds taught in this lesson;
• Knowing the *pinyin* rules for writing "i" and "y."

PRONUNCIATION BASICS

 The following activities are enhanced by an online multimedia program.

Main Features: In this lesson, we introduce numbers 1–10, basic nouns for people and things, and measure words that go between a number and a noun. We will also teach a couple of adjectives. While learning these words, we'll be looking as well at more initials and finals, including dummy finals. Some initials (e.g., z/c, zh/ch, s/x, sh/x) can be confusing for beginners and usually require more effort to learn. To learn these sounds correctly, allow yourself a little time for listening immersion; first feel these sounds, rather than hurry to repeat them multiple times. Keep in mind, the main focus of these activities is pronunciation and *pinyin* rather than memorization of words.

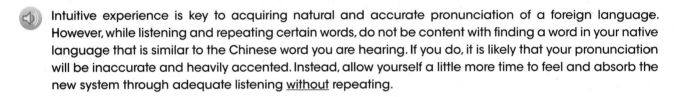

A | 2.1) EXPERIENCE THE SOUND

Intuitive experience is key to acquiring natural and accurate pronunciation of a foreign language. However, while listening and repeating certain words, do not be content with finding a word in your native language that is similar to the Chinese word you are hearing. If you do, it is likely that your pronunciation will be inaccurate and heavily accented. Instead, allow yourself a little more time to feel and absorb the new system through adequate listening <u>without</u> repeating.

Step 1   *View and Listen*   While looking at the pictures or videos, listen to the sounds and words in each group you hear and concentrate on comprehension. Do not repeat yet!

Step 2   *Listen <u>and</u> Listen*   Close your eyes and "feel" the sounds and tones. Try to hear the *differences* as well as the similarities between Chinese and your native language. Just listen!

Step 3   *Listen and Repeat*   With your eyes still closed and your mind relaxed, listen to each sound three times, and then imitate it 2–3 times.

Step 4   *Repeat and Write*   After repeating the sound, look at the screen to see the pinyin spelling of the sound or word, then write it down in the blank space under each word or on a piece of paper as you say the word 2–3 times.

1) Group 1: Numbers — 1–10 Monosyllabic sounds; The four tones (Steps 2-4)

This exercise practices single syllables and tones. The numbers are grouped so that it is easy to "feel" the tones.

1	2	3	4	5
___	___	___	___	___
one	two	three	four	five

6	7	8	9	10
___	___	___	___	___
six	seven	eight	nine	ten

2) Group 2a: Nouns — People Disyllabic sounds; Noun suffix zi (Steps 1-4)

In this group you will hear the most common noun suffix (子 zi) in three of the items. It has a neutral tone.

孩子	兒子	女兒	孫子	孫女
___	___	___	___	___
child	son	daughter	grandson	granddaughter

3) Group 2b: Nouns — Things More initials and finals (Steps 1-4)

More initials and finals are included in this group. Which words sound different to you? If you think certain sounds are similar to sounds in English, try to detect how they are different as well.

車	錢	紙	筆	桌子	椅子	鞋子	帽子
___	___	___	___	___	___	___	___
vehicle	money	paper	pen, pencil	table	chair	shoes	hat

4) Group 3: Adjectives Short phrases; Tones (Steps 1-4)

You are going to hear a few monosyllabic adjectives. They will then be combined with nouns you have just practiced so that you'll see how they sound together.

大	小	新	舊	大桌子	小椅子	新鞋子	舊車
___	___	___	___	___	___	___	___
big	small	new	old	big table	small chair	new shoes	old car

5) Group 4: Measure words — The Number-Measure-Noun (Nu-M-N) form; Tones (Steps 1-4)

When a noun is modified by a number (one child, three tables), a measure word is inserted between the number and the noun. You'll first hear a few measure words and then learn when each one is used.

個	張	輛	枝	塊
_____	_____	_____	_____	_____
一個孩子	幾張紙	一輛車	三枝筆	十塊錢
_____	_____	_____	_____	_____
one child	a few sheets	one car	three pens	ten dollars

A | 2.2) LEARN ABOUT THE PHONETIC SYSTEM

More initials

The tongue position (front, central, back) and movement (touching the back of the upper or lower teeth, curling, etc.) affect the sound utterance. In the previous lesson, we learned some front initials (b, p, m, f; d, t, n, l) and some back ones (g, k, h). Below are more initial groups, each representing a different tongue position.

1. Front: j, q, x, y
   The tongue touches the lower teeth.

   jiǔ (nine)   qī (seven)   xīn (new)   yī (one)

2. Front: z, c, s
   Approximations can be drawn from these English sounds:
   z is close to *ds* as in *clouds*, c is like *ts* in *hats*, s is like *s* in *sand*.

   zi (suffix)   cí (chinaware)   sì (four)

3. Central: zh, ch, sh
   These initials do not have exact counterparts in English, but approximations can be drawn from these English sounds, although the tongue needs to curl upward a little more:

   zh → dr in <u>dr</u>aw, ch → ch in tea<u>ch</u>, and sh → sh in <u>sh</u>awn
   zhuō (table)   chē (car)   shí (ten)

Front and Back finals   i and i-group

i (pronounced like English "ee" in flee) is a front vowel, with lips spread. a is towards the back with the mouth opening up. The sound an is a front nasal, whereas ang is a back nasal. The front i can connect an initial to a back final, as shown in the i-group compounds.

   ia   ie   iao   iu   ian   in   iang   ing   iong
              (iu=iou)   (in=ien)
      jiě (sister)   jiù (old)   qián (money)   xīn (new)

Special Spelling Rules

1. **uo** and **o**
   The compound final uo is spelled as o with the b p m f w group:

   Regular: zhuo, cuo, luo, guo

   with b p m f w: wo, bo, po

2. **y** standing for **i**
   a, o, e, and their compounds (ai, ou, ei, etc.) can stand alone without an initial, whereas the front vowels i, u, ü and their compounds (ia, ui, üe, etc.) must have an initial. Y is used as a dummy initial for the i-group, as shown below.

   The i-group includes: i, ia, ie, iao, iu, ian, in, iang, ing, iong.

   When there is no initial y, replaces i in the original form, but i stays if it is the only vowel in the final.

   i → yi   ian → yan   ie → ye   iu(iou) → you   in → yin

   When preceded by other initials, i or an i-compound remains unchanged:

   j+ia → jia   j+ie → jie   q+ian → qian   x+in → xin

3. Dummy **i** after **zh ch sh r z c s**
   i after these initials serves only as a placeholder; it is not pronounced -*ee* as it is after other initials (ni, bi, di). That means that zhi is still pronounced zh, and si, s. However, the dummy i is still important here as it receives the tone mark for the syllable.

A | 2.3) FOCUS ON FLUENCY AND ACCURACY

1) **Review the sounds and words in this lesson.**

   Listen to the sounds and write them down in pinyin without tones. Then check your answers.

   1) (Numbers)   _____   四，一，七，十，九，六

   2) (People)   _____   孩子，孫女

   3) (Things)   _____   椅子，桌子，錢，車

   4) (Adjectives) _____   小，新，舊

   5) (Measures)   _____   張，支

2) Practice: More initials   j q x y; zh ch sh; z c s

Listen to the sounds and focus on the initials. In the second round, repeat each word.

1) 家 <u>jiā</u>   掐 <u>qiā</u>   蝦 <u>xiā</u>   鴨 <u>ya</u>   Note the spelling change for y

2) 扎 <u>zhā</u>   插 <u>chā</u>   沙 <u>shā</u>   aspirated and unaspirated

3) 砸 <u>zá</u>   擦 <u>cá</u>   撒 <u>sǎ</u>

4) 家 <u>jiā</u>   扎 <u>zhā</u>   蝦 <u>xiā</u>   沙 <u>shā</u>   front vs. central tongue position

5) 插 <u>chā</u>   扎 <u>zhā</u>   擦 <u>cā</u>   砸 <u>zá</u>   aspirated and unaspirated

3) Identify initials   j q x y; zh ch sh; z c s

Listen to each group of sounds and write down the initials you hear as shown in the first item.

1) 桌 <u>zh</u>   戳 <u>___</u>   說 <u>___</u>

2) 九 <u>___</u>   肘 <u>___</u>   走 <u>___</u>

3) 擦 <u>___</u>   掐 <u>___</u>   蝦 <u>___</u>

4) 是 <u>___</u>   四 <u>___</u>   次 <u>___</u>

4) Practice: Compound finals   ia ie iao iu

Listen to the sounds and focus on the finals. In the second round, repeat each word.

(**Y-rules:** Y replaces i unless i is the only vowel in the final i (yi, yin). Change **iu** into **ou** (you).)

1) 家 jiā   街 jiē   交 jiāo   糾 jiū

2) 蝦 xiā   些 xiē   消 xiāo   休 xiū

3) 鴨 yā   耶 yē   腰 yāo   優 yōu

4) 掐 qiā   切 qiē   敲 qiāo   秋 qiū

5) 嗲 diǎ   鐵 tiě   鳥 niǎo   柳 liǔ

5) **Practice with nasal finals:**   ian in iang ing iong

1) 簡 jiǎn   緊 jǐn   講 jiǎng   景 jǐng

2) 煙 yān   因 yīn   央 yāng   英 yīng

3) 現 xiàn   信 xìn   像 xiàng   姓 xìng

4) 牽 qiān   親 qīn   槍 qiāng   清 qīng

5) 窮 qióng   雄 xióng   迥 jiǒng   勇 yǒng

6) **Compare the following pairs:**   an/ian en/in ang/iang eng/ing in/ing ong/iong

1) 沾 zhān   堅 jiān   張 zhāng   江 jiāng

2) 陳 chén   琴 qín   成 chéng   情 qíng

3) 商 shāng   香 xiāng   鬆 sōng   兄 xiōng

4) 藏 cáng   強 qiáng   從 cóng   窮 qióng

5) 隱 yǐn   影 yǐng   仰 yǎng   永 yǒng

7) **Identify the finals**

Listen to each group of sounds and write down the finals you hear next to the initials provided.

i) Non-nasals: a e i u ao ou uo ia ie iao iu

1) 車 _che_   思 _si_   七 _qi_

2) 四 _s_   色 _s_   次 _c_

3) 草 _c_   巧 _q_   左 _z_

4) 六 _l_   受 _sh_   舊 _j_

5) 寫 _x_   假 _j_   主 _zh_

ii) Nasals: an en ang eng ong; ian in iang ing iong

1) 沉 _chen_   纏 _chan_   錢 _qian_

2) 琴 _q_   先 _x_   香 _x_

3) 談 _t_   停 _t_   騰 _t_

4) 真 _zh_   今 _j_   張 _zh_

5) 兄 _x_   同 _t_   生 _sh_

The Nu-M-N form

With your eyes closed and your mind relaxed, listen to the phrases without repeating. Try to enjoy the sounds as music without thinking of the tone marks! In the second round, you may "sing along."

1) Expansion: Nu-M-Adj-N

1) 哥哥 gēge brother	大哥哥 dà gēge big brother	一個大哥哥 yí gè dà gēge one big brother	我的一個大哥哥 wǒ de yí gè dà gēge a big brother of mine
2) 姐姐 jiějie sister	大姐姐 dà jiějie big sister	三個大姐姐 sān gè dà jiějie three big sisters	他們的三個大姐姐 tāmen de sān gè dà jiějie their three big sisters
3) 孩子 háizi kid	小孩子 xiǎo háizi little kid	四個小孩子 sì gè xiǎo háizi four little kids	他們的四個小孩子 tāmen de sì gè xiǎo háizi their four little kids
4) 桌子 zhuōzi table	新桌子 xīn zhuōzi new table	七張新桌子 qī zhāng xīn zhuōzi seven new tables	我們的七張新桌子 wǒmen de qī zhāng xīn zhuōzi our seven new tables
5) 車 chē car	舊車 jiù chē old car	幾輛舊車 jǐ liàng jiù chē a few old cars	你們的幾輛舊車 nǐmen de jǐ liàng jiù chē your several old cars

2) Numbers:

1)

一	二	三	四	五	六	七		七	六	五	四	三	二	一
yī	èr	sān	sì	wǔ	liù	qī		qī	liù	wǔ	sì	sān	èr	yī
1	2	3	4	5	6	7		7	6	5	4	3	2	1

2)

四	十	十四	四十	四十四
sì	shí	shísì	sìshí	sìshísì
4	10	14	40	44

3)

四是四	十是十	十四是十四	四十是四十
sì shì sì	shí shì shí	shísì shì shísì	sìshí shì sìshí
4 is 4	10 is 10	14 is 14	40 is 40

十四不是四十	四十也不是十四
shísì búshì sìshí	sìshí yě búshì shísì
14 is not 40	40 is also not 14

INTRODUCTION

Getting Started with Writing Chinese (II): Understanding the Radicals

CHINESE WRITING BASICS

Experience the Writing

Radicals:　十　土　人　大　小　又　刀　力　口　口　月　日　目　白　田

Focus on Fluency and Accuracy

Exercises on basic radicals

OBJECTIVES
- Understanding the concept of radicals in the Chinese writing system;
- Writing the basic radicals with accuracy and appropriate stroke order;
- Memorizing the radicals covered in this part.

INTRODUCTION

Getting Started with Writing Chinese (II): Understanding the Radicals

There are 214 radicals in Chinese, which are used in Chinese dictionaries to index characters. Most radicals appear on the left side of a character, but some also appear on the top, the bottom, or the right side. Some radicals are identifiable components that appear in many characters, which can be as simple as a vertical line (e.g., 中, 串) and a hook (e.g., 了, 小). Many others, however, are meaningful characters themselves or their simplified representations, such as person (人 or 亻), water (水 or 氵), heart/emotion (心 or 忄), speech (言 or 讠), etc. These meaningful radicals serve as category labels, providing clues to the semantic classification of words. Meaningful radicals can be helpful in character learning and retention, especially for distinguishing similar characters/words. For example, 清 (qīng), 晴 (qíng), 情 (qíng), 請 (qǐng) are similar in appearance and sound as they all share the same phonetic component (青 qīng). The radical, therefore, helps correctly identify one from another, e.g., water related 清 (clear) vs. speech related 請 (invite), or sun related 晴 (sunny day) vs. heart related 情 (love, feelings).

Note that radicals may or may not provide clues to the meaning of a word. A word related to a human being does not always have a "person" radical, nor a character with a "person" radical necessarily denote a person. Sometimes, a radical does not seem to offer any clue to the meaning of the word at all. It is not necessary to memorize all 214 radicals. Rather, memorize those meaningful radicals that can stand alone as basic characters, as they also recur in many characters either as a radical or a component.

CHINESE WRITING BASICS

The following exercises are provided in full in the Workbook: Literacy Development.

B | 2.1) EXPERIENCE THE WRITING

Memorizing the meaning of frequently used radicals is key to a successful development of the literacy skills of reading and writing. To learn Chinese characters and be able to write them, it is essential that you follow the following training steps closely to establish a routine that ensures efficiency and optimal results. In this part of the lesson, 15 common radicals are introduced. Please follow this **4-step routine** to learn to write each radical/character.

1	**Know the radical**	While learning its name and meaning, take a good look at the radical so you have a mental picture.
2	**View the animation (extremely important)**	Know the stroke order, direction, and movement. The more you watch, the better you will learn and retain the character.
3	**Finger writing**	Write the radical in the air with your finger for three times, following the animation closely. Then try it again without viewing the animation. If you don't remember the stroke order, view the animation again.
4	**Trace on paper**	Reflect on the above guide and then do the tracing exercises with appropriate stroke order and method.

Reminder: Write each stroke without breaking it down into pieces. Never repair a broken stroke by patching it up or altering an imperfect shape. Rewrite it!

Trace and write:

十 土 人 大 小 又 刀 力 口 囗 月 日 目 白 田

B | 2.2) FOCUS ON FLUENCY AND ACCURACY

1) Name the following radicals/characters:

a. 大   b. 日   c. 目   d. 人   e. 土   f. 白

g. 刀   h. 月   i. 小   j. 口   k. 力   l. 田

2) Answer the questions:

1.	Which stroke should be written first for 十?	a. Heng.	b. Shu.
2.	Which stroke should be written first for 小?	a. The left one.	b. The central part.
3.	What goes first when pie and na both appear?	a. Pie.	b. Na.
4.	What's the last stroke for 日?	a. The inside heng.	b. The bottom heng.
5.	Which stroke goes first for 刀 or 力?	a. Pie.	b. Hengzhegou.
6.	Which character means "eye"?	a. 目	b. 日
7.	Which character means "power"?	a. 刀	b. 力
8.	Are all radicals based on meaning?	a. Yes.	b. No.
9.	In what position do radicals appear most often?	a. Left.	b. Top.
10.	How many strokes does 口 have ?	a. Three.	b. Four.
11.	For 因, is the frame closed before 大 is written ?	a. Yes.	b. No.
12.	Which is the last stroke for 田?	a. The inside shu.	b. The bottom heng.

3) Review radicals:

See the Workbook for more tracing and writing practices on the radicals covered in this lesson.

A PRONUNCIATION:
Polysyllables, Unique Sounds, and *Pinyin* Rules

PRONUNCIATION BASICS

Experience the Sound

Word Groups:	Proper names: countries, nationals, and languages
	Verbs: listen, speak, read, write, learn
Monosyllabic words:	人(rén), 文(wén), 語(yǔ); 聽(tīng), 説(shuō), 讀(dú), 寫(xiě)
Disyllabic:	中國(Zhōngguó), 日本(Rìběn), 中文(Zhōngwén), 日語(Rìyǔ)
Polysyllabic:	中國人(Zhōngguórén), 義大利(Yìdàlì), 西班牙語(Xībānyáyǔ)

Learn About the Phonetic System

Pinyin: The dummy initial "w" for u

The ü and ü-group of sounds and their spelling rules: ü spelled as u

Focus on Fluency and Accuracy

Exercises on pronunciation, listening, and *pinyin*

Initials: **r, w, y**

Finals: The ü sound and the ü-group

Feel the Speech: Flow of Tones and Syllables

u-ü words; people and languages

OBJECTIVES

Pronunciation: • Understanding the concept of syllables vs. words in Chinese;
  • Pronouncing r and ü correctly;
  • Distinguishing sounds: ü/u, zhu/ju, chu/qu, ru/yu;
  • Pronouncing short phrases with appropriate sounds and tones.

Pinyin: • Identifying initials and finals in the words taught in this lesson;
  • Knowing the *pinyin* rules for ü, u, and w.

PRONUNCIATION BASICS

 The following activities are enhanced by an online multimedia program.

Main Features: In this lesson, we introduce some common proper nouns, such as the names of countries, languages, and people. These words serve as good examples of disyllables and polysyllables in Chinese. While practicing these basic terms, we'll also work on some special pronunciations, such as r and ü. Perhaps the most confusing sounds in pinyin are u and ü, as the latter sometimes changes its spelling to u. We'll also introduce two groups of finals combined with u and ü. In addition, we'll continue to work on short phrases to familiarize you with the tones and tone combinations.

A | 3.1) EXPERIENCE THE SOUND

 Words are selected mainly for pronunciation; tone practice and memorization is not required.

Step 1 *View and Listen* While looking at the pictures or videos, listen to the sounds and words in each group you hear and concentrate on comprehension. Do not repeat yet!

Step 2 *Listen and Listen* Close your eyes and "feel" the sounds and tones. Try to hear the *differences* as well as the similarities between Chinese and your native language. Just listen!

Step 3 *Listen and Repeat* With your eyes still closed and your mind relaxed, listen to each sound three times, and then imitate it 2–3 times.

Step 4 *Repeat and Write* After repeating the sound, look at the screen to see the pinyin spelling of the sound or word, then write it down in the blank under each word or on a piece of paper as you say the word 2–3 times.

1) Group 1: Nouns and Verbs   Monosyllabic sounds; The four tones   (Steps 1-4)

These basic nouns and verbs will be joined with other words later in the exercises.

國	人	語	文	字
_____	_____	_____	_____	_____
country	person	language	writing	word/character

聽	說	讀	寫	學
_____	_____	_____	_____	_____
listen	speak	read	write	learn

2) Group 2a: Proper Nouns — Countries   Disyllabic sounds and tone combinations   (Steps 1-4)

These names are selected to demonstrate effectively the disyllabic sounds and tone combinations. Note that Japan and India maintain their original disyllabic names, and all other names of countries that end with **guó** represent the short names used in daily speech. That is, the character before **guó** stands for the first sound of the transliteration of a country's full name.

中國	韓國	美國	日本
_____	_____	_____	_____
China	Korea	America	Japan

英國	俄國	法國	印度
_____	_____	_____	_____
England	Russia	France	India

3) Group 2b: Proper Nouns — Countries   Polysyllabic sounds and tone combinations   (Steps 1-4)

Some polysyllabic names are not abbreviated with the -**guó** form, especially trisyllabic names, which are normally transliterations of names from their original language. Note that all proper nouns are capitalized in pinyin.

義大利	加拿大	新加坡	西班牙	澳大利亞
_____	_____	_____	_____	_____
Italy	Canada	Singapore	Spain	Australia

4) Group 3:   People — Nationals   Polysyllabic sounds and tone combinations   (Steps 1-4)

A country name can be added in front of a noun, e.g., country + person = national(s). Focus on the r-sound (e.g., in ren, person).

中國人	俄國人	美國人	日本人
_____	_____	_____	_____
Chinese (people)	Russian(s)	American(s)	Japanese (people)

義大利人	加拿大人	澳大利亞人	
_____	_____	_____	
Italian(s)	Canadian(s)	Australian(s)	

5) Group 4a: Nouns — Languages   The initial **w** and final **ü**   (Steps 1-4)

Two words are used to refer to a language: **yu** and **wen**. **Yu** (pronounced **ü**) was originally used to refer to a spoken language, while **wen** is used when talking about the written form. Both **yu** and **wen** are used with nouns for non-Chinese languages, but **wen** is used to refer to their use in formal context. For the Chinese language, four terms are used: **Zhongwen**, **Hanyu**, **Huawen**, and **Huayu**. (See Overview: The Chinese Language for details.)

語言	文字	外語	外文
_____	_____	_____	_____
language	writing/text	foreign language	foreign language

中文	漢語	華文	華語
_____	_____	_____	_____
Chinese	Chinese	Chinese	Chinese

聽中文	說中文	讀中文	寫中文
_____	_____	_____	_____
listen to Chinese	speak Chinese	read Chinese	write Chinese

6) Group 4b: Nouns — Languages   Tone combinations

Here are several languages selected for practice of tones, initials, and polysyllables. Note the third tone sandhi (in the tones for "French"). Pay special attention to the final ü (spelled as u after y).

英語/英文   俄語/俄文   法語/法文   日語/日文

_____   _____   _____   _____

English (language)   Russian (language)   French (language)   Japanese (language)

西班牙語/西班牙文   義大利語/義大利文

_____   _____

Spanish (language)   Italian (language)

聽英語   説俄語   讀法文   寫日文

_____   _____   _____   _____

listen to English   speak Russian   read French   write Japanese

---

A | 3.2) LEARN ABOUT THE PHONETIC SYSTEM

More initials
Here are two more initials to learn: r and w

1. Central: r
   We have already introduced three central initials: zh, ch, and sh. The initial r is the fourth, which completes the group. Just like zhi, chi, shi, i in ri is not pronounced (e.g., the dummy i).
   Unlike the English r, the Chinese r is mostly pronounced without rounded or protruded lips.

   rì (sun)   rén (person)   ròu (meat)

2. w in place of u
   w is like y in that it is not a real initial but a dummy in place of u in the u-group of finals. See below for spelling rules.

Compound finals   u and u-group   ü and ü-group
1. u and the u-group:
   u as a single vowel: It is pronounced like "oo" in English, with lips rounded and protruded.

   wǔ (five)   shūshu (uncle)   gūgu (aunt)

   u also serves as a medial to join another sound to form a compound final:

   ua   uo   uai   ui   uan   un   uang   ueng
   (=uei)   (=uen)

uo	I, me	uai	foreign	uen	writing/text
	(wǒ)		(wài)		(wén)

(See spelling rules on next page.)

2. ü and the ü-group:

ü as a single vowel: To pronounce ü, round your lips slightly as you say the sound i (ee), or the French "y."

(See spelling rules below.)

nǚ female   yǔ (language/speech)
(yǔ)

ü also serves as a medial to join another sound to form a compound final:

(See spelling rules below.)

üe   üan   ün (=üen)
lüe (omit)   jüan (roll)   yün (cloud)
(juan)   (yun)

Special spelling rules

1. Dummy Initial: **w** replaces **u**

W replaces u unless u is the only vowel; special rules apply to uo, ui, and un:

u → wu   uan → wan   uo → wo   ui → wei   un → wen

When preceded by another initial, u or a u-compound remains unchanged:

l+uan → luan   k+uan → kuan   sh+uo → shuo   h+ui → hui   z+un → zun

2. Dummy **i** after **r**

i, when following an initial r, is not pronounced, just as it is not after zh, ch, or sh.

3. Spelling rules with the ü and ü-group compounds: ü, üe, üan, ün

With the initials l and n: ü and u sounds are both possible; ü must keep its original form:

lü   nü   lüe   nüe

Compare: lü vs. lu   nü vs. nu

With initials j, q, x, and y, the u and u-group sounds are not used and only ü-sounds are used. All ü's are spelled as u without changing the ü sound.

y+ü → yu   q+üè → que   x+üan → xuan   j+ün → jun

(They are still pronounced yü, qüe, xüan, and jün respectively)

Compare: ü vs. u   yu vs. ru   ju vs. zhu   qu vs. chu   xu vs. shu

A | 3.3) FOCUS ON FLUENCY AND ACCURACY

1) **Review the sounds and words in this lesson.**

Listen to the sounds and write them down in pinyin without tones. Then check your answers.

1) (Countries) _____ 美國，日本，中國，俄國

2) (People) _____ 法國人，加拿大人，印度人

3) (Languages) _____ 英語，日語，中文，西班牙文

4) (V + language) _____ 說俄語，聽日語，讀法文，寫英文，學中文

2) Practice: Initials   **r, w**, and their corresponding finals

Listen to the sounds focusing on initial r. In the second round, repeat each word.

1) 日 <u>rì</u>   熱 <u>rè</u>   人 <u>rén</u>   仍 <u>rēng</u>   嚷 <u>rǎng</u>   冗 <u>rǒng</u>

2) 染 <u>rǎn</u>   軟 <u>ruǎn</u>   若 <u>ruò</u>   肉 <u>ròu</u>   潤 <u>rùn</u>   瑞 <u>ruì</u>

Note the spelling adjustments: w replaces u unless u is the only vowel; also, ui → wei; un → wen

u ua uo uai ui uan un uang ueng

3) 五 <u>wǔ</u>   外 <u>wài</u>   我 <u>wǒ</u>   偉 <u>wěi</u>

4) 頑 <u>wán</u>   文 <u>wén</u>   汪 <u>wāng</u>   翁 <u>wēng</u>

3) Identify initials   r y sh zh j w

Listen to each group of sounds and write down the appropriate initials as shown in the first item.

1) 演 <u>y</u>   染 <u>   </u>   晚 <u>   </u>

2) 熱 <u>   </u>   社 <u>   </u>   這 <u>   </u>

3) 銀 <u>   </u>   人 <u>   </u>   文 <u>   </u>

4) 日 <u>   </u>   至 <u>   </u>   記 <u>   </u>

5) 又 <u>   </u>   肉 <u>   </u>   受 <u>   </u>

4) Practice: Finals   u / ü / i;   uan / üan / ian;   un / ün / in;   üe / ie

Listen to each group. Pay special attention to the spelling rules for ü and the ü-group finals.
(**Rule:** Following the initials j, q, x, or y, ü is spelled as u but still pronounced ü.)

1) 魯 lú   旅 lú   語 yǔ (ü)

2) 努 nǔ   女 nǔ   你 nǐ

3) 船 chuán   全 quán (ü)   錢 qián

4) 順 shùn   迅 xùn (ü)   運 yùn (ü)

5) 謝 xiè   略 lüè   越 yuè (ü)

5) Identify finals　　　　u uan un; ü üan üe ün; i ian ie in

Listen to each group of sounds and write down the finals that you hear next to the initials provided.

1) 簡 jian_____　　卷 j_____　　晚 w_____

2) 綠 l_____　　路 l_____　　去 q_____

3) 酸 s_____　　宣 x_____　　先 x_____

4) 銀 y_____　　元 y_____　　雲 y_____

5) 學 x_____　　寫 x_____　　也 y_____

A | 3.4) FEEL THE SPEECH: FLOW OF TONES AND SYLLABLES

u-ü words; people and languages

With your eyes closed and your mind relaxed, listen to the phrases without repeating. Try to enjoy the sounds as music without thinking of the tone marks! In the second round, you may "sing along."

1) u-ü Combinations

Pay special attention to the ü, which is sometimes spelled u.

		出去	呼籲	陸續	數據
1)	u + ü	chūqù	hūyù	lùxù	shùjù
		go out	invoke	successively	data
		居住	綠樹	旅途	敘述
2)	ü + u	jūzhù	lùshù	lǚtú	xùshù
		reside	green tree	journey	narrate

2) People and Languages

Feel the natural flow of syllables and tones.

一個中國人
yí gè Zhōngguórén
a Chinese person

五個美國人
wǔ gè Měiguórén
five Americans

十個日本人
shí gè Rìběnrén
ten Japanese

1)
聽中文
tīng Zhōngwén
listen to Chinese

聽俄語
tīng Éyǔ
listen to Russian

説法語
shuō Fǎyǔ
speak French

説日語
shuō Rìyǔ
speak Japanese

2)
讀英文
dú Yīngwén
read English

讀義大利文
dú Yìdàlì wén
read Italian

寫西班牙文
xiě Xībānyá wén
write Spanish

3)
中國人説漢語
Zhōngguórén shuō Hànyǔ
Chinese people speak Chinese.

韓國人説韓語
Hánguórén shuō Hányǔ
Korean people speak Korean.

日本人説日語
Rìběnrén shuō Rìyǔ
Japanese people speak Japanese.

4)
我爸爸説英語
Wǒ bàba shuō Yīngyǔ
My dad speaks English.

我姐姐學日語
wǒ jiějie xué Rìyǔ
My sister is studying Japanese.

我弟弟學法語
wǒ dìdi xué Fǎyǔ
My brother is learning French.

3) Learning foreign languages

人人都在學外語,
rénren dōu zài xué wàiyǔ
Everyone studies a foreign language.

英語法語和日語,
Yīngyǔ Fǎyǔ hé Rìyǔ
English, French, and Japanese

漢語韓語西班牙語;
Hànyǔ Hányǔ Xībānyá yǔ
Chinese, Korean, Spanish

聽一句, 説一句,
tīng yí jù, shuō yí jù
Listen to a sentence, (then) say
a sentence,

讀幾句再寫幾句,
dú jǐ jù zài xiě jǐ jù
read a few sentences and
also write a few

聽説讀寫學外語
tīng shuō dú xiě xué wàiyǔ
listen, speak, read, write (to)
learn a foreign language

B CHARACTER WRITING:
Character Components and Composition

INTRODUCTION

Getting Started with Writing Chinese (III): Character Components and Composition

CHINESE WRITING BASICS

Experience the Writing

Radicals   辶 阝 宀 言 子 手 水 木 火 父 心 女 馬 糸 金

Focus on Fluency and Accuracy

Exercises on basic radicals

OBJECTIVES

- Knowing the basic concept of radical positioning;
- Knowing the basic concept of character composition;
- Writing radicals with accuracy and using appropriate stroke order;
- Memorizing at least 10 basic radicals covered in this section including their names and meanings.

INTRODUCTION

Getting Started with Writing Chinese (III): Character Components and Composition

Chinese characters are also called square characters, as each one is shaped like a square or block. Irrespective of the complexity of strokes and structures, each character occupies the same amount of space.

Components: Complex characters are formed by components. These components, which may include a number of radicals, are either independent characters when used alone or blocks that recur in many other characters. To memorize Chinese characters effectively, the learner should make an effort to memorize individual components, "building blocks," rather than just individual strokes. This is very much like building a house: it is easier to build a house using prefabricated materials than using loose bricks.

Composition of a character: Four composition types are most common: unitary, top-bottom, left-right, and enclosing.

Structure	Formation	Examples
Unitary		人 大 日 月 山
Top-bottom		早 分 花 笑 字 草 芬 京 藍 意
Left-right		你 好 北 江 吃 樹 班 謝 湖 腳
Enclosing		回 四 圖 因 國 醫 風 同 區 閃

(Introduction by Yong Ho)

The following exercises are provided in full in the Workbook: Literacy Development.

B 3.1) EXPERIENCE THE WRITING

Just like radicals, many commonly used components are equally important in the learning of Chinese characters. It takes a day-to-day effort to build a component base. You can make progress by studying just a few minutes a day. In this part of the lesson you are going to practice 15 common components that often serve as radicals as well. Follow the **4-step routine** to learn to write each character.

Trace and write:

辶 阝 宀 言 子 手 水 木 火 父 心 女 馬 糸 金

B 3.2) FOCUS ON FLUENCY AND ACCURACY

1) Name the following characters/radicals in Chinese and provide the English meaning:

a. 金　　b. 木　　c. 水　　d. 火　　e. 糸　　f. 子

g. 手　　h. 心　　i. 言　　j. 女　　k. 父　　l. 馬

2) Match the radical variation form on the right to each character on the left:

1. 火 _____　　a. 忄

2. 水 _____　　b. 糹

3. 言 _____　　c. 釒

4. 心 _____　　d. 訁

5. 手 _____　　e. 灬

6. 金 _____　　f. 氵

7. 糸 _____　　g. 扌

3) Answer the questions:

Stroke order and radical position:

1. For 火, which part should be written first?   a. The two dots   b. The 人 part
2. For 水, which part should be written first?   a. The left part   b. The central part
3. For 女, which stroke should be written first?   a. Heng   b. Piedian
4. For 進 (enter), which part should be written first?   a. 井   b. 辶
5. Which radical should be placed on the side?   a. 心   b. 忄
6. Which position is ⺣ normally taken in a character?   a. Top   b. Bottom
7. Which radical is nornally positioned on top?   a. 宀   b. 又

Components and functions:

8. What composition type is 想?   a. Top-bottom   b. Left-right
9. What composition type is 生?   a. Top-bottom   b. Unitary
10. What composition type is 家?   a. Top-bottom   b. Unitary
11. Which 阝 suggests "place", left (陳) or right(都)?   a. The left 阝   b. The right 阝
12. For 媽 (mā: mom), which part suggests meaning?   a. 女   b. 馬
13. What does 馬 (mǎ: horse) suggest in 罵 (mà: scold)?   a. Category   b. Sound
14. Identify the character denoting "feelings."   a. 晴   b. 情
15. Which word is likely indicating a physical action?   a. 拉   b. 垃

4) Review the following radicals/components:

See the Workbook for more tracing and writing practices on the components, radicals and independent characters covered in this lesson.

PRONUNCIATION BASICS

Experience the Sound

Words:	Miscellaneous
Monosyllabic:	多(duō), 少(shǎo), 好(hǎo), 難(nán), 忙(máng), 累(lèi), 對(duì)
	很(hěn), 也(yě); 不(bù), 太(tài), 天(tiān), 年(nián), 點(diǎn), 次(cì), 這(zhè)
ér:	兒(ér); 這兒(zhèr), 那兒(nàr), 小孩兒(xiǎoháir)
yī, bù:	一天(yì tiān), 一次(yí cì), 不多(bù duō), 不累(bú lèi)
Phrases:	一天一次(yì tiān yí cì), 不多不少(bù duō bù shǎo),
	我很好(wǒ hěn hǎo)

Learn About the Phonetic System

The er sound; -er as a suffix
Tone sandhi: yi and bu; serial third tones
Pronunciation and spelling rules for er sounds
Pinyin: How to indicate tones

Focus on Fluency and Accuracy

er words	二, 兒, 這兒, 那兒, 一點兒, 小孩兒
Similar pronunciation	睡覺/水餃 shuijiao; 試用/使用 shiyong; 練習/聯繫 lianxi
Finals	you/niu; jia/ya, guo/wo, yu/lu…

Feel the Speech: Flow of Tones and Syllables

Tone sandhi with yi and bu
Phrases with serial third tones

OBJECTIVES

Pronunciation:	• Understanding the basic concept of the noun suffix -**er**;
	• Pronouncing **er** words correctly;
	• Knowing the rules for the tone sandhi with **yi** and **bu**;
	• Pronouncing phrases with appropriate tone adjustment for **yi**, **bu**, and third tones.
Pinyin:	• Knowing the *pinyin* rules for **er**;
	• Knowing the rules for indicating tones in writing.

PRONUNCIATION BASICS

 The following activities are enhanced by an online multimedia program.

Main Features: This lesson concludes the pre-units. We'll introduce the last final, the er sound, which is a prominent feature of Beijing speech. We'll work more on tone combinations and tone sandhi with two common sounds, yi (one) and bu (not) as well as with consecutive third tones. In addition, you'll hear some words that sound the same except for their tone. Tones often hold the key to the meaning of spoken words. As pairs of words such as these are numerous in Chinese, the accuracy of tones cannot be overstressed. If you are serious about learning Chinese, you must take tones seriously! To be able to pronounce tones correctly in the long run, do not hurry to pronounce words quite yet. The first step is to immerse yourself in the language as you do with a new song: listen, listen, and listen!

A | 4.1) EXPERIENCE THE SOUND

 Words in these exercises are selected for pronunciation and tone practice. Memorization is not required.

Step 1 **View and Listen** While looking at the pictures or videos, listen to the sounds and words in each group you hear and concentrate on comprehension. Do not repeat yet!

Step 2 **Listen <u>and</u> Listen** Close your eyes and "feel" the sounds and tones. Try to hear the *differences* as well as the similarities between Chinese and your native language. Just listen!

Step 3 **Listen and Repeat** With your eyes still closed and your mind relaxed, listen to each sound three times, and then imitate it 2–3 times.

Step 4 **Repeat and Write** After repeating the sound, look at the screen to see the *pinyin* spelling of the sound or word, then write it down in the blank under each word or on a piece of paper as you say the word 2–3 times.

1) Group 1: Miscellaneous Words   -er as a suffix

The er sound serves as a final which can stand alone without an initial, e.g., èr (two). Er is also used as a suffix (-兒), mostly for nouns, but it can also be used with other words. The suffix er is common in northern dialects, especially in Beijing speech, although not commonly used in formal text.

First listen to the words without -er and then to the second group with -er added.

without -er	這	那	點	玩	小孩
	zhè	nà	diǎn	wán	xiǎo hái
	this/here	that/there	bit, dot	to play	little kid

When -er is used, it is blended with the sound before it rather than pronounced by itself in full.

with -er	這兒	那兒	點兒	玩兒	小孩兒
	(zhè'ér)	(nà'ér)	(diǎn'ér)	(wán'ér)	(xiǎo hái'ér)
	zhèr	nàr	diǎnr	wánr	xiǎo háir

Note that when *typing* Chinese using *pinyin*, use -er rather than -r.

2) Group 2:   Adjectives and Adverbs   Monosyllabic; The four tones   (Steps 2-4)

Can you recognize the initials and the finals by listening? Can you recognize tones?

Listen to each group first. Then listen to each word, repeat it and write it down in *pinyin*.

多	少	忙	累	好	對
_____	_____	_____	_____	_____	_____
many	few	difficult	tired	good	correct

很	也	太	不
_____	_____	_____	_____
very	also	too (much)	not

3) Group 3:   Adverb-Adjective Phrases   Third tone sandhi   (Steps 2-3)

Review the third tone sandhi. When the third tone is followed by any tone but T3, it is a half/short third tone. What happens when it is followed by another T3?

Listen to each group focusing on the tones. Then listen to each item again and repeat.

很多	很少	很忙	很累	Which *hen* has a different tone? Higher or lower?
hěn duō	hěn shǎo	hěn máng	hěn lèi	
a lot	very few	(very) busy	(very) tired	
3-1	3-3 → **2-3**	3-2	3-4	

What if there are multiple T3s in a row? (Indicate the tones you hear.)

你很好	我也很好	你寫法語	我也寫法語
nǐ hěn hǎo	wǒ yě hěn hǎo	nǐ xiě Fǎyǔ	wǒ yě xiě Fǎyǔ
You are good/fine.	I'm also good/fine.	You write French.	I also write French.
3-3-3 → _____	3-3-3-3 → _____	3-3-3-3 → _____	3-3-3-3-3 → _____

4) Group 4:   Miscelloneous Words   Tone sandhi with *yi* and *bu*   (Steps 2-3)

Yi (one) and **bu** (not) have different tones when spoken, depending on the tone that follows. However, in the written form the tone never changes.

Listen to each group for the tones. Then listen to each item again and repeat.

一天	一年	一點兒	一個	Which **yi** is different in tone?
yi tian	yi nian	yi dianr	yi ge	Does it go lower or higher?
one day	one year	a little bit	one __	What tone causes the change?

The same tone adjustment applies to bu when it is followed by the fourth tone.

不多	不少	不忙	不累	不好	不壞
bu duo	bu shao	bu mang	bu lei	bu hao	bu huai
Not many	(lit.) not a few	not busy	not tired	not good	not bad

There are numerous homophones in Chinese, i.e., words sharing the same pronunciation but having different meanings. There are even more words that differ only in their tone. For the latter, the correct tone is often the key to one's understanding of the meaning. Obviously, it is important to develop a sensitive ear for the tone in Chinese!

Listen to each pair focusing on the tones. Then listen to each item again and repeat. Mark the tones yourself.

舊	九	四	死
jiu	jiu	si	si
old	nine	four	dead/death

一千	以前	問她	吻她
yi qian	yiqian	wen ta	wen ta
one thousand	before/formerly	ask her	kiss her

睡覺	水餃	聯繫	練習
shuijiao	shuijiao	lianxi	lianxi
to sleep	boiled dumplings	to contact	to practice

鞋子	寫字	韓語	漢語
xiezi	xiezi	Hanyu	Hanyu
shoes	to write characters	Korean	Chinese

The syllable er:

1. The er sound
   - er serves as a final, which can stand alone without an initial: èr (two), érzi (son).
   - If er is the second syllable, an apostrophe is used to separate the two syllables, e.g., nü'er.

2. er as a suffix
   - In speech, -er (兒) is sometimes used as a suffix, abbreviated as r in *pinyin*.
   - As a suffix, -er is blended into the syllable immediately before it rather than pronounced in full.
         zhèr/nàr (here/there)   **xiǎo háir** (little kid)   **wánr** (to play)
   - The suffix -er (兒) is mostly used in speech, and is normally absent in formal written texts except in a few specific instances (e.g., 一點兒，一會兒).

Tone sandhi

1. Tone sandhi rules for serial T3
   - Single words/syllables or a stressed last syllable: → regular T3 (i.e., low rising)
         wǒ, hǎo, méiyǒu (The rising part may be rather light and short.)

   T3 followed by another syllable: → half T3 (i.e., low without rising)
       Měiguó, xiǎochē, hěn dà (There is no rising at all.)

   - Two T3s together: → 2–3 instead of 3–3 (that is, rising, then low tone)
         Fǎyǔ → Fáyǔ   hén hǎo → hén hǎo

   - Multiple T3s in a row: → 2–2–3, 3–2–3, or 2–3–2–3 (i.e., rising–rising-low, or rising-low–rising-low)
         wǒ hěn hǎo → (2-2-3) **wó hén hǎo**, (or 3-2-3) **wǒ hén hǎo**
         wǒ yé hén hǎo → (2-2-2-3) **wó yé hén hǎo**, (or 2-3-2-3) **wó yě hén hǎo**

   - In writing the *pinyin* text, the third tone mark remains <u>unchanged</u> in any case.

2. Tone sandhi rules for yi and bu
   - As a single syllable, 一 (one) is pronounced with the <u>first</u> tone (yī), while 不 (not) is pronounced with the <u>fourth</u> tone (bù). However, the tone changes when yi or bu is followed by another syllable.
     Rule 1: Falling before anything but falling
         yī and bù = T4 before T1, T2, and T3
           yì tiān, yì nián, yì diǎnr   bù duō, bù máng, bù hǎo
     Rule 2: Rising before falling:
         yī and bù = Tone 2 before Tone 4 (i.e., rising–then–falling)
           yí gè, yí kuài, bú lèi, bú duì, bú huài
   - Regardless of which tone yi or bu changes to in natural speech, the *pinyin* tone mark remains unchanged in writing.
         In pronunciation → yì tiān, yí gè, bù máng, bú lèi
         In *pinyin* → yī tiān, yī gè, bù máng, bù lèi

Note: In this book, yi and bu are marked with the changed tones to guide beginning learners to the natural pronunciation.

3. How to mark *pinyin* tones
   - The tone mark falls on these vowels only: a, o, e, i, u, ü, such as wǒ, rì, ér, méng.
   - When the vowel i carries a tone mark, it replaces the dot: zhi → zhǐ, jin → jīn
   - For compound finals, the tone mark is assigned to the dominant vowel in this order:

   a o e i u ü (with the exception of ui)

lai → líi	jia → jiā	duo → duō	gou → gǒu
mei → měi	xie → xiè	yue → yuè	lue → luè
qiu → qiú	dui → duì	ao → ào	ian → yān

A | 4.3) FOCUS ON FLUENCY AND ACCURACY

1) Review the sounds/words in this lesson

Listen to the sounds and write them down in *pinyin* without tones. Then check your answers.

1) (er sound) 　　二，兒子，這兒，那兒，小孩兒

2) (Adjectives) 　　多，少，好，壞，忙，累，對

3) (Adverbs) 　　很，太，不，也

4) (yi/bu phrases) 　　一天，一個，不多，不對

2) Practice: er sounds   words with er; the er suffix

Listen and repeat.

1) 二 ___èr___　　兒子 ___érzi___　　女兒 ___nǚ'ér___

The suffix -er needs to be blended with the sound before it.

2) 這兒 ___zhèr___　　那兒 ___nàr___　　小孩兒 ___xiǎo háir___

花兒 ___huār___　　歌兒 ___gēr___　　一點兒 ___yìdiǎnr___

3) Identify er sounds: a word or a suffix?

Listen to each item and write down the appropriate er-sound.

1) 　　而 ___ér___　　　女兒　　　　　哪兒

2) 　　兒子　　　　　畫兒　　　　　男孩兒

4) Distinguish Initials   j q x y zh ch sh r z c s

Listen to each group. Pay special attention to the difference betwen initials.

a) Monosyllabic

1) 支 zhī   吃 chī   機 jī

2) 師 shī   西 xī   思 sī

3) 字 zì   記 jì   次 cì

4) 易 yì   日 rì   利 lì

5) 起 qǐ   幾 jǐ   止 zhǐ

b) Disyllabic

1) 支持 zhīchí   機器 jīqì   日記 rìjì

2) 實際 shíjì   實質 shízhì   襲擊 xíjī

3) 尺子 chǐzi   起子 qǐzi   侄子 zhízi

4) 曲子 qǔzi   橘子 júzi   廚子 chúzi

5) 書架 shūjià   虛假 xūjiǎ   出家 chūjiā

6) 收拾 shōushi   休息 xiūxi   就是 jiùshì

5) Identify sounds

Listen to each word and choose the appropriate sound with correct *pinyin* spelling.

1)   a. xi   b. shi   c. si

2)   a. ci   b. ji   c. zi

3)   a. qi   b. chi   c. zhi

4)   a. ri   b. re   c. er

5)   a. chi   b. zhe   c. zhi

6)   a. zhichi   b. jichi   c. jiqi

7)   a. chishi   b. chixu   c. qixu

8)   a. shoushi   b. xiuxi   c. xiushi

9)   a. zhichi   b. chizhi   c. jiqi

10) a. qizi   b. zhuzi   c. quzi

6) Distinguish Finals

Listen to each group. Pay special attention to the difference in finals or spelling rules.

1)	你 ni	女 nü	努 nu			
2)	日 ri	熱 re	二 er			
3)	説 shuo	收 shou	休 xiu			
4)	談 tan	堂 tang	同 tong			
5)	記 ji	句 ju	住 zhu	(ju=jü)		
6)	對 dui	貴 gui	為 wei	(wei=ui)		
7)	藍 lan	郎 lang	良 liang			
8)	走 zou	左 zuo	九 jiu			
9)	借 jie	這 zhe	業 ye	(ye=ie)		
10)	過 guo	末 mo	破 po	(mo=muo, po=puo)		
11)	印 yin	運 yun	硬 ying	(=in, ün, ing)		
12)	煞 sha	下 xia	薩 sa			
13)	又 you	肉 rou	就 jiu	(you=iu/iou)		
14)	學 xue	鞋 xie	雄 xiong	(xue=xüe)		
15)	王 wang	頑 wan	文 wen	(wen=un)		

7) Identify sounds

Listen to each word and choose the appropriate sound with correct *pinyin* spelling.

1)	a. yin	b. yun	c. un
2)	a. nü	b. lu	c. nu
3)	a. zou	b. zuo	c. cou
4)	a. zhe	b. jie	c. qie
5)	a. po	b. puo	c. bo
6)	a. gan	b. kang	c. gang
7)	a. xie	b. xue	c. shuo
8)	a. lan	b. lang	c. len
9)	a. shou	b. shuo	c. xiu
10)	a. shou	b. sou	c. xiu

11)	a. uei	b. hui	c. wei
12)	a. ri	b. re	c. ye
13)	a. you	b. rou	c. yong
14)	a. xia	b. sa	c. sha
15)	a. wan	b. wang	c. wen
16)	a. ju	b. zhu	c. chu

8) Mark tones

Determine which letter in each final should be assigned a tone mark.

1)	wei	a. e	b. i		
2)	xie	a. i	b. e		
3)	jiu	a. i	b. u		
4)	gui	a. u	b. i		
5)	mai	a. a	b. i		
6)	piao	a. i	b. a	c. o	
7)	xue	a. u	b. e		
8)	xiong	a. i	b. o	c. n	d. g
9)	zhuo	a. u	b. o		
10)	you	a. o	b. u		

A **4.4** **FEEL THE SPEECH**

🔊 Tone adjustments and similar pronunciations

With your eyes closed and your mind relaxed, listen to the phrases without repeating. Try to enjoy the sounds as music without thinking of the tone marks! In the second round, you may "sing along."

1) *yi*-combinations

Rules: In speech, the word "一" (yī) naturally changes to yì when followed by Tone 1, 2, or 3 and becomes yí before Tone 4. However, in *pinyin* the tone mark is always written yī, regardless of how it is pronounced. (We use the actual pronunciation here as a guide.)

1)
一天	一年	一點兒	一次	一個	一夜
yì tiān	yì nián	yì diǎnr	yì cì	yí gè	yí yè
one day	one year	one bit	once	one __	one night

2)
一天一夜	一年一次	一次一點兒	一次一個
yì tiān yí yè	yì nián yí cì	yí cì yì diǎnr	yí cì yí gè
around the clock	once a year	a bit at a time	one at a time

2) *bu*-combinations

Rules: In speech, bù naturally changes to bú when followed by Tone 4. However, in *pinyin* text the tone mark remains bù regardless of changes in pronunciation. (We use the actual pronunciation here as a guide.)

1)
不多	不聽	不忙	不難	不好	不少	不小
bù duō	bù tīng	bù máng	bù nán	bù hǎo	bù shǎo	bùxiǎo
not many	not listen	not busy	not hard	not good	not few	not small

2)
不大	不對	不錯	不累	不壞
bú dà	bú duì	bú cuò	bú lèi	bú huài
not big	not right	not wrong	not tired	not bad

3)
不多不少	不大不小	不好不壞
bù duō bù shǎo	bú dà bù xiǎo	bù hǎo bú huài
not too much or too little	not too big or too small	neither good nor bad; so-so

4)
不聽也不説	不忙也不累	不對也不錯
bù tīng yě bù shuō	bù máng yě bú lèi	bú duì yě bú cuò
neither listen nor speak	neither busy nor tired	neither right nor wrong

3) Multiple third tones

1)
你很好	我也很好	他也很好
nǐ hěn hǎo	wǒ yě hěn hǎo	tā yě hěn hǎo
You're fine.	I'm fine too.	He's also fine.
2-2-3 or 3-2-3	2-3-2-3	1-3-2-3

2)
你有狗	我也有狗	你的狗很小	我的狗也很小
nǐ yǒu gǒu	wǒ yě yǒu gǒu	nǐ de gǒu hěn xiǎo	wǒ de gǒu yě hěn xiǎo
You have a dog.	I have a dog too.	Your dog is small.	My dog is small too.
2-2-3	2-3-2-3	3-0-3-2-3	3-0-3-2-2-3

3)
你的小狗跑	我的狗不跑	狗跑你也跑	狗不跑，我也不跑
nǐ de xiǎo gǒu pǎo;	wǒ de gǒu bù pǎo;	gǒu pǎo nǐ yě pǎo;	gǒu bù pǎo, wǒ yě bù pǎo
Your small dog runs.	My dog doesn't run.	When the dog runs, you also do.	[My] dog doesn't run, I also don't.
3-0-2-2-3	3-0-3-2-3	2-3-2-2-3	3-4-3, 2-3-4-3

4) Distinguishing tones and meaning

Listen to each pair of words multiple times before trying to pronounce them yourself.

1) 我想問你
    wǒ xiǎng wèn nǐ
    I want to ask you.

    我想吻你
    wǒ xiǎng wěn nǐ
    I want to kiss you.

2) 我要睡覺
    wǒ yào shuìjiào
    I'm going to sleep.

    我要水餃
    wǒ yào shuǐjiǎo
    I want to have boiled dumplings.

3) 我跟他聯繫
    wǒ gēn tā liánxì
    I contact him.

    我跟他練習
    wǒ gēn tā liànxí
    I practice with him.

4) 我説韓語
    wǒ shuō Hányǔ
    I speak Korean.

    我説漢語
    wǒ shuō Hànyǔ
    I speak Mandarin Chinese.

PRE—UNIT
4 基礎訓練

B CHARACTER WRITING:
Distinguishing Characters

INTRODUCTION

Getting Started with Writing Chinese (IV): Chinese Input Methods and Character Recognition Skills

CHINESE WRITING BASICS

Experience the Writing

Distinguishing radicals:　八 / 入 ，儿 / 几 ，己 / 已 ，厂 / 广 ，
又 / 文 ，土 / 士 ，日 / 曰 ，亻 / 彳 ，
冫 / 氵 ，辶 / 廴 ，扌 / 犭 ，弋 / 戈 ，
艹 / 竹 ，木 / 禾 ，衤 / 礻

Focus on Fluency and Accuracy

Exercises on radicals and character recognition

OBJECTIVES

- Understanding the basic concept of the Chinese input methods (IME);
- Knowing how to type Chinese words using a computer keyboard or a cellphone;
- Distinguishing the similar radicals, components, and characters in this lesson;
- Memorizing and reproducing the pairs covered in this part, including their names and meanings.

Getting Started with Writing Chinese (IV): Chinese Input Methods and Character Recognition Skills

As introduced so far in this course, the Chinese writing system is a complex one which requires tremendous effort to master. With the development of new technologies, the burden of writing character by character by hand is greatly reduced through various input methods, e.g., key board typing in *pinyin*, using a cell phone writing pad with a finger, or even using voice conversion.

Chinese skill requirement: On the other hand, these new input methods bring along new requirements for text production: the ability to correctly recognize and distinguish characters. For instance, most people today use the *pinyin* input method to type Chinese. However, there are over a hundred characters with the "yi" sound. When you enter the *pinyin*, you will be given numerous candidates to pick from, ranging from 3 to 20 at a time! With mobile devices, you can finger-write characters one by one. After writing a character, rows of candidates similar in look are provided for you to pick from. Even with the voice recognition input method, the wrong characters from the conversion will need manual correction with a similar process.

Distinguishing similar characters: In addition, many characters look similar with tiny differences that may be hard for learners to recognize, e.g., 已 vs. 己, and 衤 vs. 礻 . Needless to say, skills for character recognition pose great challenges and have become more important than ever! It means that, besides building a list of radicals/components needed to learn characters more effectively, learners must also develop the sensitivity to every single detail that differentiates one character from another from the very beginning.

CHINESE WRITING BASICS

The following exercises are provided in full in the Workbook: Literacy Development.

B | 4.1) EXPERIENCE THE WRITING

In this part of the lesson you are going to work on common components/characters that look similar. Make an effort to develop a method to remember them. Many learners find it helpful to create simple hints or associations, but you may try different ways to find something that works for you.

Trace and write:

八 / 入 , 儿 / 几 , 已 / 巳 , 厂 / 广 ,
又 / 文 , 土 / 士 , 日 / 曰 , 亻 / 彳 ,
冫 / 氵 , 辶 / 廴 , 扌 / 犭 , 弋 / 戈 ,
艹 / 竹 , 木 / 禾 , 礻 / 衤

1) Identify the characters: Which answer is correct?

    1. 己   a. ji/self   b. yi/already

    2. 八   a. ru/enter   b. ba/eight

    3. 士   a. tu/earth   b. shi/scholar

    4. 文   a. wen/text, language   b. you/again

2) Name the radicals in each pair :

    a. 艹 竹   b. 扌 犭   c. 木 禾   d. 衤 礻

3) Answer the questions on radicals:

Radical: form and/or meaning

    1. Which word is likely an animal?   a. 拘   b. 狗

    2. What radical is used in this character: 聲?   a. 士   b. 土

    3. What is the word 秋 related to?   a. wood and tree   b. grains and crops

    4. Which radical should be used for clothing items?   a. 礻   b. 衤

    5. Which word is associated with ice?   a. 江   b. 凍

Character recognition

Choose the correct character for the meaning indicated.

6. **ba** (dad)   a. 八   b. 巴   c. 爸   d. 吧

7. **ta** (she)   a. 它   b. 他   c. 她   d. 塔

8. **gou** (dog)   a. 構   b. 狗   c. 溝   d. 勾

9. **yu** (language)   a. 玉   b. 與   c. 于   d. 語

10. **meimei** (sister)   a. 梅梅   b. 每每   c. 妹妹   d. 美眉

4) Typing exercises:

Type the following groups of characters using the Chinese Input Method built into your computer operating system. Enter the word in *pinyin* without tone marks. Type each item twice. For the ü sound, type v instead of u or ü.

1. ni 你   wo 我   ta 他   ta 她

2. ru 入   ren 人   ba 八   da 大

3. ji 幾   ji 已   yi 已

4. ri 日   yue 月   bai 白

5. tian 田   li 力   nan 男

6. fu 父   zi 子   nü 女   (type nv for nü)

7. jin 金   mu 木   shui 水   huo 火   tu 土

For each word, type the syllables together without breaking them into separate words.

8. baba 爸爸   mama 媽媽   meimei 妹妹   gege 哥哥

9. nüer 女兒   erzi 兒子   haizi 孩子

10. nühaier 女孩兒   nanhaier 男孩兒   xiaohaier 小孩兒

Main Units

Units 8-14 and the Concluding Unit are available in Volume 2.

我和家人

Me and My Family

The Story

As our story opens, you'll meet a Chinese student and his family . . .

FUNCTIONS & GLOBAL TASKS	CORE VOCABULARY	GRAMMAR	CULTURE
• Introducing yourself • Asking for someone's personal information • Telling about your family	• Personal pronouns • Family members • Surnames • School terms	• Personal pronouns • Equative verbs • Question words and interrogative forms	• Chinese names

Communication

Interpretive

Understand listening and reading passages related to someone's personal information.

Interpersonal

Exchange greetings and personal information.

Presentational

Introduce yourself; describe your family.

A 第一課

我叫林小東
My name is LIN Xiaodong

| A | 1.1 | 詞語預習 cíyǔ yùxí | PREVIEW THE VOCABULARY |

 Use the **online audio flashcards** to familiarize yourself with the new vocabulary in this section.

Personal Pronouns (Pron)

我	wǒ	I, me
你	nǐ	you
他/她	tā	he/she, him/her
們	men	(a suffix used to make plural forms of personal pronouns and nouns)
您	nín	you (polite form of 你)

Verbs (V)

姓	xìng	be surnamed
叫	jiào	call, be called

Nouns (N)

Names

名字	míngzi	name
林	Lín	Lin (a Chinese surname)
王	Wáng	Wang (a Chinese surname)
于	Yú	Yu (a Chinese surname)
李	Lǐ	Li (a Chinese surname)

Family

爸爸	bàba	father, dad
媽媽	māma	mother, mom

孩子	háizi	child
兒子	érzi	son
女兒	nǚ'ér	daughter

Titles

老師	lǎoshī	teacher
先生	xiānsheng	Mr., Sir
小姐	xiǎojiě	Miss, young lady

Directions

東/東方	dōng/dōngfāng	east/Orient
西/西方	xī/xīfāng	west/Occident

Adjectives (Adj)

大	dà	big
中	zhōng	middle, medium
小	xiǎo	small
對	duì	yes, right
好	hǎo	fine, good

Adverb (Adv)

不	bù	not

Question Words (QW)

誰	shéi/shuí	who, whom
誰的	shéi de	whose
什麼	shénme	what

Particles (P)

| 嗎 | ma | (used to form a simple yes/no question) |
| 的 | de | (used to indicate possession, modify a noun, etc.) |

Expressions (Exp)

你好! Nǐ hǎo!	(A common greeting) Hello! Hi!
請問…… Qǐngwèn……	Could you tell me . . . ; Excuse me . . .
您貴姓? Nín guìxìng?	What's your (family) name, please?

Structures

- 你姓什麼?
- 叫什麼名字?
- 我姓……
- 我叫……
- 你……嗎?
- 我不姓……

A 1.2 詞句聽說 cíjù tīngshuō FOCUS ON GRAMMAR

Aural-Oral Exercises: Do the online exercises to further familiarize yourself with the new vocabulary and grammar when it is used in sentences.

Main Features: This lesson introduces the basic expressions and forms used for <u>greetings and simple introductions</u>. Note that the order of <u>Chinese names</u> is different from that used in English; the last name (family name) comes first. Pay special attention to the verbs used when telling someone your surname and given name. <u>Question words and forms</u> are also presented. The word order used with these expressions is quite different from what you are used to in English.

1 Usage of 的   modifier + 的 + noun

 的 is a modifier marker. It joins the modifier with the noun that follows it. The modifier can be a noun, a pronoun, or another descriptive word. When the modifier is a pronoun or refers to a person, 的 joins it with the noun to form a possessive noun phrase indicating ownership or a certain relationship.

1) 她的爸爸媽媽, 他的孩子, Mary的老師
   tā de bàba māma   tā de háizi   ... de lǎoshī

2) 他的名字, 老師的名字
   tā de míngzi   lǎoshī de míngzi

■ 的 is commonly omitted before kinship expressions when it is preceded by a monosyllabic personal pronoun.

3) 我爸爸， 他媽媽， 她孩子
    wǒ bàba   tā māma   tā háizi

4) 我們爸爸、Mary媽媽   ✗   我們的爸爸， Mary的媽媽   ✓
                                                      wǒmen de bàba   de māma

2   Greetings   你好；title + 好

■ 你好 is perhaps the most common form of greeting when you meet someone for the first time or during daily encounters. To respond, simply say back 你好. To greet a teacher or someone of higher rank, use their title, e.g., 老師好.

Initial greeting: *Response:*

1) 你好！   →   你好！   (general greeting)
   Nǐ hǎo!   Nǐ hǎo!

2) 老師好！   →   你好！   (a student greeting a teacher)
   Láoshī hǎo!   Nǐ hǎo!

3) 王東，你好！   →   老師好！ (a teacher greeting a student)
   Wáng Dōng, nǐ hǎo!   Lǎoshī hǎo!

4) (Surname +) Title好！   →   你好！   (greeting someone of higher rank)
                hǎo!   Nǐ hǎo!

   (Surname +) Title，您好！ →   你好！
                   nín hǎo!   Nǐ hǎo!

5) 你好！   →   你好！   (greeting a peer or someone of the same rank)
   Nǐ hǎo!   Nǐ hǎo!

6) 你們好！   →   你好！   (greeting a group)
   Nǐmen hǎo!   Nǐ hǎo!

2 — 1)

2 — 2)

3   Giving one's name   姓 + family name; 叫 + full/given name

■■■ Use 姓 and 叫 together or separately when introducing yourself or someone else.

1) 我姓王，他姓林。
    Wǒ xìng Wáng, tā xìng Lín.

2) 她爸爸姓李，她媽媽姓于。
    Tā bàba xìng Lǐ,   tā māma xìng Yú.

3) 你好！我姓王，我叫王小名。 → 你好，我叫李東。
    Nǐ hǎo! Wǒ xìng Wáng, wǒ jiào Wáng Xiǎomíng.   Nǐ hǎo, wǒ jiào Lǐ Dōng.

4   Asking a yes/no question   statement + 嗎

A)   statement + 嗎

■■■ Adding 嗎 at the end of a statement turns the statement into a yes/no question. To answer positively, 對 (correct) can be used, followed by a short statement.

1) 你姓李嗎？   → 對，我姓李。
    Nǐ xìng Lǐ ma?   Duì,   wǒ xìng Lǐ.

2) 你叫李大林嗎？   → 對，我叫李大林。
    Nǐ jiào Lǐ Dàlín ma?   Duì,   wǒ jiào Lǐ Dàlín.

B) 不姓 + family name; 不叫 + full/given name

■■■ To answer in the negative, place 不 before the verb. An additional 不 (no) may be placed at the start of the sentence.

1) 你姓王嗎？   → 我不姓王，我姓李。
    Nǐ xìng Wáng ma?   Wǒ bú xìng Wáng, wǒ xìng Lǐ.

2) 他媽媽姓林嗎？   → 不，他媽媽不姓林，姓于。
    Tā māma xìng Lín ma?   Bù,   tā māma bú xìng Lín, xìng Yú.

3) 他的名字叫王子名嗎？ → 他不叫王子名，他叫王小名。
    Tā de míngzi jiào Wáng Zǐmíng ma?   Tā bú jiào Wáng Zǐmíng, tā jiào Wáng Xiǎomíng.

5   Asking someone's name using QWs   什麼，誰，誰的

■ The word order in a wh-question remains the same as in a reply statement. The answer in the reply statement will replace the question word in the question.

1) 你姓什麼？她姓什麼？她媽媽姓什麼？   (Asking for someone's family name)
Nǐ xìng shénme? Tā xìng shénme? Tā māma xìng shénme?

2) 你叫什麼名字？（你的名字叫什麼？）   (Asking for someone's full name)
Nǐ jiào shénme míngzi? (Nǐ de míngzi jiào shénme?)

3) 你的老師姓什麼？叫什麼名字？ → 我的老師姓王，叫王子名。
Nǐ de lǎoshī xìng shénme? Jiào shénme míngzi?   Wǒ de lǎoshī xìng Wáng, jiào Wáng Zǐmíng.

4) 誰姓王？ → 我的老師姓王。
Shéi xìng Wáng?   Wǒ de lǎoshī xìng Wáng.

5) 誰的名字叫王子名？ → 老師的名字叫王子名。
Shéi de míngzi jiào Wáng Zǐmíng?   Lǎoshī de míngzi jiào Wáng Zǐmíng.
（他的名字叫王子名。）
(Tā de míngzi jiào Wáng Zǐmíng.)

5 — 3)

5 — 4)

6   Polite forms   請問 + question；貴姓

A) 請問 + question

■ 請問 ("May I ask" or "Excuse me") is a polite form used to initiate an information question. A comma can be used between 請問 and the question, especially when the question is a little long.

1) 請問你叫什麼名字？ → 我叫李小東。
Qǐngwèn nǐ jiào shénme míngzi?   Wǒ jiào Lǐ Xiǎodōng.

2) 請問，你的老師姓什麼？ → 我的老師姓王。
Qǐngwèn, nǐ de lǎoshī xìng shénme?   Wǒ de lǎoshī xìng Wáng.

B) 貴姓

■ 貴姓 is more formal and is used to show respect when asking for the surname of someone older or of higher rank. It should not be used to address a person who is younger or of lower rank, to ask for the surname of a third party, or to answer the question about the surname.

1) 先生/小姐，請問您貴姓？　　　→　　　我姓王。
Xiānsheng/xiǎojiě, qǐngwèn nín guìxìng?　　　　　Wǒ xìng Wáng.

2) Asking for the surname of a peer, of someone younger, or of lower rank:

（請問）你姓什麼？　✓　　　　　　　你貴姓？　✗
(Qǐngwèn) nǐ xìng shénme?

3) Asking for the surname of a third party:

（請問）她姓什麼？　✓　　　　　　　她貴姓？　✗
(Qǐngwèn) tā xìng shénme?

4) Giving your surname in a statement or in reply:

我姓王。　　　✓　　　　　　　我貴姓王。　✗
Wǒ xìng Wáng.

7　**Telling one's name in detail /with clarification**

■ Many words in Chinese sound the same, but have different meanings and are written differently. When telling one's name, it is usually necessary to define the characters using common words or compounds.

1) 他叫王小名。 "大小" 的小， "名字" 的名。(小 as in 大小, and 名 as in 名字)
Tā jiào Wáng Xiǎomíng. "Dàxiǎo" de xiǎo, "míngzi" de míng.

2) 我叫李一林。 木子李， 一二三的一， 雙木林。
Wǒ jiào Lǐ Yìlín. Mù zǐ Lǐ, yī èr sān de yī, shuāng mù Lín.

Before viewing . . .

1) In your culture, what do high school seniors normally do in the summer after they graduate?

2) How about high school graduates in China: what do you imagine they will be busy with?

While viewing . . .

1) During your first viewing, focus on meaning.

2) During your second viewing, pay special attention to speech forms and tones.

3) Finally, practice saying the sentences by answering the questions below.

Who are these people?

What are they so excited about?

What is his name?

"我姓＿＿＿＿＿＿＿，
Wǒ xìng……

叫＿＿＿＿＿＿＿＿＿＿。"
jiào……

How does he clarify his given name the first time?

"_____ 的小，_____ 的東。"
　　　 ……de xiǎo,　　　　 ……de dōng.

How does he clarify his name "dong" the second time?

"不，_____ 的東。
Bù,　　　　 ……de dōng.

對，_____ 的東！"
Duì,　　　 ……de dōng!

 U1-A2

What can he say when he meets a peer the first time?

"你好！我_____。
Nǐ hǎo!　Wǒ……

請問，_____？"
Qǐngwèn……

What can he say when he meets a teacher the first time?

"_____！_____。

請問_____？"
Qǐngwèn……

1 **Forms and structures**
See 1.2 for more notes and examples.

1) 你好！
Nǐ hǎo!

(General greeting)

2) 我姓林，(我)叫林小東。
Wǒ xìng Lín, (wǒ) jiào Lín Xiǎodōng.

(A comma is used between the two parts.)

3) "大小"的小，"東方"的東。
"Dàxiǎo" de xiǎo, "dōngfāng" de dōng.

(Use commas to allow sentences to flow.)

Question Forms:

4) 請問，你叫什麼名字？
Qǐngwèn, nǐ jiào shénme míngzi?

(A polite way to initiate a question for information)

5) 請問您貴姓？
Qǐngwèn nín guìxìng?

(A formal way to address someone older or of higher rank)

2 **Interrogative and negative forms**

Practice the following interrogative and negative sentences.

A) 嗎 - questions

Use 不 to negate these simple "嗎- questions". Remember 不 changes to the second tone when followed by the fourth tone.

1) 他姓王嗎？   _____

2) 他叫王一東嗎？   _____

3) 你的名字叫林小東嗎？   _____

B) More question words: 什麼 (what)，誰 (who)，誰的 (whose)

Change the following statements into questions using the question words provided.
Note that the word order remains unchanged.

1) <u>他</u>不姓李。 　　　　　(誰)　_____

2) 他姓<u>林</u>。 　　　　　　(什麼)　_____

3) <u>他</u>叫林小東。 　　　　(誰)　_____

4) <u>小東的</u>媽媽不姓林。 (誰的)　_____

1 **Pair work**

Take turns assuming the roles in the pictures and role play a conversation with your partner. Greet each other and exchange names. Use the polite form if necessary.

Note:
- A person's title is placed after his/her surname.
- In Chinese it is considered rude to ask a person's given name if the person is a teacher, or someone older or of higher rank.

Greeting:

你好！/ 您好！
Nǐ hǎo! / Nín hǎo!

老師好！/ 王老師好！
Lǎoshī hǎo! / Wáng lǎoshī hǎo!

王先生(王小姐、王媽媽)好！
Wáng xiānsheng (Wáng xiǎojiě, Wáng māma) hǎo!

Asking someone's name:

請問您貴姓?
Qǐngwèn nín guìxìng?

請問你姓什麼?
Qǐngwèn nǐ xìng shénme?

請問，你叫什麼名字?
Qǐngwèn, nǐ jiào shénme míngzi?

請問，你姓王嗎?
Qǐngwèn, nǐ xìng Wáng ma?

王小姐, 22
Wáng xiǎojiě

Lín lǎoshī, 25
林老師

李東, 19
Lǐ Dōng

于先生, 40
Yú xiānsheng

王媽媽, 50
Wáng māma

Frank, 20

2 Interview and report

1) **Interview:** Move around the classroom and speak to at least two classmates. Greet the classmates and ask and answer questions about their names. Be prepared to share the information with the class.

2) **Report:** The teacher will ask students their names or their classmates' names.

3) **Quiz:** The teacher may quiz students on the information shared in the reports, e.g.,

誰姓……? 誰的名字叫……? 他姓……，對嗎?

Students are expected to answer questions and correct the information if it is wrong, e.g.,

他不姓…… / 不叫……

A 1.6 語法鞏固 yǔfǎ gǒnggù　　　**REINFORCE THE GRAMMAR**

🌐 These exercises are also available online with automatic feedback.

Question Words: 什麼 (what)，誰 (who)，誰的 (whose)

1 Replace the underlined word in each sentence
Use an appropriate question word listed above.

1) 我的老師姓<u>李</u>。　→　你的老師姓_____?

2) <u>我的老師</u>姓李。　→　_____姓李?

3) <u>我的</u>老師姓李。　→　_____老師姓李?

4) <u>他的</u>名字叫王東。　→　_____名字叫王東?

5) 他的名字叫<u>王東</u>。　→　他的名字叫_____?

2 Give the Chinese equivalent for each question
Pay attention to the Chinese structures and avoid word-for-word translation. Pinyin may be used.

1) What's your last name?　→　_____

2) What's his name? (full name)　→　_____

3) Who is (called) Lin Xiaodong?　→　_____

4) Is your name Lin Xiaodong?　→　_____

5) Whose last name is Yu?　→　_____

A 1.7 聽答對話 tīngdá duìhuà　　　**LET'S CHAT**

🌐 In this listening-speaking activity you'll be asked to answer questions about the **video** segment as well as about **yourself.** You may be asked to record and submit your answers to the teacher.

UNIT 1

B 第二課

我 的 家 人
My family

B 1.8 詞語預習 cíyǔ yùxí

PREVIEW THE VOCABULARY

 Use the **online audio flashcards** to familiarize yourself with the new vocabulary in this section.

Nouns (N)

Family

家	jiā	family
人	rén	person
哥哥	gēge	older brother
姐姐	jiějie	older sister
弟弟	dìdi	younger brother
妹妹	mèimei	younger sister
男孩	nánhái	boy
女孩	nǚhái	girl
兄弟姐妹	xiōngdì jiěmèi	siblings

School

學校	xuéxiào	school
大學	dàxué	college, university
中學	zhōngxué	secondary school
高中	gāozhōng	high school
小學	xiǎoxué	elementary school

年級	niánjí	grade, year
學生	xuésheng	student
小學生	xiǎoxuéshēng	elementary school student
中學生	zhōngxuéshēng	secondary school student
高中生	gāozhōngshēng	high school student
大學生	dàxuéshēng	college student
同學	tóngxué	schoolmate, classmate
新生	xīnshēng	new student, freshman

Directions

南/南方	nán/nánfāng	south
北/北方	běi/běifāng	north

Verbs (V)

是	shì	(verb to be) is, am, are
有	yǒu	have, possess

Adverbs (Adv)

也	yě	also
沒	méi	(negative of 有) not having, be without

Question Word (QW)

幾	jǐ	how many, which (grade, etc)

Measure Words (M)

個	gè	(generic measure word used for concrete nouns)
口	kǒu	(used for family members)

Conjunctions (Conj)

和	hé	and
可是	kěshì	but

Structures

- 誰是我爸爸?
- 她是誰?
- 他(不)是⋯⋯
- 有/沒有⋯⋯
- 有幾個?

B | 1.9) 詞句聽説 cíjù tīngshuō   **FOCUS ON GRAMMAR**

Aural-Oral Exercises: Do the online exercises to further familiarize yourself with the new vocabulary and grammar when it is used in sentences.

Main Features: In this lesson we'll expand on basic personal information to include <u>family and school information</u>. Two important verbs - 是 (to be) and 有 (to have) are introduced to help build your personal profile. You'll notice that 是, different from 叫, is used to confirm or identify someone's name. You'll also learn a new <u>question word</u> for numbers and quantity.

---

1 Terms relating to school and question words

A) 什麼

1) 什麼學校? → 小學, 中學, 高中, 大學
Shénme xuéxiào?   xiǎoxué, zhōngxué, gāozhōng, dàxué

2) 什麼學生? → 小學生, 中學生, 高中生, 大學生, 大學新生
Shénme xuésheng?   xiǎoxuéshēng, zhōngxuéshēng, gāozhōngshēng, dàxuéshēng, dàxué xīnshēng

B) 幾

 幾 is a question word used to ask for information represented by numbers. It is also a number word itself (several, a few). When 幾 is used as a question word, always end the sentence with a question mark.

1) 幾年級? → 一年級, 二年級; 一年級的學生, 大學一年級的學生
Jǐ niánjí?   yī niánjí,   èr niánjí;   yì niánjí de xuésheng, dàxué yì niánjí de xuésheng
Which grade?

2) 幾個同學？ ➡ 兩個同學，三個高中同學，四個大學同學
Jǐ gè tóngxué?　　liǎng gè tóngxué, sān gè gāozhōng tóngxué, sì gè dàxué tóngxué
How many classmates?

3) 幾個老師？ ➡ 四個老師， 四個大學老師；王老師，李老師，
Jǐ gè lǎoshī?　　sì gè lǎoshī,　 sì gè dàxué lǎoshī,　 Wáng lǎoshī, Lǐ lǎoshī,

林老師，于老師
Lín lǎoshī,　 Yú lǎoshī

4) 幾個新生？ ➡ 兩個新生；兩個大學一年級(的)新生
Jǐ gè xīnshēng?　　liǎng gè xīnshēng; liǎng gè dàxué yì niǎnjí (de) xīnshēng

---

2 | **Giving one's identity**　　　　　person + 是 + identity (name, occupation)

1) 他是一個大學生，是一個大一的新生；李老師是一個中學老師。
Tā shì yí gè dàxuéshēng,　 shì yí gè dàyī de xīnshēng;　 Lǐ lǎoshī shì yí gè zhōngxué lǎoshī.

2) 他是幾年級的學生？ ➡ 不是，他是大學二年級的學生(大二的學生)。
Tā shì jǐ niǎnjí de xuésheng?　　Bú shì, tā shì dàxué èr niǎnjí de xuésheng (dà'èr de xuésheng).

是新生嗎？
Shì xīnshēng ma?

3) 李老師是大學老師嗎？ ➡ 不是，他是中學老師。
Lǐ lǎoshī shì dàxué lǎoshī ma?　　Bú shì,　 tā shì zhōngxué lǎoshī.

▰ Note that 誰 is in the final position of the sentence when a person's identity information is asked for.

4) 他是誰？ ➡ 他叫王小名，他是一個大學生。
Tā shì shéi?　　Tā jiào Wáng Xiǎomíng, tā shì yí gè dà xuéshēng.

5) 王小名是誰？ ➡ 王小名是一個大學生。
Wáng Xiǎomíng shì shéi?　　Wáng Xiǎomíng shì yí gè dà xuéshēng.

2 – 4)

3   Confirming one's identity   personal pron + 是 + full or given name

■■■ 是 is not normally used when you give your name. Rather, it is used to confirm or identify someone's name, assuming the person's identity is known.

1) 誰是王小名？   →   我是王小名。(Identifying 王小名 from a group of people)
    Shéi shì Wáng Xiǎomíng?   Wǒ shì Wáng Xiǎomíng.

2) 你是李小名嗎？   →   不是，我是王小名，不是李小名。
    Nǐ shì Lǐ Xiǎomíng ma?   Bú shì,   wǒ shì Wáng Xiǎomíng, bú shì Lǐ Xiǎomíng.

3 – 1)

4   Explaining one's relationship to another person   person + 是 + relationship

1) 小西的爸爸，小東的妹妹，小南的老師，小北的同學，王老師的學生
    Xiǎoxī de bàba,   Xiǎodōng de mèimei, Xiǎonán de lǎoshī, Xiǎoběi de tóngxué, Wáng lǎoshī de xuésheng

2) 小西是小北的妹妹嗎？   →   不是，小西是姐姐，小北是妹妹。
    Xiǎoxī shì Xiǎoběi de mèimei ma?   Bú shì,   Xiǎoxī shì jiějie,   Xiǎoběi shì mèimei.

3) 李先生是小西的什麼人？   →   不是，李先生是小西的爸爸。
    Lǐ xiānsheng shì Xiǎoxī de shénme rén?   Bú shì,   Lǐ xiānsheng shì Xiǎoxī de bàba.

    是小西的老師嗎？
    Shì Xiǎoxī de lǎoshī ma?

■■■ Note that 誰 is in the final position of the sentence when a person's identity information is asked for.

4) 李小西是誰？   →   李小西是李先生的女兒，她是一個高中生。
    Lǐ Xiǎoxī shì shéi?   Lǐ Xiǎoxī shì Lǐ xiānshēng de nǚ'ér, tā shì yí gè gāozhōngshēng.

5 Telling about one's family   我有……；我家有__口人

有 suggests existence, condition, status, or possession. The negative form is 没有 (méiyǒu).

1) 我家有五口人：爸爸、媽媽、哥哥、姐姐和我。
   Wǒ jiā yǒu wǔ kǒu rén: bàba,   māma,   gēge,   jiějie hé wǒ.

2) 她有一個弟弟和兩個妹妹。
   Tā yǒu yí gè dìdi hé liǎng gè mèimei.

3) 我没有弟弟妹妹。
   Wǒ méiyǒu dìdi mèimei.

4) 她家有幾口人?   →   有五口人。
   Tā jiā yǒu jǐ kǒu rén?   Yǒu wǔ kǒu rén.

5 — 1)

6 Word usage examples   和，也，可是

A) 和 (and)

和 joins short parallel pronouns or noun phrases. It does NOT join clauses or introduce a sentence. Also note that in the "A 和 B" form, the first-person pronoun (我) normally comes first.

1) 我和他，我和我媽媽   (Uncommon: 他和我，我媽媽和我)
   wǒ hé tā,   wǒ hé wǒ māma

2) 爸爸和媽媽，哥哥、姐姐和妹妹；我有一個哥哥和兩個妹妹。
   bàba hé māma,   gēge,   jiějie,   hé mèimei;   Wǒ yǒu yí gè gēge hé liǎng gè mèimei.

3) 我有一個哥哥，没有姐姐。 ✔   我有一個哥哥和我没有姐姐。 ✘
   Wǒ yǒu yí gè gēge,   méiyǒu jiějie.

6 — 3)

B) 也 (*also*)

▬▬ 也 is an adverb that always appears <u>before</u> a verb, an adverb, or an adjective phrase. Often the verb after 也 duplicates the verb in the first part of the sentence.

1) 她是一個學生，也是一個老師。 (A comma is normally used.)
   Tā shì yí gè xuésheng, yě shì yí gè lǎoshī.

2) 她有一個哥哥，我也有一個哥哥。 (……<u>也我有</u>…… ✗)
   Tā yǒu yí gè gēge, wǒ yě yǒu yí gè gēge.

3) 我沒有弟弟，也沒有妹妹。 (我沒有弟弟<u>和</u>我沒有妹妹。 ✗)
   Wǒ méiyǒu dìdi, yě méiyǒu mèimei.

C) 可是 (*but*)

▬▬ 可是 joins two parts of a sentence following a comma.

1) 我有一個哥哥，可是沒有姐姐。 (A comma is normally used before 可是.)
   Wǒ yǒu yí gè gēge, kěshì méiyǒu jiějie.

2) 她是一個老師，可是她也是一個學生。
   Tā shì yí gè lǎoshī, kěshì tā yě shì yí gè xuésheng.

6 – C) – 2)

Before viewing . . .

1) Recall the previous scenes, do you remember how many family members Xiaodong has?

2) Do you think all the members have the same family name?

While viewing . . .

1) During your first viewing, focus on meaning.

2) During your second viewing, pay special attention to speech forms and tones.

3) Finally, practice saying the sentences by answering the questions below.

▶ U1-B1

小東是學生嗎?
Xiǎodōng shì xuéshēng ma?

"我是＿＿＿＿＿＿＿＿。"
Wǒ shì……

他家有幾口人?
Tā jiā yǒu jǐ kǒu rén?

"我們家有＿＿＿＿＿＿＿＿。"
Wǒmen jiā yǒu……

誰是他爸爸?　爸爸叫什麼名字?
Shéi shì tā bàba?　Bàba jiào shénme míngzi?

"他是我爸爸, 他叫＿＿＿＿＿＿＿。"
Tā shì wǒ bàba,　tā jiào……

媽媽姓林嗎?
Māma xìng Lín ma?

"她＿＿＿＿＿林, 她姓＿＿＿＿＿。"
Tā……　　　　Lín,　tā xìng……

她是誰？是小東的姐姐嗎？
Tā shì shéi? Shì Xiǎodōng de jiějie ma?

"我姐姐？不，她＿＿＿＿＿＿＿＿＿＿，
Wǒ jiějie?　Bù,　tā……

她是＿＿＿＿＿＿＿＿＿＿。"
tā shì……

▶ U1-B2

她叫什麼名字？
Tā jiào shénme míngzi?

"我叫林小南。小是＿＿＿＿＿＿＿＿，
Wǒ jiào Lín Xiǎonán. Xiǎo shì……

南是＿＿＿＿＿＿＿＿＿＿。"
nán shì……

她是學生嗎？是幾年級的學生？
Tā shì xuésheng ma? Shì jǐ niánjí de xuésheng?

"我是＿＿＿＿＿＿＿＿＿＿＿＿。"
Wǒ shì……

小南有幾個哥哥？
Xiǎonán yǒu jǐ gè gēge?

"我有＿＿＿＿＿＿，名字叫＿＿＿＿＿＿。"
Wǒ yǒu……　　　　míngzi jiào……

小南有姐姐、弟弟和妹妹嗎？
Xiǎonán yǒu jiějie,　dìdi hé mèimei ma?

"我＿＿＿＿＿＿＿＿＿＿，
Wǒ……

也＿＿＿＿＿＿＿＿＿＿＿＿＿。"
yě……

1 **Forms and structures**
See 1.9 for more notes and examples.

1) 我是大學新生。
Wǒ shì dàxué xīnshēng.

(是 is used for giving one's identity.)

2) 我叫林小南，小是 "大小" 的小，
Wǒ jiào Lín Xiǎonán, xiǎo shì "dàxiǎo" de xiǎo,

南是 "南方" 的南。
nán shì "nánfāng" de nán.

(The introduction of the given name can be shortened: 大小的小，南方的南.)

3) 我是高二的學生。
Wǒ shì gāo èr de xuésheng.

(是一個 can also be used.)

■ Note the use of the comma and the omission of the pronoun in the second part of a sentence.

1) 她是我媽媽，她不姓林，(她)姓于。
Tā shì wǒ māma, tā bú xìng Lín, (tā) xìng Yú.

(她 can be omitted in the final clause.)

2) 她不是我姐姐，(她)是我妹妹。
Tā bú shì wǒ jiějie, (tā) shì wǒ mèimei.

(Use a comma to separate the clauses.)

3) 他也是學生，可是(他)不是高中生，
Tā yě shì xuésheng, kěshì (tā) bú shì gāozhōngshēng,

是大學生。
shì dàxuéshēng.

(The pronoun 他 can be omitted after the first clause.)

■ Note the use of the Nu-M-N form.

1) 我們家有四口人。
Wǒmen jiā yǒu sì kǒu rén.

(口 is a measure word for the number of family members.)

2) 我有一個哥哥。
Wǒ yǒu yí gè gēge.

(個 is a generic measure word for people.)

3) 我沒有姐姐，也沒有弟弟和妹妹。
Wǒ méiyǒu jiějie, yě méiyǒu dìdi hé mèimei.

(Measure words are not used when there is no number. 也 must be followed by a verb, which is often a repeated verb.)

■ Note the different positions of the question word 誰.

1) 誰是我爸爸?
Shéi shì wǒ bàba?

(誰 in front of the sentence asks for an identification, i.e, who among these people is . . . ?)

2) 她是誰?
Tā shì shéi?

(誰 at the end of the sentence asks for a person's identity, such as name, occupation, etc.)

2 Interrogative and negative forms 　　是，有，幾

Practice the following interrogative and negative sentences. Note that the word order in a QW-queston (wh-question) remains the same as in a statement.

1)　林小東是高二的學生嗎？

_____
（大一）

2)　小東有一個姐姐嗎？

_____
（沒有）

3)　小南有姐姐、弟弟和妹妹嗎？

_____
（也沒有）

4)　小東家有幾口人？有五口人嗎？

_____
（四口）

5)　小東有幾個妹妹？有兩個嗎？

_____
（一個）

3 Story narration

Note the use of punctuation marks.

林小東是一個大學新生。他家有四口人：爸爸、媽媽、他，
Lín Xiǎodōng shì yí gè dàxué xīnshēng. Tā jiā yǒu sì kǒu rén:　bàba、　māma、　tā,

還有一個妹妹。他爸爸叫林子新，媽媽姓于，妹妹叫林小南。
hái yǒu yí gè mèimei.　Tā bàba jiào Lín Zǐxīn,　　māma xìng Yú,　mèimei jiào Lín Xiǎonán.

小南也是學生，可是她不是大學生，她是一個高二的學生。
Xiǎonán yě shì xuésheng, kěshì tā bú shì dàxuéshēng,　tā shì yí gè gāo èr de xuésheng.

小南有一個哥哥，可是沒有姐姐，也沒有弟弟和妹妹。
Xiǎonán yǒu yí gè gēge,　　kěshì méiyǒu jiějie,　yě méiyǒu dìdi hé mèimei.

1 Pair work

Ask your partner questions about the people in the pictures: **name**, **relationship**, and **occupation** or **status** of each person. In each question, use a question word or question form:

什麼，誰，誰的，幾，嗎

Wang Xiaoxi   Wang Xiaonan   Wang Xiaobei

1) [person] 的[姐姐/弟弟]叫 X 名字？
2) [person]是 X 年級的學生？
3) X 是[大二/高二]的學生？
4) [person] 是 X 的[弟弟/妹妹/姐姐]？
5) [person] 也是……嗎？
6) [person] 有……嗎？

Li Xueming   Wang Lin   Li Xiaoming

1) X 的名字叫[李學名/王林/李小名]？
2) [person]有 X 個孩子？
3) [爸爸/媽媽/兒子]的名字叫 X？
4) X 是[大學老師/中學老師]？
5) [person] 是 X 年級的學生？
6) [person]是 X 的[兒子/爸爸/媽媽]？

2 Tell about a family

1) **Family Profile:** Fill in the table with real or fictional information. (Pinyin or English is allowed).

	Family name	Given name	Occupation
Father			
Mother			
Child 1			
Child 2			

2) **Presentation:** In groups of three or four, present your profile to the group in 4-5 sentences, including at least one negative sentence.

Hints: Pick one family member as a primary person and explain the relationship of other members with him or her. You may begin your presentation using one of the following:

我有一個同學，他/她的名字叫……

[name]家有[四]口人，……

3) **Quiz:** End your presentation by asking 3-4 quiz questions to the group.

For example:

誰姓……? 誰的名字叫……?

[name] 是誰? 是誰的哥哥? 是幾年級的學生?

[name] 家有幾口人? 他有兄弟姐妹嗎?

B | 1.13 語法鞏固 yǔfǎ gǒnggù REINFORCE THE GRAMMAR

These exercises are also available online with automatic feedback.

Question Words: 什麼(what)，誰(who)，誰的(whose)，幾(how many)

1 **Replace the underlined word in each sentence**
Use an appropriate question word listed above.

1) 她是大學二年級的學生。 → 她是大學_____年級的學生?

2) 她有三個哥哥。 → 她有_____個哥哥?

3) 她的一個哥哥也是大學生。 → _____也是大學生?

4) 她還有一個妹妹。 → 她還有一個_____?

5) 她沒有姐姐和弟弟。 → _____沒有姐姐和弟弟?

2 **Give the Chinese equivalent for each question**
Pay attention to the Chinese structures and avoid word-for-word translation. Pinyin may be used.

1) Who is he? → _____

2) Is he your older brother? → _____

3) Do you have sisters? → _____

4) How many sisters do you have? → _____

5) Who also isn't a college student? → _____

B | 1.14 聽答對話 tīngdá duìhuà LET'S CHAT

In this listening-speaking activity you'll be asked to answer questions about the **video** segment as well as about **yourself.** You may be asked to record and submit your answers to the teacher.

CHINESE NAMES

Chinese names are customarily written with the family name first. General Yang Liwei (楊利偉), for example, China's first man in space, would be General Yang, not General Liwei. Most Chinese family names consist of one syllable. There are also a few two-syllable names like Ouyang (歐陽) and Situ (司徒), but these are not common. Since a syllable is represented in writing by a single character (again, with very few exceptions), most surnames are single-character surnames.

Given names, which follow family names, often consist of two characters; thus, most Chinese names consist of three syllables (and three characters), e.g., Deng Xiaoping (鄧小平). However, there is a growing trend for more and more Chinese to use given names of only one syllable, so that a significant number of people have names consisting of two syllables, the first being the family name and the second the given name. Basketball star Yao Ming (姚明) typifies this trend.

Most English given names, like Katherine and William, are not commonly used meaningful words. Chinese names, however, are often meaningful, and when parents choose a name for their child, they prefer those that are auspicious or are somehow related to the child's life or situation. Thus, the word **míng** (明), meaning "bright," is a common element in boys' names. Words widely used in females' names include **qín** (琴), meaning "a stringed musical instrument," and **tíng** (婷), meaning "graceful."

In the past, parents often gave their children, particularly their sons, names that would identify their generation. That is, of the two elements in a son's given name, one would typically be shared by all his brothers—and even by those of his cousins related to him through his father's side. Characters in Ba Jin's 1933 novel *Family* illustrate this.

The novel takes place during the dramatic events of the May Fourth Movement and tells the story of China's modernizing youth in rebellion against their traditional parents. The central characters in the novel are three brothers of the Gao (高) family; they are named Gao Juexin (高覺信), Gao Juemin (高覺民), and Gao Juehui (高覺慧). The three parts of their names serve to identify them by family, by generation, and as unique individuals within a given family and generation. Family names in China are inherited from one's father, so the boys shared their family name with their father and his brothers, but, of course, not their generation name. The father and his brothers had the generation name of Ke (克), and their names were Gao Keming (高克明), Gao Ke'an (高克安), and Gao Keding (高克定).

The use of generation names in traditional China reflected cultural concerns with the individual male's place within his lineage. Generation names were not as common for females, since a daughter would leave her own lineage at marriage and join her husband's family; she would add her husband's surname to her own. A woman named Gao Xiuying (高秀英) would become Li Gao Xiuying (李高秀英) once she

married to Mr. Li. This practice, however, has become almost obsolete on the mainland, although it can still be found in Hong Kong, Taiwan, and Macau.

Ba Jin (巴金) is actually a pen name, the original name of this author being Li Yaotang (李尧棠). This highlights another common Chinese tradition: the custom among prominent men of changing their names at life milestones or for particular sociopolitical reasons, as was the case for the Nobel Literature laureate Mo Yan (莫言).

Confucius

Ba Jin

Mo Yan

Yao Ming

Jeremy Lin

DISCUSSION QUESTIONS

1. If you know any Chinese friends, find out who chose their name or names for them (it isn't always the parents). Then find out if there is a story behind their names. You might also ask them if they had any nicknames, either in school or in the household.

2. Korean culture has borrowed very heavily from Chinese culture over the centuries. Even Korean names are Korean-language versions of Chinese words or names. The popular Korean name Kim, for example, comes from the Chinese word Jīn (金) meaning "gold" or "metal." Im is a Korean surname that means "forest" and is simply the Korean version of the Chinese name Lín (林). If you are acquainted with any Korean friends, ask them if in their family the brothers and/or sisters share a common "generation name."

FOR FURTHER RESEARCH

1. Confucius is the most famous Chinese person who ever lived, yet "Confucius" is not a Chinese name. What was the real name of the philosopher we call Confucius? What was his family name?

2. As mentioned above, Mo Yan, the winner of the 2012 Nobel Prize for Literature, is not this writer's real time. What is his real time?

3. The Chinese-American basketball star Jeremy Lin was born to a Taiwanese immigrant family. He and his two brothers all have Chinese names. What is Jeremy Lin's Chinese name? What is the generation name of him and his brothers?

1.16 主課復習 zhǔkè fùxí　　　　**REVIEW THE STORY**

Read the following passages as fast as you can. Follow these steps:

1) Do not stop to check the meaning of words you don't recognize. Mark them and keep reading.
2) Read the passage again and guess the meaning of the marked words on a separate piece of paper.
3) Finally, look up the words in a dictionary or the vocabulary index and verify their meanings.

你好！我姓林，叫林小東。"大小"的小，"東方"的東。請問你叫什麼名字？

她姓林，叫林小南，小是"大小"的小，南是"南方"的南。她是高中二年級的學生。她有一個哥哥，名字叫林小東。他也是學生，可是不是高中生，是大學生。她沒有姐姐，也沒有弟弟和妹妹。

他們家有四口人：爸爸姓林，叫林子新。媽媽姓于，叫于南。他們有兩個孩子，一個兒子和一個女兒。兒子小東是大學一年級的新生，女兒小南是高中二年級的學生。

Quickly provide the Chinese equivalents for the following phrases and sentences. Do not translate them word for word.

1 **Greetings:** How to greet people appropriately

You want to greet . . .   *In Chinese you say . . .*

1) a teacher without knowing his/her name.   _____

2) a teacher whose last name is Wang.   _____

3) someone you are unfamiliar with.   _____

4) an older person or a person of higher rank, known or unknown to you.   _____

5) a group of people   _____

2 **Giving information:** How to give your or someone else's name

You want to . . .

1) introduce yourself or someone for the first time.   _____

2) give your or someone else's full name as new information.   _____

3) give your name, assuming your identify is known.   _____

3 **Asking for information:** How to ask someone's name

You want to ask . . .

1) the name of an older person.   _____

2) the name of a teacher.   _____

3) the name of a teacher (by asking someone else),   _____

4) the full name of a peer (politely).   _____

5) the last name of a person (politely).   _____

6) the full name of a person younger or of lower rank.   _____

4 **Question Words:** Which question word should be used and where should it be placed?
(什麼, 誰, 誰的, 幾, 嗎)

Questions to be formulated: *Corresponding answers:*

1) _____   對，她姓王。

2) _____   她叫王林。

3) _____   她叫王林。

4) _____   她家有五口人。

5) _____   她没有妹妹。

6) _____   王東是王林的哥哥。

7) _____   王新是王林的姐姐。

1 **Correct the sentences**

Identify the error(s) in each sentence and then rewrite the sentence correctly.

1) 請問他貴姓? ✘

_____
(What's his last name?)

2) 他/我貴姓王。 ✘

_____
(His/My last name is Wang.)

3) 什麼是你的名字? ✘

_____
(What's your name?)

4) 誰的爸爸是他? ✘

_____
(Whose dad is he?)

5) 幾個哥哥她有? ✘

_____
(How many older brothers does she have?)

6) 誰是他? ✘

_____
(Who is he?)

7) 他不有姐姐妹妹。 ✘

_____
(He doesn't have any sisters.)

2 **Choose the appropriate answer**

1) 她是大學生_____我也是大學生。   a. 和   b. ，(comma)

2) 他有一個哥哥_____一個妹妹。   a. 也   b. 和

3) 他有一個哥哥，_____有一個妹妹。   a. 也   b. 和

4) 他有哥哥，_____沒有姐姐。   a. 也   b. 可是

The following activities allow you to further practice your interpretive, interpersonal, and presentational communication skills in a meaningful, communicative context.

Interpretive

1 **Listening** （U1.19_1：我叫Katie）

Take notes as you listen to the audio clip. Then tell whether each statement is true (T) or false (F).

True or False?

1) ☐ The girl's name is not Chinese.

2) ☐ The girl is a first-year college student.

3) ☐ She has an older brother, who is a college junior.

4) ☐ Her younger sister is going to a small school.

5) ☐ Her family has three more children.

2 **Reading**

Read the passage and answer the questions that follow:

我姓方(Fāng)，是一個大學老師。我有三個孩子，一個是女兒，兩個是兒子。老大是女兒，名字叫李芳(Lǐ Fāng)，是中學生。老二和老三都是兒子，哥哥叫李新，上小學四年級，弟弟叫李南，上小學二年級。

© Cengage Learning 2015

1) What is this person's identity?

    a. a college student

    b. a high school teacher

    c. a college teacher

2) What is the person's role in the family?

    a. mother

    b. father

    c. foster mother

3) How many children does this person have? Are they boys or girls?

    a. three; a girl and two boys

    b. two; a daughter and a son

    c. three; a boy and two girls

4) What is the children's family name?

    a. Li

    b. Fang

    c. Nan

5) What does "老大" refer to?

    a. the biggest child

    b. the oldest child

    c. the tallest child

6) Regarding the child named 李芳, which description is correct?

    a. a boy who is a fourth-grader in elementary school; his given name is Fang.

    b. a girl who goes to middle school and whose given name is Li.

    c. a girl who goes to middle school and whose family name is Li.

7) Which one of the following describes the child named 李新?

    a. the youngest son, who is a second-grader and has a brother and a sister.

    b. the oldest child, a boy, who goes to middle school and has a sister and brother.

    c. a second child, a boy, who is a fourth-grader and who has an older sister and a younger brother.

Interpersonal

3 Speaking

1) Speak with at least three classmates and exchange your personal information including your Chinese name. Introduce two of them to others.

2) Visit the Chinese Students' Club in your school and introduce yourself in Chinese. Ask for the members' names.

3) Greet a Chinese international student when you see him or her on campus. Try to make conversation by exchanging names and other personal information.

Presentational

4 Speaking

1) **Self-introduction:** Introduce yourself to the class.

2) **Show and tell:** Show some photos of your family and friends (e.g. siblings, former classmates), and tell about them to the class or to a small group.

5 Writing

Personal profile: Create a personal profile online in Chinese through a blog or other social media. (You'll use it to update your personal information and write journals later on.)

City Highlights

Beijing 北京

Temple of Heaven

National Stadium (also known as the Birds Nest)

UNIT 2

第 二 單 元

認 識 新 朋 友

Meeting New Friends

The Story

Who is Xiaodong going to meet on his first day at school? While Xiaodong is arriving at his college, Katie is arriving in China and meeting her host family . . .

© Cengage Learning 2015

FUNCTIONS & GLOBAL TASKS	CORE VOCABULARY	GRAMMAR	CULTURE
• Introducing yourself • Exchanging personal information • Describing your language ability • Telling where you live	• Cities and countries • Dorm furniture • Nationalities • Languages • Names and social titles	• Pronouns/Specifiers • Place Words • Verb 在 • Yes/No and alternative questions • Auxiliary Verb 會 • Adverb 都	• Forms of address

© Cengage Learning 2015

© Cengage Learning 2015

© Cengage Learning 2015

Communication

Interpretive

Understand listening and reading passages related to where one is originally from, where one's home is, and where one currently lives.

Interpersonal

Talk about your nationality, language skills, and your school.

Presentational

Describe yourself by providing basic information.

A 第一課 這是我的宿舍
This is my dorm room

A 2.1 詞語預習 cíyǔ yùxí — PREVIEW THE VOCABULARY

 Use the **online audio flashcards** to familiarize yourself with the new vocabulary in this section.

Pronouns (Pron)/Specifiers (Sp)

這	zhè/zhèi	this
那	nà/nèi	that

Place Words (PW)

Generic

這裡/這兒	zhèlǐ/zhèr	here
那裡/那兒	nàlǐ/nàr	there
本地	běndì	local, this locality
外地	wàidì	a place other than where one is

Proper Names

北京	Běijīng	Beijing
臺北	Táiběi	Taipei
廣州	Guǎngzhōu	Guangzhou
廣東	Guǎngdōng	Guangdong (Canton)
上海	Shànghǎi	Shanghai
南京	Nánjīng	Nanjing
加州	Jiāzhōu	California

Measure Words (M)

棟	dòng	(used for buildings)
張	zhāng	(used for tables, paper, beds, etc.)
把	bǎ	(used for chairs, umbrellas, etc.)

Nouns (N)

			M
朋友	péngyou	friend	個
室友	shìyǒu	roommate	個
號	hào	number (for rooms, phones, etc.)	
宿舍	sùshè	dormitory	
樓	lóu	storied building	棟
床	chuáng	bed	張
桌子	zhuōzi	table	張
椅子	yǐzi	chair	把
書架	shūjià	bookcase	個

Verbs (V)

在	zài	be (at a place)
住(在)	zhù (zài)	reside, live (at)

Question Words (QW)		
哪	nǎ, něi	which
哪裡/哪兒	nǎlǐ/nǎr	where, which place

Conjunction (Conj)		
還是	háishi	or

Adverbs (Adv)		
都	dōu	all, both
還	hái	also, still

Expressions (Exp)	
你是哪裡人/哪兒人？ Nǐ shì nǎlǐ rén / nǎr rén?	Where are you from?
你是哪裡/哪兒來的？ Nǐ shì nǎlǐ / nǎr lái de?	Where do you come from?

Structures

- 是哪裡(哪兒)人
- 是哪裡(哪兒)來的
- 這是……
- 家在……
- 住在……
- 都是……
- 是……還是……

 Aural-Oral Exercises: Do the online exercises to further familiarize yourself with the new vocabulary and grammar when it is used in sentences.

Main Features: As you have seen in the vocabulary section, a new category called <u>Place Words</u> (PW) is introduced in this unit. In this lesson we will focus on expressions and forms of <u>telling about a place</u>: where one is originally from, where one's home is, and where one currently lives. Along with the listening-speaking exercises, you'll continue to learn corresponding <u>question words and forms</u> as well as new <u>adverbs</u>. To begin, we'll first practice the words essential for our questions and statements, i.e., <u>這</u>,<u>那</u> and <u>哪</u>.

1   **Introducing/Identifying people and things**

zhè nà
這/那+是……
This/That is . . .

■■■ The pronoun in this form, 這/那, normally appears at the front of the sentence as a stand-alone element (the subject).

1) 這是我哥哥，這是我的宿舍，那是我的床，那是我(的)室友的桌子
   Zhè shì wǒ gēge, zhè shì wǒ de sùshè, nà shì wǒ de chuáng,nà shì wǒ (de) shìyǒu de zhuōzi

2) 這是誰? 是你哥哥嗎?
   Zhè shì shéi? Shì nǐ gēge ma?
   → 不是，那是我哥哥。
     Bú shì, nà shì wǒ gēge.

3) 這是誰的宿舍?
   Zhè shì shéi de sùshè?
   → 這是王小名的宿舍。
     Zhè shì Wáng Xiǎomíng de sùshè.

2 Specifying people and things

這/那 + Nu-M-N
this/these, or that/those + noun

▬ When 這/那/哪 is followed by a noun / quantified noun phrase (Number-Measure-Noun), it acts as a specifier and is often pronounced zhèi / nèi / něi in everyday speech. When the noun is singular, the number "一" is usually omitted, e.g., 那(一)个人, unless "一" is emphasized.

A) 這/那 + Nu-M-N

1) 這(一)個朋友，這兩個朋友，那(一)棟樓，那幾棟樓 (幾 as a vague number "a few")
zhèi (yí) gè péngyou, zhèi liǎng gè péngyou, nèi (yí) dòng lóu, nèi jǐ dòng lóu

B) 哪 + Nu-M-N

▬ 哪 is a question word meaning "which".

1) 哪個朋友？ 那個朋友； 哪兩棟樓？ 那兩棟樓 (The tones change the meaning.)
něi gè péngyou? nèi gè péngyou; něi liǎng dòng lóu? nèi liǎng dòng lóu

C) 這/那 + (Nu)-M-N

▬ Note the measure word can stand for the understood noun to avoid repetition.

1) 那兩棟樓是學生宿舍嗎？   →   這棟是宿舍，那棟不是。 (樓 is omitted.)
Nèi liǎng dòng lóu shì xuéshēng sùshè ma?   zhèi dòng shì sùshè, nèi dòng bú shì.

2) 那兩個人，哪個是你的室友？   →   那個是(我的室友)。 (人 is omitted.)
Nèi liǎng gè rén, něi ge shì nǐ de shìyǒu?   nèi gè shì (wǒ de shìyǒu).

3 Talking about a place

這裡/兒，那裡/兒，哪裡/兒

▬ These words are generic place words (PW) indicating a location, position, or space. 這裡 means here or this place, and 那裡 there or that place. The corresponding question word is 哪裡 nǎlǐ (where).

1) 這裡/這兒是我的家。   *(This place over here is my home.)*
Zhèlǐ/zhèr shì wǒ de jiā.

2) 那裡/那兒是一棟學生宿舍樓。 *(That place over there is a student dorm.)*
Nàlǐ/nàr shì yí dòng xuéshēng sùshè lóu.

A) 在 + PW

▬ 在 as the main verb means "to be in [place]". The negative form is 不在.

1) 在哪裡/哪兒？
zài nǎlǐ / nǎr?
→ 在這裡，在我家，在北京，在上海
zài zhèlǐ,   zài wǒ jiā,   zài Běijīng,   zài Shànghǎi

2) 你們(的)家在哪裡？
Nǐmén de jiā zài nǎlǐ?
→ 我家在北京，她家不在北京，在臺北。
Wǒ jiā zài Běijīng,   tā jiā bú zài Běijīng,   zài Táiběi.

3) 你的學校在這兒嗎？
Nǐ de xuéxiào zài zhèr ma?
→ 不在這兒，在那兒。
Bú zài zhèr,   zài nàr.

4 – A) – 2)

B) 住在 + PW

▬ 住在 is always followed by a PW, meaning "live in/at [place]". To negate, use 不住在 [place].
在 is optional in the spoken form (informal).

1) 住在哪裡/哪兒？
Zhù zài nǎlǐ / nǎr?
→ 住在那兒，住在學校，住在3號樓，住在3號宿舍樓
zhù zài nàr, zhù zài xuéxiào, zhù zài sān hào lóu, zhù zài sān hào sùshè lóu

2) 你們住在這裡嗎？
Nǐmen zhù zài zhèlǐ ma?
→ 我們不住在這裡，我們住在5號學生宿舍樓。
Wǒmen bú zhù zài zhèlǐ, wǒmen zhù zài wǔ hào xuéshēng sùshè lóu.

4 – B) – 1)

A) 是 [Place] 人

This form is normally used to identify the city or region of a country that a person is from.

1) 是哪裡人/哪兒人?
shì nǎlǐ rén/nǎr rén?

→ 是北京人，廣東人，臺北人，加州人
shì Běijīngrén, Guǎngdōngrén, Táiběirén, Jiāzhōurén

2) 你的兩個室友是哪裡人?
Nǐ de liǎng gè shìyǒu shì nǎlǐ rén?

→ 一個是加州人，一個是臺北人。
Yí gè shì Jiāzhōurén, yí gè shì Táiběirén.

3) 于老師是北京人，李老師也是北京人嗎?
Yú lǎoshī shì Běijīngrén, Lǐ lǎoshī yě shì Běijīngrén ma?

→ 他不是北京人，是廣東人。
Tā bú shì Běijīngrén, shì Guǎngdōngrén.

B) 是 [Place] 來的

come from [place]

This form is used to specify the place someone comes from, which may or may not be the original place where he/she was raised.

1) 你的老師是上海人嗎?
Nǐ de lǎoshī shì Shànghǎirén ma?

→ 他是上海來的，可是不是上海人。
Tā shì Shànghǎi lái de, kěshì bú shì Shànghǎirén.

2) 李先生是哪兒人?
Lǐ xiānsheng shì nǎr rén?

→ 他是廣東人，是廣州來的。
Tā shì Guǎngdōngrén, shì Guǎngzhōu lái de.

5 – B) – 2)

6 Review: Similar situation

也 + Verb Phrase; 也不 + Verb Phrase
also / both

■ Remember 也 is an unmovable adverb and always appears before the main verb (or the main adjective) phrase. It never takes an initial or final position in the sentence as its equivalent (also) does in English.

1) 她是加州來的，她的室友也是加州來的。
Tā shì Jiāzhōu lái de, tā de shìyǒu yě shì Jiāzhōu lái de.

2) 他不住在北京，他的朋友也不住在北京。
Tā bú zhù zài Běijīng, tā de péngyou yě bú zhù zài Běijīng.

7 Emphasizing the same situation

[plural item] 都 + Verb Phrase
both/all . . .

■ 都 is an unmovable adverb, so it can only appear before the main verb phrase (or the main adjective phrase) and never appears in the initial or final position of a sentence. 都 refers to the item(s) in front, which must be plural.

1) 我和他都是學生。/我和他都不是學生。 （都我和他……。✗）
Wǒ hé tā dōu shì xuésheng. /Wǒ hé tā dōu bú shì xuésheng.

2) 他們都是北京人。/他們都不是北京人。
Tāmen dōu shì Běijīngrén. /Tāmen dōu bú shì Běijīngrén.

3) 我家和她家都在北京。/我家和她家都不在北京。
Wǒ jiā hé tā jiā dōu zài Běijīng. /Wǒ jiā hé tā jiā dōu bú zài Běijīng.

■ For partial negation, **不都** is used.

4) 你們都是大學生嗎？ ➔ 不都是(大學生)，我是大學生，他是高中生。
Nǐmen dōu shì dàxuéshēng ma?   Bù dōu shì (dàxuéshēng), wǒ shì dàxuéshēng, tā shì gāozhōngshēng.

5) 他們都是臺北來的嗎？ ➔ 不都是，一個是，一個不是。
Tāmen dōu shì Táiběi lái de ma?   Bù dōu shì, yí gè shì, yí gè bú shì.

8 Asking an alternative question

[Verb] A 還是 B?
. . . or . . .

1) 李先生是本地人還是外地人？   ➔   他是外地人。
Lǐ xiānsheng shì běndìrén háishi wàidìrén?   Tā shì wàidìrén.

2) 他住在3號樓還是5號樓？   ➔   他住在5號樓。
Tā zhù zài sān hào lóu háishi wǔ hào lóu?   Tā zhù zài wǔ hào lóu.

Before viewing . . .

1) Name some Chinese cities you know. Which city do you think Xiaodong lives in?

2) In your culture, how are college dorms arranged for the incoming first-year students?

While viewing . . .

1) During your first viewing, focus on meaning.

2) During your second viewing, pay special attention to speech forms and tones.

3) Finally, practice saying the sentences by answering the questions below.

▶ U2-A1

小東是哪兒人？
Xiǎodōng shì nǎr rén?

"我是＿＿＿＿＿人。"
Wǒ shì........   rén

他的家在哪兒？ 大學在哪兒？
Tā de jiā zài nǎr?   Dàxué zài nǎr?

"我家在＿＿＿＿＿＿，
Wǒ jiā zài......

我們大學＿＿＿＿＿＿。"
wǒmen dàxué......

© Cengage Learning 2015

小東住在哪裡？
Xiǎodōng zhù zài nǎlǐ?

"我住在＿＿＿＿＿＿。"
Wǒ zhùzài......

© Cengage Learning 2015

這是誰的宿舍？小東有什麼？
Zhè shì shéi de sùshè? Xiǎodōng yǒu shénme?

"這是＿＿＿＿＿＿＿＿＿＿＿＿。
Zhè shì……

我有＿＿＿＿＿＿、＿＿＿＿＿＿、
Wǒ yǒu……

＿＿＿＿＿＿和＿＿＿＿＿＿。"
　　　　　　hé

小東有幾個室友？他們是幾年級的學生？
Xiǎodōng yǒu jǐ gè shìyǒu? Tāmen shì jǐ niánjí de xuésheng?

"我還有＿＿＿＿＿＿＿＿，
Wǒ háiyǒu……

我們＿＿＿＿＿＿＿＿＿。"
Wǒmen……

這幾個室友是哪裡來的？
Zhè jǐ gè shìyǒu shì nǎlǐ lái de?

"他們是＿＿＿＿＿＿？
Tāmen shì……

是＿＿＿＿＿＿還是＿＿＿＿＿＿？"
shì……　　　　　　háishi……

1 **Forms and structures**
See 2.2 for more notes and examples.

1) 我是北京人。
Wǒ shì Běijīngrén.

(This statement tells the original place where someone was raised.)

2) 我家在北京，我們大學也在北京。
Wǒ jiā zài Běijīng, wǒmen dàxué yě zài Běijīng.

(在 functions as the main verb meaning "to be in/at".)

3) 這是我們大學。
Zhè shì wǒmen dàxué.

(我們+ N refers to a community one belongs to.)

4) 我住在這棟樓。
Wǒ zhù zài zhèi dòng lóu.

(住在 + Place: *to live in/at [a place]*)

5) 這是我的宿舍。
Zhè shì wǒ de sùshè.

(這 appears at the front of the sentence as the subject.)

6) 我有一張床、一張桌子、一把椅子……
Wǒ yǒu yì zhāng chuáng, yì zhāng zhuōzi, yì bǎ yǐzi……

(When listing items, the pausing mark "、" is used.)

7) 我還有三個室友。
Wǒ hái yǒu sān gè shìyǒu.

(還 is an adverb that only appears before the verb. It introduces additional details to what has been said.)

8) 我們都是新生。
Wǒmen dōu shì xīnshēng.

(都 only appears before the verb.)

9) (他們)是本地人還是外地人？
(Tāmen) shì běndìrén háishi wàidìrén?

(還是 is used to ask a question about alternatives.)

2 Interrogative and negative forms　哪個，哪兒，哪裡，幾，誰的，還是

Practice these sentences to familiarize yourself with word order in questions and negations. Answer the questions accordingly.

1) 小東是哪兒人？是上海人嗎？　小東不是上海人，是……人。

2) 他的大學在哪裡？在廣州嗎？
　_____
　(城市名)

3) 他住在哪兒？住在家裡嗎？
　_____
　(學校)

4) 他住在哪棟樓？住在這棟嗎？
　_____
　(那棟)

5) 這是誰的宿舍？是小南的嗎？
　_____
　(小東)

6) 他有幾張桌子、幾把椅子？
　_____
　(1，1)

7) 這幾個室友是本地人還是外地人？_____
　(外地)

3 Review the negative forms of 有

1) **Negate all:** 没有 + N
   Simply use 没有 + N when the number is 0 (none).

   小東有(一個)哥哥嗎？ ➡ 他没有哥哥。(没有一個哥哥 ✗)

2) **Negate the incorrect number:** 不 / 不是
   Use 不 or 不是 in front.

   小東有兩個室友嗎？ ➡ 不(是)，他有三個。(不是 here means "No" or "Incorrect".)

3) **Negate the incorrect number if it's larger than the fact:** 没有 + Nu-M-N
   It means "not have that many."

   小東有四個室友嗎？ ➡ 他没有四個室友，他有三個。
   He doesn't have four roommates; he only has three.

1 Pair work

 Ask and answer questions based on the following pictures. English may be used for names (person, city, building, etc.)

Questions about Images 1—4:

Jack是哪裡人？是哪裡來的？
… shì nǎlǐ rén?   Shì nǎlǐ lái de?

Jack在哪裡？
… zài nǎlǐ?

Jack住在哪裡？
… zhù zài nǎlǐ?

Jack有室友嗎？有幾個？
… yǒu shìyǒu ma? Yǒu jǐ gè?

Questions about Images 5—6:

Mary也是一年級新生嗎？
… yě shì yì niánjí xīnshēng ma?

Mary也住在……嗎？
… yě zhù zài…… ma?

Mary也有一個室友嗎？
… yě yǒu yí gè shìyǒu ma?

Mary有幾張桌子和幾把椅子？
… yǒu jǐ zhāng zhuōzi hé jǐ bǎ yǐzi?

Jack (Jiékè)

Mary (Mǎlì)

2 Interview and report

1) **Interview:** Move around the classroom and speak to at least two classmates. Greet the classmates and ask and answer questions about where they are from, where they live, how many roommates they have, etc.

2) **Report:** The teacher will ask students to report what they learned about the classmates they interviewed. The teacher may also invite students to ask him/her questions.

3) **Quiz:** The teacher may quiz students on the information shared in the reports, e.g.,
誰是…人？誰的家在X？X是哪兒人？他住在X樓，對嗎？
Students should answer questions and correct any wrong information, such as 他家不在X，他不住在X。

These exercises are also available online with automatic feedback.

Verbs, PWs, and Adverbs

1 Choose the best word to complete the sentence

1) 你的宿舍＿＿＿＿哪兒？   a. 住在   b. 是   c. 在

2) ＿＿＿＿是她的家嗎？   a. 這裡/兒   b. 哪裡   c. 在這兒

3) 我們＿＿＿＿3號樓。   a. 都是   b. 那裡   c. 住在

4) 北京＿＿＿＿哪裡？   a. 是   b. 在   c. 住

5) 她＿＿＿＿哪裡人？   a. 是   b. 在   c. 住

2 Rewrite the sentence
Insert the adverb in the appropriate place.

1) 我的家在這兒。   ＿＿＿＿＿＿＿＿＿＿＿
（不）

2) 她不是高中生，我不是高中生。   ＿＿＿＿＿＿＿＿＿＿＿
（也）

3) 我們不是高中生。   ＿＿＿＿＿＿＿＿＿＿＿
（都）

4) 我們不是高中生。（三個是，一個不是）   ＿＿＿＿＿＿＿＿＿＿＿
（都）

5) 我有兩個室友。   ＿＿＿＿＿＿＿＿＿＿＿
（還）

3 Give the Chinese equivalent for each question
Pay attention to the Chinese structures. Avoid word-for-word translation. Pinyin may be used.

1) Where is he from?   → ＿＿＿＿＿＿＿＿＿＿＿

2) Where is his school?   → ＿＿＿＿＿＿＿＿＿＿＿

3) Where does he live?   → ＿＿＿＿＿＿＿＿＿＿＿

4) How many roommates does he have?   → ＿＿＿＿＿＿＿＿＿＿＿

5) Is his roommate a native of Shanghai or of Taipei?   → ＿＿＿＿＿＿＿＿＿

A | 2.7) 聽答對話 tīngdá duìhuà   LET'S CHAT

In this listening-speaking activity you'll be asked to answer questions about the **video** segment as well as about **yourself.** You may be asked to record and submit your answers to the teacher.

你是哪裡人？
Where are you from?

B | 2.8 詞語預習 cíyǔ yùxí | PREVIEW THE VOCABULARY

 Use the **online audio flashcards** to familiarize yourself with the new vocabulary in this section.

Nouns (N)

Countries

國家	guójiā	country
外國	wàiguó	foreign country
中國	Zhōngguó	China
美國	Měiguó	United States
英國	Yīngguó	United Kingdom

People from a country

外國人	wàiguórén	foreigner
中國人	Zhōngguórén	Chinese
美國人	Měiguórén	American
英國人	Yīngguórén	British

Languages

語言	yǔyán	language
文字	wénzì	written language; script
母語	mǔyǔ	mother tongue
雙語	shuāngyǔ	bilingual

外語/文	wàiyǔ/wén	foreign language
漢語	Hànyǔ	Chinese (referring to spoken Chinese, used in mainland China)
中文	Zhōngwén	Chinese language, Chinese
英語/文	Yīngyǔ/wén	English language

Spoken languages/Dialects

話 huà		speech, spoken words
普通話 Pǔtōnghuà		common speech (a term used in mainland China)
國語 guóyǔ		national language/standard Chinese (a term used in Taiwan)
北京話 Běijīnghuà		Beijing dialect
上海話 Shànghǎihuà		Shanghainese, Shanghai dialect
廣東話 Guǎngdōnghuà		Cantonese, Guangdong dialect

Names

陳 Chén		a Chinese surname
劉 Liú		a Chinese surname
白 Bái		a Chinese surname (also means white)

龍 lóng		dragon (used as a given name, usu. for males)
英 yīng		flower, talent (used as a given name)
雪 xuě		snow (used as a given name)

Social Titles

阿姨 āyí		aunt; a term of address for a woman of one's mother's generation
叔叔 shūshu		uncle; a term of address for a man of one's father's generation
先生 xiānsheng		a polite form used for male adults in general; husband
太太 tàitai		a polite form of address for a married woman; wife

Verbs (V) / Auxiliary Verbs (AV)

認識	rènshi	know, meet (new people)
會	huì	know how to, can
說	shuō	speak
學	xué	learn

Conjunctions (Conj)

| 因為 | yīnwèi | because |
| 所以 | suǒyǐ | so, therefore |

Particle (P)

| 呢
ne | | (a marker for abbreviated questions or a tone softener) |

School Terms

學院	xuéyuàn	college or school in a university
文學院	Wénxuéyuàn	School of Liberal Arts
外語學院	Wàiyǔxuéyuàn	School of Foreign Languages
商學院	Shāngxuéyuàn	School of Business

Expressions (Exp)

來，認識一下。 Lái, rènshi yíxià.	Let's get acquainted. (Let's introduce ourselves.)
很高興認識你! Hěn gāoxìng rènshi nǐ!	It is a pleasure to meet you!
謝謝! —不謝! Xièxie! Búxiè!	Thank you! — You are welcome!
再見! Zàijiàn!	Goodbye! (See you again.)
會說一點兒…… Huì shuō yìdiǎnr……	Can speak a little . . .

Structures

- 你呢?
- 會不會……?
- 因為…，所以…

Aural-Oral Exercises: Do the online exercises to further familiarize yourself with the new vocabulary and grammar when it is used in sentences.

Main Features: This lesson continues to teach the vocabulary you will need for basic self-descriptions. You will learn the names of countries and languages. These terms can be tricky as they do not share the same form as they do in English. For instance, in English, the terms "Chinese people" and "Chinese language" can be expressed using the same word "Chinese"; in Chinese, these two terms are expressed by 中國人 and 中文 respectively. In terms of sentence structures, we'll introduce two new question forms: abbreviated questions with 呢 and the choice-type (or V不V) questions. Finally, you will learn expressions to use when meeting people.

1　**Identifying someone's nationality or native country**　　是 + country name + 人

▰ Note the term X國人 is often used broadly and may not accurately reflect a person's citizenship.

1) 哪國人？　　　　　→ 中國人，美國人，英國人，日本人
   Nǎ guó rén?　　　　　Zhōngguórén, Měiguórén, Yīngguórén, Rìběnrén,

2) 他是中國人嗎？　　　→ 不是，他不是中國人，他是日本人。
   Tā shì Zhōngguórén ma?　　　Bú shì, tā bú shì Zhōngguórén, tā shì Rìběnrén.

3) 他的老師是美國人嗎？　→ 不是，他的老師不是美國人，是英國人。
   Tā de lǎoshī shì Měiguórén ma?　　Bú shì, tā de lǎoshī bú shì Měiguórén, shì Yīngguórén.

2　**Describing someone's language ability**　　説/會説 + language
　　　　　　　　　　　　　　　　　　　　　speak/ can speak [language]

▰ Both –文 and –語 are used for the language spoken within a culture. Generally speaking, 語 is considered less formal and sometimes is limited to the spoken form only. For the Chinese language, the term "中文" is more commonly used outside of China than "漢語", although the latter is mostly used within China.

1) 説英語/文，學中文/漢語，會説外語，會説三種語言
   shuō Yīngyǔ/wén, xué Zhōngwén/Hànyǔ, huì shuō wàiyǔ, huì shuō sān zhǒng yǔyán

2) 王小名會説什麼外語？　→ 他會説一點兒英語，他也學日語(Japanese)。
   Wáng Xiǎomíng huì shuō shénme wàiyǔ?　　Tā huì shuō yìdiǎnr Yīngyǔ, tā yě xué Rìyǔ.

3) 李先生的母語是中文還是英語？→ 他是雙語，中文、英文，他都會説。
   Lǐ xiānsheng de mǔyǔ shì Zhōngwén háish Yīngyǔ?　　Tā shì shuāngyǔ, Zhōngwén, Yīngwén, tā dōu huì shuō.

1) 北京人說北京話，廣東人說廣東話，上海人說上海話。
Běijīngrén shuō Běijīnghuà, Guǎngdōngrén shuō Guǎngdōnghuà, Shànghǎirén shuō Shànghǎihuà.

2) 李小姐是上海人，她說上海話 → 上海話、普通話，她都說。
Lǐ xiǎojiě shì Shànghǎirén, tā shuō Shànghǎihuà   Shànghǎihuà, Pǔtōnghuà, tā dōu shuō.
還是普通話?
háishi Pǔtōnghuà?

3) 王老師會說廣東話還是上海話? → 她不會說廣東話，也不會說上海話。
Wáng lǎoshī huì shuō Guǎngdōnghuà háishi   Tā bú huì shuō Guǎngdōnghuà, yě bú huì shuō
Shànghǎihuà?   Shànghǎihuà.

3 – 1)

■ 中國老師 refers to a teacher either teaching in China or who has Chinese nationality. The teacher may or may not teach Chinese. 中文老師 means "a teacher of Chinese", regardless of his or her nationality.

1) 這個學校有中國老師嗎? → 沒有中國老師，可是有中國學生。
Zhè gè xuéxiào yǒu Zhōngguó lǎoshī ma?   Méi yǒu Zhōngguó lǎoshī, kěshì yǒu Zhōngguó xuésheng.

2) 你們的中文老師是哪國人? → 一個是中國人，一個是美國人。
Nǐmen de Zhōngwén lǎoshī shì nǎ guó rén?   Yí gè shì Zhōngguórén, yí gè shì Měiguórén.

4 – 1)

A) Choice-Type Yes/No Questions: V不V (是不是? 有没有? 會不會?)

▀▀ This is perhaps the most widely-used form for yes/no questions in daily conversation. The form V不V indicates in the sentence that a positive verb (e.g., 是, 有, 會) or no (不是, 没有, 不會) is expected in the answer.

1) 李先生是不是北京人?　→　不是，他是上海人。 *(No, he is from Shanghai.)*
   Lǐ xiānsheng shì bú shì Běijīngrén?　Bú shì, tā shì Shànghǎirén.

2) 李先生有没有孩子?　→　有，他有一個女兒。 *(Yes, he has a daughter.)*
   Lǐ xiānsheng yǒu méiyǒu háizi?　Yǒu, tā yǒu yí gè nǚ'ér.

3) 李先生會不會説英文?　→　會説。/他會説英文。 *(Yes. / He can speak English.)*
   Lǐ xiānsheng huì bú huì shuō Yīngwén?　Huì shuō. / Tā huì shuō Yīngwén.

5 — A) — 1)

▀▀ If an adverb is present, either switch to the 嗎-form or use 是不是+Verb Phrase:

4) 李先生是不是也説普通話?　✓　李先生也説不説普通話?　✗
   Lǐ xiānsheng shì bú shì yě shuō Pǔtōnghuà?
   (Is it the case that Mr. Li also speaks standard Chinese?)

5) 李先生和太太是不是都是上海人?　✓　李先生和太太都是不是　✗
   Lǐ xiānsheng hé tàitai shì bú shì dōu shì Shànghǎirén?　上海人?
   (Is it correct that Mr. and Mrs. Li are both from Shanghai?)

B) Abbreviated Questions: Person/Topic + 呢?
How/What about [person/topic]?

5 — A) — 5)

▀▀ This form is commonly used in conversation when someone asks a follow-up question on the preceding statement.

1) 我是中國人，你呢?　*(I'm Chinese. How about you?)*
   Wǒ shì Zhōngguórén, nǐ ne?

2) 她會説英文。中文呢?　*(She can speak English. What about Chinese?)*
   Tā huì shuō Yīngwén. Zhōngwén ne?

6   Connecting cause and effect in a sentence

因為……，所以……
Because . . . , (so) . . .

▬▬ Normally in a cause and effect sentence, the cause (因為) is stated first and then the effect (所以). 因為 can sometimes be omitted. However, once 因為 initiates a statement, 所以 must be used in the second part. Note that a comma is normally used to separate the two clauses.

1) 因為他媽媽是中國人，所以他會說中文。
     Yīnwèi tā māma shì Zhōngguórén, suǒyǐ tā huì shuō Zhōngwén.

(所以 and a comma before it are both required.)

2) (因為)小東是大學生，所以他住在學校。
     (Yīnwèi) Xiǎodōng shì dàxuéshēng, suǒyǐ tā zhù zài xuéxiào.

6 – 2)

7   Meeting people: Common expressions

1) 來，認識一下。我姓李，叫李新。　➔　你好，李新，很高興認識你！
     Lái, rènshi yíxià.   Wǒ xìng Lǐ,   jiào Lǐ Xīn.   Nǐ hǎo,   Lǐ Xīn,   hěn gāoxìng rènshi nǐ!

2) 我也很高興認識你！/認識你，我也很高興！
     Wǒ yě hěn gāoxìng rènshi nǐ! /Rènshi nǐ,   wǒ yě hěn gāoxìng!

3) 謝謝！　➔　不謝！
     Xièxie!   Búxiè!

4) 再見！　➔　再見！
     Zàijiàn!   Zàijiàn!

7 – 1)

Before viewing . . .

1) In your culture, what would you say when you meet a roommate for the first time?

2) Would you prefer sharing a room with a person who was from the same part of the country as you are?

3) If you participated in a study abroad program, what would you choose: to stay with a local family or to have a Chinese roommate? Why?

While viewing . . .

1) During your first viewing, focus on meaning.

2) During your second viewing, pay special attention to speech forms and tones.

3) Finally, practice saying the sentences by answering the questions below.

▶ U2-B1

這個室友說:
Zhège shìyǒu shuō:

"來, 認識一下。 ⋯⋯ 我姓_____,
Lái, rènshi yíxià.   Wǒ xìng⋯⋯

_____。"

小東說:
Xiǎodōng shuō:

"你好你好! ⋯⋯ 很高興_____!"
Nǐ hǎo nǐ hǎo!   Hěn gāoxìng⋯⋯

▶ U2-B2

阿龍說他是哪裡人?
Ā Lóng shuō tā shì nǎlǐ rén?

"我是_____人, 是_____來的。"
Wǒ shì⋯⋯   rén, shì⋯⋯   lái de.

小東說:
Xiǎodōng shuō:

"因為_____, 所以_____!"
Yīnwèi⋯⋯   suǒyǐ⋯⋯

阿龍說什麼？小東呢？
Ā Lóng shuō shénme? Xiǎodōng ne?

"認識一下吧，　我叫陳一龍，
Rènshi yíxià ba, 　wǒ jiào Chén Yīlóng,

是＿＿＿＿＿＿的。"
shì…… 　　　　de.

"我叫林小東，是＿＿＿＿＿的。
Wǒ jiào Lín Xiǎodōng, shì…… 　　de.

我們＿＿＿＿＿，
Wǒmen……

很高興＿＿＿＿＿！"
hěn gāoxìng……

這兩個女生說什麼？
Zhè liǎng gè nǚshēng shuō shénme?

"我們也＿＿＿＿＿＿＿！
Wǒmen yě……

我叫劉英，是＿＿＿＿＿的學生。"
Wǒ jiào Liú Yīng, shì…… 　　de xuésheng.

"我叫白曉雪，也是＿＿＿＿＿的，
Wǒ jiào Bái Xiǎoxuě, yě shì…… 　　de,

我是＿＿＿＿。"
wǒ shì……

小南說那個外國女孩是誰？
Xiǎonán shuō nèige wàiguó nǚhái shì shéi?

"她叫＿＿＿＿，是＿＿＿＿，
Tā jiào…… 　　shì……

＿＿＿＿＿＿來的。"
……lái de.

"她是＿＿＿＿，她住在＿＿＿＿。"
Tā shì…… 　　tā zhù zài……

"她會說＿＿＿＿＿。"
Tā huì shuo……

1   Forms and structures

See 2.9 for more notes and examples.

1) 來，認識一下。我是……
   Lái, rènshi yíxià. Wǒ shì……

   (an expression to initiate a self-introduction)

2) 朋友們都叫我阿龍。
   Péngyou dōu jiào wǒ Ā Lóng.

   (阿 is a term of endearment that is used as a name prefix in some areas such as Guangdong and Shanghai.)

3) 你好你好！
   Nǐ hǎo nǐ hǎo!

   (Short, polite forms can be repeated to show hospitality.)

4) (我)很高興認識你！
   (Wǒ) hěn gāoxìng rènshi nǐ!

   (我 is usually omitted at the beginning of a sentence.)

5) 我也很高興認識你！
   Wǒ yě hěn gāoxìng rènshi nǐ!

   (我/我們 cannot be omitted when 也 is used. Another way to say this is: 認識你，我也很高興！)

6) 因為你是廣東人，所以叫阿龍！
   Yīnwèi nǐ shì Guǎngdōngrén, suǒyǐ jiào Ā Lóng!

   (If 因為 is used in the first clause, 所以 must be used in the second clause. The two clauses should be separated by a comma.)

7) 我是商學院的。
   Wǒ shì Shāngxuéyuàn de.

   (The 的 at the end stands for 的學生 or 的人.)

8) 我是外語學院(的)大二的學生。
   Wǒ shì Wàiyǔxuéyuàn (de) dà èr de xuésheng.

   (The first 的 is omitted.)

▨ Question Forms (QF)

1) 我是本地人。你呢？
   Wǒ shì běndìrén,   Nǐ ne?

   (你呢 is an abbreviated question meaning "How about you"?)

2) 她是哪國人？
   Tā shì nǎ guó rén?

   (*Which country is she from?*)

3) 她會不會說中國話(中文)？
   Tā huì bú huì shuō Zhōngguóhuà (Zhōngwén)?

   (**V**不**V**-Question: to be used with the main verb.)
   (她會說不說中文？ ✘)

2 Interrogative and negative forms

Practice these sentences. Remember, the word order in a question remains the same as in a statement.

A) 呢–Questions: 你呢？他呢？你的室友呢？
Give negative answers.

1) 我不是中國人。你呢？　＿＿＿＿＿＿＿＿＿＿

2) 他不説日語。你呢？　＿＿＿＿＿＿＿＿＿＿

3) 他沒有中國朋友。他的室友呢？　＿＿＿＿＿＿＿＿＿＿

B) V不V–Questions: 是不是，説不説，會不會説，有沒有
Answer each question with "No," then supply the correct information based on the hints provided.

1) 那個人是不是美國學生？　　（中國）＿＿＿＿＿＿＿＿＿

2) 他會不會説日語？　　（英語）＿＿＿＿＿＿＿＿＿

3) 他有沒有一個美國朋友？　　（英國）＿＿＿＿＿＿＿＿＿

3 Story narration　　他們是誰？

Pay special attention to the verb forms and the use of punctuation marks.

那個男生是小東的室友，姓陳，叫陳一龍，他的朋友都叫他
Nàge nánshēng shì Xiǎodōng de shìyǒu,　xìng Chén, jiào Chén Yīlóng,　tā de péngyou dōu jiào tā

阿龍。他不是本地人，是廣東人，是廣州來的。他是商學院的學生。
Ā Lóng.　Tā bú shì běndìrén, shì Guǎngdōngrén, shì Guǎngzhōu lái de.　Tā shì shāng xuéyuàn de xuésheng.

那兩個女生一個叫劉英，一個叫白曉雪，她們都是外語學院的。劉英
Nà liǎng gè nǚshēng yí gè jiào Liú Yīng, yí gè jiào Bǎi Xiǎoxuě, tāmen dōu shì wàiyǔ xuéyuàn de.　Liú Yīng

是大二的學生，白曉雪是一年級新生。她們很高興認識阿龍和小東。
shì dà èr de xuésheng,　Bǎi Xiǎoxuě shì yī niánjí xīnshēng.　Tāmen hěn gāoxìng rènshi Ā Lóng hé Xiǎodōng.

那個外國女孩叫Katie，她是一個美國高中生，是華盛頓來的。她
Nàge wàiguó nǚhái jiào … ,　tā shì yí gè Měiguó gāozhōngshēng, shì Huáshèngdùn lái de. Tā

住在小南家。她會説中文。
zhùzài Xiǎonán jiā. Tā huì shuō Zhōngwén.

1 **Pair Work**

Preparation: Fill in the middle column of the Chinese info sheet with real or imaginary data (in pinyin or English). Ask the teacher for unknown vocabulary if necessary.

Ask and Answer questions: Students work in pairs to ask and answer questions and use the info sheet to take notes in the right column. Finish with one person and then reverse the role to ask about another.

Chinese Information Sheet

1) 姓名 (Name):
   xìngmíng

2) 學院 (School):
   xuéyuàn

3) 宿舍 (Dorm):
   sùshè

4) X 國人 (Nationality):
   ⋯ guó rén

5) X 來的 (City/State):
   ⋯ lái de

6) 會說 X 語:
   huì shuō ⋯ yǔ
   (Language spoken)

7) 學 X 語:
   xué ⋯ yǔ
   (Language studied currently)

Ask Questions:

1) 他/她姓什麼？ 叫什麼名字？
   Tā/tā xìng shénme? Jiào shénme míngzi?
   (What's X's name?)

2) 他/她是哪個學院的？
   Tā/tā shì nǎ gè xuéyuàn de?
   (Which school is X enrolled in?)

3) 他/她住在哪棟樓？
   Tā/tā zhù zài nǎ dòng lóu?
   (Which building does X live in?)

4) 他/她是哪國人？
   Tā/tā shì nǎ guó rén?
   (Which country is X from?)

5) 他/她是哪裡來的？ 本地人還是外地人？
   Tā/tā shì nǎlǐ lái de? Běndìrén háishi wàidìrén?
   (Which area is X from? Local or non-local?)

6) 他/她會不會說外語？
   Tā/tā huì bú huì shuō wàiyǔ?
   (Does X speak a foreign language?)

7) 他/她學什麼外語？ A還是B？
   Tā/tā xué shénme wàiyǔ? A háishi B?
   (What language(s) does X study? A or B?)

2 **Interview and report**

1) **Interview:** Interview a classmate to learn about his or her personal information, such as, nationality, region, language skills, school, and dorm.

2) **Report:** The teacher will ask some students to report their interview results.

3) **Quiz:** After each report, the teacher or the presenter may quiz students on the information shared in the report. Students are expected to confirm or correct the information to practice positive and negative sentences.

B **2.13** 語法鞏固 *yǔfǎ gǒnggù*   **REINFORCE THE GRAMMAR**

These exercises are also available online with automatic feedback.

1 **Change the statements into questions**

1) 那個人不是老師。 （哪個） _____

2) 他是外國學生。 （v不v） _____

3) 他是文學院的。 （哪個） _____

4) 他住在5號樓。 （哪棟） _____

5) 他是日本人。 （哪國） _____

6) 他是東京來的。 （哪裡） _____

7) 他會說英語。 （v不v） _____

8) 他也學中文和英語。 （什麼） _____

2 **Correct the sentences**
Identify the error in each sentence and then rewrite it correctly.

1) 你是不是外國學生嗎？ ✘ → _____

2) 你是哪學院的？ ✘ → _____

3) 你會說不說外語？ ✘ → _____

4) 你學中文也英文嗎？ ✘ → _____

5) 你有不有中國朋友？ ✘ → _____

6) 因為他是美國人，他說英語。✘ → _____

B **2.14** 聽答對話 *tīngdá duìhuà*   **LET'S CHAT**

In this listening-speaking activity you'll be asked to answer questions about the **video** segment as well as about **yourself.** You may be asked to record and submit your answers to the teacher.

FORMS of ADDRESS

Forms of address can be complex and idiosyncratic in the greater China region, but there are some commonly followed rules of etiquette observed on the mainland, on Taiwan, in Hong Kong, and in Macau. For instance, on a formal occasion, such as a business meeting or during introductory greetings, a full name (the family name followed by a given name) is expected to be used. In addition, xiānsheng (先生, Mr.), which follows either the family name or the full name) would be used to address adult males; nǚshì (女士, Madam) is used for adult females. For a married woman, tàitai (太太, Mrs.) is added to her husband's surname (e.g., 王太太).

Unlike in the English-speaking world, kinship terms are distinguished along the lines of lineage with a specific term for each type of relationship. Here is a list of some of the most commonly used kinship-related terms:

yéye (爺爺, paternal grandfather), nǎinai (奶奶, paternal grandmother), wàigōng (外公, maternal grandfather), wàipó (外婆, maternal grandmother).

shūshu (叔叔, paternal uncle), gūgu (姑姑, paternal aunt), jiùjiu (舅舅, maternal uncle), āyí (阿姨, maternal aunt);

gēge (哥哥, older brother), jiějie (姐姐, older sister), dìdi (弟弟, younger bother), mèimei (妹妹, younger sister).

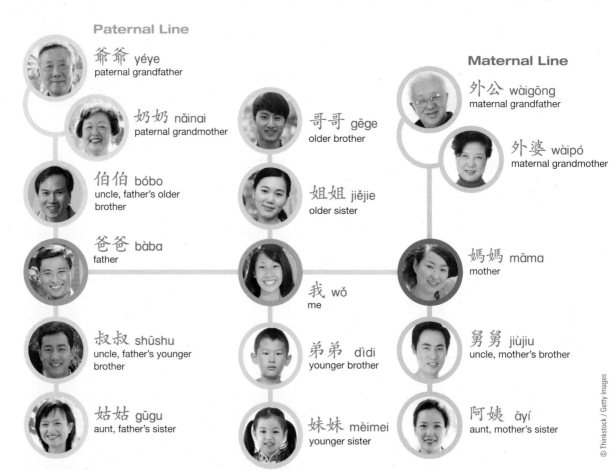

Paternal Line

爺爺 yéye
paternal grandfather

奶奶 nǎinai
paternal grandmother

伯伯 bóbo
uncle, father's older brother

爸爸 bàba
father

叔叔 shūshu
uncle, father's younger brother

姑姑 gūgu
aunt, father's sister

哥哥 gēge
older brother

姐姐 jiějie
older sister

我 wǒ
me

弟弟 dìdi
younger brother

妹妹 mèimei
younger sister

Maternal Line

外公 wàigōng
maternal grandfather

外婆 wàipó
maternal grandmother

媽媽 māma
mother

舅舅 jiùjiu
uncle, mother's brother

阿姨 āyí
aunt, mother's sister

© Thinkstock / Getty Images

Some of these kinship terms can also be used for nonrelatives. Close friends often address each other using gē (older brother) or jiě (older sister) to show intimacy and congeniality. By extension, their children may use "uncle," "aunt," and other kinship terms to address their parents' friends.

Among professionals, people address each other by their title, adding the title (e.g., jīnglǐ 經理, Manager; gōngchéngshī 工程師, Engineer) after the family name. Thus, one might say **Wáng Jīnglǐ** (王經理, Manager Wang) or **Lǐ Gōngchéngshī** (李工程師, Engineer Li). However, there are a few exceptions where professional nomenclature goes beyond conventional usage. For

instance, **lǎoshī** (老師) is commonly used to address someone who is a teacher or professor. **Lǎoshī**, literally "old teacher," does not necessarily mean the teacher is "old" in years; this is merely a cultural symbol of respect. Thus, a senior journal editor might well be addressed as **lǎoshī** by a junior member. In the workplace, especially on the mainland, a form of **lǎo** + family name (e.g., 老張) is a common form referring to an old or older colleague or friend. In Hong Kong, a polite form would be "given name + older brother" for an adult male. For instance, a friend of Mr. Wong Chi-Wah (王志華, in Cantonese spelling) might call him Chi-Wah Go (志華哥). For casual address of young people on the mainland, a common form is **xiǎo** ("little" or "young") + family name (e.g., 小張).

王經理
Wáng jīnglǐ
(lit.) Manager Wang

李工程師
Lǐ gōngchéngshī
(lit.) Engineer Li

林老師
Lín lǎoshī
(lit.) Teacher Lin

老張
Lǎo Zhāng
(lit.) Old Zhang

小張
Xiǎo Zhāng
(lit.) Young Zhang

QUIZ

1. What is the correct order of address for a man in Chinese?
   a. Mr., family name, given name
   b. Mr., given name, family name
   c. Family name, given name, Mr.
   d. Given name, family name, Mr.

2. What is the correct term of address for a paternal grandfather? maternal grandmother? paternal uncle? maternal aunt?

DISCUSSION QUESTIONS

1. Use of kinship terms for nonrelatives is not uniquely Chinese. For instance, the terms for "brother" and "sister" are also used for people outside the family in many cultures. Discuss the context in which these terms are used in your culture. If possible, compare and contrast their use with that of their Chinese counterparts.

2. The word lao (老) in laoshi means "old" in Chinese. But a teacher is not necessarily "old" in years. What does this tell you about Chinese sensibility regarding age? Is this the point of view of other traditional societies?

單元復習
Review and Integration

2.16 主課復習 zhǔkè fùxí　　　　**REVIEW THE STORY**

Read the following passages as fast as you can. Follow these steps:

1) Do not stop to check the meaning of words you don't recognize. Mark them and keep reading.
2) Read the passage again and guess the meaning of the marked words on a separate piece of paper.
3) Finally, look up the words in a dictionary or the vocabulary index and verify their meanings.

我是北京人，我的家在北京，我們大學也在北京。我住在這棟樓。這是我的宿舍。我有一張床、一張桌子和一把椅子。我還有三個室友，我們都是新生。

我是新生，我姓陳 (Chén)，叫陳一龍 (Chén Yīlóng)，朋友都叫我阿龍。我不是本地人，我是廣東人，是廣州來的。我住在3號樓，是林小東的室友，他是文學院的，我是商學院的。

這兩個女生一個叫劉英 (Liú Yīng)，一個叫白曉雪 (Bái Xiǎoxuě)，她們都是外語學院的。劉英是大二的學生，白曉雪是一年級新生。她們很高興認識阿龍和小東。

這個外國女孩叫Katie，是一個美國高中生，是華盛頓 (Huáshèngdùn) 來的。她住在小南家。她會說中文。

Quickly provide the Chinese equivalents for the following phrases and sentences. Do not translate them word for word.

1   Forms of Address: How to address people appropriately

In China, if you want to address . . .   *Which form is more appropriate?*

1) LI Nan (李南), a young woman who works in the office

   a. 李小姐 Lǐ xiǎojiě   b. 李南 Lǐ Nán

2) Alice Wang, a teacher in her twenties

   a. Alice   b. 王老師 Wáng lǎoshī

3) Mr. Liu (劉), the father in your host family

   a. 劉先生 Liú xiānsheng   b. 劉叔叔 Liú shūshu

4) Jane Wang (王), Mr. Liu's wife

   a. 劉太太 Liú tàitai   b. 王阿姨 Wáng āyí

5) YU Xin (于新), a school administrator

   a. 于老師 Yú lǎoshī   b. 于先生 Yú xiānsheng

6) WANG Wen (王文), your Chinese roommate

   a. 王文 Wáng Wén   b. 文 Wén

2   Meeting people: Beginning and ending a conversation

What is the Chinese equivalent of . . .   *You say . . .*

1) "Hi, my name is . . ." _____

2) "How do you do? " _____

3) "Nice to meet you!" _____

4) "Nice to meet you, too!" _____

5) "Thank you!" → "You're welcome." _____

6) "Goodbye!" → "See you again." _____

3   Question Forms: How to ask for personal information

You want to ask . . .   *In Chinese you say . . .*

1) a person's nationality _____

2) what part of the country a person is from _____

3) where a person's home is (permanent) _____

4) where a person currently lives (temporary) _____

5) whether or not a person has a roommate _____

6) whether or not a person can speak a foreign language _____

7) whether a person studies Chinese or Japanese _____

8) whether a person's older sister also studies Chinese _____

9) whether a person's roommates are all freshmen _____

4 **Question Words (QWs):** How to ask questions using appropriate QWs
Form questions asking about the underlined information.

1) 小東(Xiǎodōng)是<u>北京</u>人。 _____

2) 小東住在<u>3</u>號樓。 _____

3) <u>那個女生</u>叫劉英(Liú Yīng)。 _____

4) 劉英是<u>大二</u>的學生。 _____

5) <u>這三個</u>學生都是外地人。 _____

6) <u>小東</u>不會說廣東話。 _____

7) 阿龍(Ā Lóng)是<u>小東的</u>室友。 _____

8) 于阿姨(āyí)是林叔叔(shūshu)的<u>太太</u>。 _____

9) <u>Katie</u>會說一點兒中文。 _____

10) <u>這3</u>棟(dòng)樓都是學生宿舍。 _____

2.18 語法小測驗 yǔfǎ xiǎo cèyàn　**CHECK FOR ACCURACY**

1 **Correct the sentences**

Identify the error(s) in each sentence and then rewrite the sentence correctly.

1) 你家是哪裡? ✘ _____

2) 幾個室友你有? ✘ _____

3) 他們住在中國裡。 ✘ _____

4) 都我們會說中文。 ✘ _____

5) 他有一個室友也。 ✘ _____

6) 因為他是美國人，他說英語。 ✘ _____

7) 他們都是不是中國人? ✘ _____

8) 哪樓是你的宿舍? ✘ _____

9) 你有不有一個室友? ✘ _____

10) 我有三中文朋友。 ✘ _____

The following activities allow you to further practice your interpretive, interpersonal, and presentational communication skills in a meaningful, communicative context.

Interpretive

1 **Listening**

(U2.19_1_1：你是北京人嗎？)

Take notes as you listen to each audio clip. Then tell whether each statement is true (T) or false (F).

True or False?

1) [ ] The man is from Beijing but lives in Shanghai.

2) [ ] He is currently going to Beijing University and living on campus.

3) [ ] The woman assumes that the man knows Wang laoshi.

4) [ ] Li Wen, Wang laoshi's child, is also studying at Beijing University.

5) [ ] The man is not acquainted with Li Wen, who doesn't live on campus.

(U2.19_1_2：你是不是紐約大學的學生？)

True or False?

1) [ ] The girl is a student in New York University.

2) [ ] She lived on campus because her home is not in New York.

3) [ ] She has a roommate who is from Guangdong, China.

4) [ ] Her roommate speaks Cantonese and English.

5) [ ] Since the girl doesn't understand Cantonese, she and her roommate communicate in English.

2 Reading

Read the passage and indicate if the following statements are true (T) or false (F).

我叫劉雲(Liú Yún)，我家在上海。
我是廣東人，所以我會説廣東話，也
會説上海話和普通話。我先生是北京
人，他不會説廣東話，也不會説上海
話，所以我和他都説普通話。我們有
一個女兒，叫芳芳(Fāngfang)，上小學三
年級。她有一個英文老師，是美國人，他也會説一點中文。芳芳有一
個同學，爸爸是中國人，媽媽是日本人，所以他日語和中文都會説。

© Cengage Learning 2015

True or False?

1) ☐ The person lives in both Guangdong and Shanghai.

2) ☐ Her husband is from Beijing and speaks neither Cantonese nor Shanghainese.

3) ☐ Her daughter is currently a college junior.

4) ☐ Her daughter is studying English with a teacher from America.

5) ☐ Her daughter's English teacher is proficient in Chinese.

6) ☐ Her daughter has a classmate, who speaks both Japanese and Chinese.

3 Speaking

1) **Role play:**

Role A: You are traveling to Beijing, and you have just gotten off the plane at the airport. You hand over your passport to a passport officer and answer the officer's questions.

Role B: You are a passport officer. You need to ask the person for the following information:

- Nationality
- Language skills
- Permanent residency (permanent address)
- Occupation: college student?
- What school he/she attends
- Where his/her school is located (city, state)

2) **Interview:** Ask a Chinese international student on campus for the following information:

- Chinese name and English name
- Where he/she is from
- Size of family; whether he/she has siblings?
- Status: undergraduate or graduate student (研究生 yánjiūshēng); what year of college
- Where he/she lives: on or off-campus, with roommates, etc.
- Language skills: which languages he/she speaks

(Please use an online translator to learn more country names and foreign language names in Chinese. Also find out how to say the names of common educational institutions in Chinese.)

Presentational

4 Speaking

Describe to the class what you have learned about the Chinese student you interviewed.

5 Writing (Choose one of the topics)

1) Imagine you will study abroad and will stay with a Chinese family. Write a description of yourself accompanied by a photo, which will serve as a self-introduction to the host family.

2) Write an email message to the Chinese student who will be staying with your family, providing basic information about yourself (or your family).

UNIT 3

第三單元

我的東西

My Things

The Story

Xiaonan needs to buy some new things. Her backpack is worn out and her clothes no longer fit . . .

FUNCTIONS & GLOBAL TASKS	CORE VOCABULARY	GRAMMAR	CULTURE
• Describing and commenting on things • Stating a change of situation	• School supplies • Clothing items • Measure words • Adjectives to describe objects	• Subject + Adj phrases • Particle 了 for changed status • Adjectives as modifiers • Adj-的 as noun phrases • 要 as Aux Verb and Verb	• Expenses in college

Communication

Interpretive

Understand listening and reading passages on describing items and change of state.

Interpersonal

Discuss the items you need to buy for your room and state why.

Presentational

State the items on your wish list and explain your choices.

UNIT 3

A 第一課

我 的 書 包 太 小 了
My backpack is too small

A 3.1 詞語預習 cíyǔ yùxí — PREVIEW THE VOCABULARY

Use the **online audio flashcards** to familiarize yourself with the new vocabulary in this section.

Nouns (N) · M

房間	fángjiān	room	個
東西	dōngxi	thing, object	個
本子	běnzi	notebook, exercise book	本
筆	bǐ	writing instrument (pen, pencil, etc.)	支
紙	zhǐ	paper	張
書	shū	book	本
書包	shūbāo	school bag, backpack	個
衣服	yīfu	clothes	件
褲子	kùzi	trousers, pants	條

Verb (V)

看	kàn	see, watch, look at

Measure Words (M)

些 xiē	some, a few (used to indicate an indefinite amount or a very small amount)
本 běn	(used for books)
支 zhī	(used for long, thin, inflexible objects)
件 jiàn	(used for luggage, clothes, furniture, matters, etc.) piece
條 tiáo	(used for something long, narrow, or thin)

Numerals (Nu)

很多	hěn duō	a lot, many, much
一些	yìxiē	a number of, some
幾個	jǐ gè	a few

Adjectives (Adj)/Stative Verbs (SV)

多	duō	many, much, more
少	shǎo	few, little, scarce
長	cháng	long
短	duǎn	(of length) short, low
高	gāo	tall, high
矮	ǎi	(of height) short
漂亮	piàoliang	pretty, good-looking
老	lǎo	old, aged
舊	jiù	used, worn
貴	guì	expensive
便宜	piányi	cheap, inexpensive
好	hǎo	good
壞	huài	bad, broken
高興	gāoxìng	happy, glad
不錯	búcuò	impressive

72 | UNIT 3: My Things

Adverbs (Adv)

很	hěn	very, quite
太	tài	too, extremely
不夠	búgòu	not enough
有(一)點兒 yǒu (yì) diǎnr		a bit, a little

Time Words (TW)

| 以前 | yǐqián | before, previously |
| 現在 | xiànzài | now, currently |

Particle (P)

| 了 | le | (a marker for change of state) |

Question Words (QW)

| 怎麼樣 | zěnmeyàng | how is/about |
| 為什麼 | wèishénme | why |

Structures

- 東西很多
- 太…了
- 現在我高了，衣服小了
- 這個書包怎麼樣？
- 為什麼……？

A 3.2 詞句聽説 cíjù tīngshuō **FOCUS ON GRAMMAR**

 Aural-Oral Exercises: Do the online exercises to further familiarize yourself with the new vocabulary and grammar when it is used in sentences.

Main Features: In this lesson we will focus on the <u>predicative use of adjectives</u>, that is, adjectives that comment on or describe the subject/topic of the sentence, which is normally a person or an object. As you will see in the following exercises, most Chinese adjectives act like verbs. That is, the verb "to be" 是 is normally absent. To facilitate describing people and things, you will need to be familiar with <u>words for objects</u> and their corresponding <u>measure words</u>. So get ready! Let's first work on the <u>Sp-Nu-M-N</u> form used with the new vocabulary.

1 Review the Sp-Nu-M-N form

A) Phrases with a specific quantity:

1) 一個房間，兩本書，三張書桌，四個書包，五張紙，六件衣服
   yí gè fángjiān, liǎng běn shū; sān zhāng shūzhuō; sì gè shūbāo; wǔ zhāng zhǐ; liù jiàn yīfu

2) 這個房間，這兩本書，那三張書桌
   zhège fángjiān, zhè liǎng běn shū, nà sān zhāng shūzhuō

3) 哪幾本書是你的？ → 這三本是我的。
   Nǎ jǐ běn shū shì nǐ de? Zhè sān běn shì wǒ de.

B) Phrases with a nonspecific quantity: 幾，些

■ 幾 here is not a question word, but rather an unspecified number in the range of 3–9. Use a measure word after 幾 as usual.

1) 幾本書 (*a few books*)，這幾本書 (*these few books*)，那幾張書桌 (*those few desks*)
    jǐ běn shū   zhè jǐ běn shū   nà jǐ zhāng shūzhuō

■ 些 is used to refer to an unspecific quantity of two or more: 一些，這些，那些，哪些.

2) 一些書，這些書，那些筆，那些學生
    yìxiē shū,   zhèxiē shū, nàxiē bǐ,   nàxiē xuésheng

3) 這些書，哪幾本是中文書?   →   這幾本是中文書。
    Zhèxiē shū, nǎ jǐ běn shì Zhōngwén shū?   Zhè jǐ běn shì Zhōngwén shū.

■ Measure words are not required when numbers (including 幾) and specifiers (這/那/哪) are absent.

4) 我的書   （我的本書 ✗）
    wǒ de shū

5) 我有筆和紙，沒有本子。
    wǒ yǒu bǐ hé zhǐ,   méiyǒu běnzi.

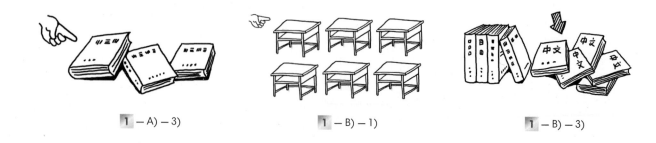

1 – A) – 3)   1 – B) – 1)   1 – B) – 3)

▭▭ These adverbs of degree can modify an adjective. They always precede the adjectives they modify.

1) 很 [+ Adj] (*really, very*) for emphasis :

很新/舊，很高/矮，很長/短，很貴/便宜，很好，很漂亮
hěn xīn/jiù,   hěn gāo/ǎi,   hěn cháng/duǎn, hěn guì/piányi, hěn hǎo, hěn piàoliang

2) 太 [+ Adj] (*too ...*) :

太小(了)，太舊(了)，太貴(了)，太長(了)，太矮(了)
tài xiǎo (le),   tài jiù (le),   tài guì (le),   tài cháng (le),   tài ǎi (le)

3) 不太 [+ Adj] (*not very*) :

不太大，不太舊，不太貴，不太長
bú tài dà,   bú tài jiù,   bú tài guì,   bú tài cháng

2 – 2)

4) 不夠 [+ desirable quality] (*not ... enough*) :

不夠大，不夠好，不夠新，不夠長
búgòu dà,   búgòu hǎo,   búgòu xīn,   búgòu cháng

5) 有點兒 [+ an undesirable quality] (*a bit too ...*) :

有點兒大，有點兒舊，有點兒短
yǒudiǎnr dà,   yǒudiǎnr jiù,   yǒudiǎnr duǎn

很新/舊

2 – 1)

很高/矮

2 – 1)

3 **Describing people and things using adjectives** **Subject + Adj Phrase**

■ Chinese adjectives (also called stative verbs) follow the subject (or topic) of the sentence without including the verb to be (是).

A) Using a single adjective to suggest a contrast or a comparison: Sb/Sth + (不) + Adj

1) 你們兩個人哪個高? → 我高。 ✔
   Nǐmen liǎng gè rén nǎge gāo?

   我是高。 ✘

2) 哪個書包便宜? → 這個(書包)便宜，那個不便宜。 ✔   **3** – A) – 1)
   Nǎge shūbāo piányi?   Zhège (shūbāo) piányi,   nàge bù piányi.

   那個是不便宜。 ✘

B) Using an adjective phrase for a descriptive comment: 很 X, 不 X, 不太 X, 不夠 X, 有點兒 X

■ This is the regular form. 很 is often unstressed, i.e., without emphasizing "very".

1) 她很好，她不太高，她很漂亮
   tā hěn hǎo,   tā bú tài gāo,   tā hěn piàoliang

2) 這個房間很新，這張桌子很大，我的書很多，這些東西很便宜
   zhège fángjiān hěn xīn, zhè zhāng zhuōzi hěn dà, wǒ de shū hěn duō, zhèxiē dōngxi hěn piányi

■ To describe undesirable qualities, 不太, 不夠, and 有點兒 can be used.

3) 這張書桌不太好，不夠大，有點兒貴。
   Zhè zhāng shūzhuō bú tài hǎo, búgòu dà, yǒudiǎnr guì.

3 – B) – 2)

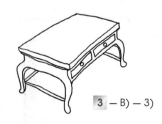

3 – B) – 3)

    Illustrations © Cengage Learning 2015

C) Using an emotive emphasis: 太⋯⋯了！

[It's] great! . . . too big! so pretty!

1) 這本書太好了！
Zhè běn shū tài hǎo le!

2) 這個書包太大了！
Zhège shūbāo tài dà le!

3 – C) – 1)

3 – C) – 2)

3) 這支筆太漂亮了！
Zhè zhī bǐ tài piàoliang le!

4) 這兩本書太便宜了！
Zhè liǎng běn shū tài piányi le!

3 – C) – 3)

3 – C) – 4)

---

4 **Expressing a change of state**   **Sentence 了**

A) Using 了 at the end of a sentence indicates an updated or changed state or situation with reference to the past.

1) 以前王老師的兒子很小，現在大了。
Yǐqián Wáng lǎoshī de érzi hěn xiǎo, xiànzài dà le.

(Professor Wang's son used to be little. Now he is all grown up.)

2) 以前東西很便宜，現在貴了。
Yǐqián dōngxi hěn piányi, xiànzài guì le.

(Things used to be inexpensive, but they are now expensive.)

4 – A) – 1)

B) 不⋯⋯了 means "not . . . anymore."

1) 以前東西很便宜，現在不便宜了。
Yǐqián dōngxi hěn piányi, xiànzài bù piányi le.

(Things are no longer inexpensive/affordable.)

C) Time words are often absent, and 了 at the end signifies a contrast to the previous situation.

1) 他很高了。   vs.   他很高。
Tā hěn gāo le.   Tā hěn gāo.
(He has become tall./He is tall now.)   *(He is tall.)*

4 – C) – 1)

Before viewing . . .

1) Do you often buy things online?

2) What is your favorite store for school supplies?

3) What items (school supplies or clothing) would you like to buy more of? Why?

While viewing . . .

1) During your first viewing, focus on meaning.

2) During your second viewing, pay special attention to speech forms and tones.

3) Finally, practice saying the sentences by answering the questions below.

 U3-A1

小南說什麼?
Xiǎonán shuō shénme?

"我＿＿＿＿＿＿!"
　Wǒ……

因為現在小南高了，所以她的衣服
Yīnwèi xiànzài Xiǎonán gāo le, suǒyǐ tā de yīfu
怎麼樣了?
zěnmeyàng le?

"所以我的衣服＿＿＿＿＿＿，
　Suǒyǐ wǒ de yīfu……

褲子也＿＿＿＿＿＿!"
kùzi yě……

小南的什麼東西很多？
Xiǎonán de shénme dōngxi hěn duō?

"我的＿＿＿＿＿＿＿＿＿＿＿＿＿＿＿。"
Wǒ de……

她說她的書包怎麼樣？
Tā shuō tā de shūbāo zěnmeyàng?

"這個書包＿＿＿＿＿＿＿＿！
Zhège shūbāo……

這兒也＿＿＿＿＿＿。"
Zhèr yě……

 U3-A2

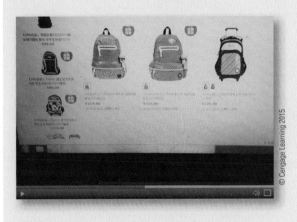

小南覺得新書包怎麼樣？
Xiǎonán juéde xīn shūbāo zěnmeyàng?

"這個＿＿＿＿＿＿＿＿＿，
Zhège……

這個也＿＿＿＿＿＿＿＿，
zhège yě……

可是＿＿＿＿＿＿＿＿＿＿。"
kěshì……

衣服怎麼樣？　貴不貴？
Yīfu zěnmeyàng?　Guì bú guì?

"衣服呢？＿＿＿＿＿＿＿＿＿。"
Yīfu ne?……

1 Forms and structures

See 3.2 for more notes and examples.

1) 我的書和本子都很多。
   Wǒ de shū hé běnzi dōu hěn duō.

(是 is not required before the adjective.)

2) 這個書包太小了!
   Zhège shūbāo tài xiǎo le!

太……了
(This structure adds an emotive tone.)

3) 這個書包很漂亮, 這個也不錯!
   Zhège shūbāo hěn piàoliang, zhège yě bú cuò!

這個…, 這個…
(rather than 這個…, 那個…)

4) 可是(這)兩個書包都有點兒貴。
   Kěshì (zhè) liǎng gè shūbāo dōu yǒudiǎnr guì.

有點兒 + Adj
(undesirable quality)

5) 衣服呢? 衣服也不便宜。
   Yīfu ne? Yīfu yě bù piányi.

(Do not put 也 at the beginning or the end of a clause.)

Change of situation: Use sentence-final 了

1) 我高了, 所以我的衣服小了。
   Wǒ gāo le, suǒyǐ wǒ de yīfu xiǎo le.

(*I'm taller now, so my jacket has become too small.*)

2) 我的褲子也不夠長了。
   Wǒ de kùzi yě búgòu cháng le.

不……了
(*not . . . anymore*)

3) 這兒也壞了。
   Zhèr yě huài le.

(*It's also broken here.*)

Interrogative and negative forms

Remember, 不 changes to the second tone when it is followed by the fourth tone.

不 X , 不太 X , 不夠 [+ desirable]

A) Comments and related questions: *Negative answers:*

1) 這個書包很大，那個呢？   那個不大(不太大、不夠大)。

2) 衣服有點兒貴，褲子也貴嗎？   _____

3) 王新很高，他弟弟也高嗎？   _____

B) Indicating changed situation with 了:

1) 以前小南的書包小不小？
   現在夠大嗎？   以前她的書包不小，現在不夠大了。

2) 以前小南矮不矮？ 現在還矮嗎？   _____

3) 以前小南的褲子短不短？ 現在呢？   _____

1 Pair work

First, review the new vocabulary, then ask and answer questions based on the following pictures.

Adjectives:	大/小，多/少，新/舊，高/矮，貴/便宜，好/壞，漂亮，高興
New Question Words:	怎麼樣，為什麼
New Adverbs:	很X，太X了，不太X，不夠X，有點兒X
Time Words:	以前，現在

1

Mike是大三的學生，他的宿舍大不大？
… shì dà sān de xuésheng, tā de sùshè dà bú dà?

他的室友多不多？
Tā de shìyǒu duō bù duō?

2

Mike 的房間怎麼樣？書桌呢？（大？ 好？ 新？）
… de fángjiān zěnmeyàng? Shūzhuō ne? (Dà? Hǎo? Xīn?)

他的東西多不多？ 什麼很多？
Tā de dōngxi duō bù duō? Shénme hěn duō?

3

他妹妹Mary是大一的學生。她的室友也很多嗎？
Tā mèimei … shì dà yī de xuésheng. Tā de shìyǒu yě hěn duō ma?

她的房間怎麼樣？
Tā de fángjiān zěnmeyàng?

4

Mary 的室友好不好？ 為什麼？
… de shìyǒu hǎo bù hǎo? Wèishénme?

Mary高興不高興？
… gāoxìng bù gāoxìng?

5

Mary現在高興了嗎？ 為什麼？
… xiànzài gāoxìng le ma? Wèishénme?

她的房間還小嗎？ 東西新還是舊？
Tā de fángjiān hái xiǎo ma? Dōngxi xīn háishi jiù?

2 Interview and report

1) **Interview:** Move around the classroom and speak to several classmates. Ask and answer questions about where they live, their roommates, and the quality and conditions of their rooms.

2) **Report:** The teacher will ask students to report what they learned about the classmates they interviewed. The teacher may also invite students to ask questions about his/her office.

3) **Quiz:** The teacher may quiz students on the information shared in the reports.

A 3.6 語法鞏固 yǔfǎ gǒnggù   **REINFORCE THE GRAMMAR**

These exercises are also available online with automatic feedback.

Predicative adjectives reflecting changed situations

1 **Give the Chinese equivalent for each sentence**
Remember not to use 和 for "and." Instead, use a comma and 也.

1) He is a student. <u>He is tall</u>. → _____

2) This book <u>is good</u> and <u>inexpensive</u>. → _____

3) This backpack is good, but <u>it is a little old</u>. → _____

4) <u>Which</u> desk is <u>big</u>? — That one is. (contrastive) → _____

5) He <u>has aged</u>. (changed situation) → _____

6) She <u>is not pretty anymore</u>. (changed situation) → _____

2 **Correct the sentences**
Identify the error in each sentence and write it correctly.

1) 我的宿舍是新和是大。✗ _____

2) 這本書一點貴。✗ _____

3) 因為她的宿舍小，她的床也小。✗ _____

4) 以前她的東西很少，東西多了。✗ _____

5) 那張桌子很大不大？✗ _____

A 3.7 聽答對話 tīngdá duìhuà   **LET'S CHAT**

In this listening-speaking activity you'll be asked to answer questions about the **video** segment as well as about **yourself.** You may be asked to record and submit your answers to the teacher.

B 第二課

買 一 個 新 的
Let's buy a new one

B 3.8 詞語預習 cíyǔ yùxí — PREVIEW THE VOCABULARY

🌐 Use the **online audio flashcards** to familiarize yourself with the new vocabulary in this section.

Numerals (Nu)

十	shí	ten
百	bǎi	hundred
千	qiān	thousand

Nouns (N)   M

錢	qián	money	
運動服	yùndòngfú	sweatsuit, tracksuit	套/件
電腦	diànnǎo	computer	個/臺
手機	shǒujī	mobile phone	個/臺

Measure Words (M)

元 yuán	dollar, *yuan*
塊 kuài	dollar, *yuan*
套 tào	set
臺 tái	(used for machines, equipment, etc.)

Verbs (V)

要	yào	want, need, be going to
想要	xiǎng yào	want to, intend to, desire
覺得	juéde	feel, think
應該	yīnggāi	should, ought to
買	mǎi	buy
賣	mài	sell
問	wèn	ask

Question Word (QW)

多少	duōshao	how much/many

Conjunction (Conj)

而且	érqiě	and also, moreover

Specifier (Sp)

這麼	zhème	so, such, in this way, like this

Expressions (Exp)

夠了/不夠
gòu le/búgòu
enough / not enough

有什麼事？
Yǒu shénme shì?
What's up?

那好吧！/好吧！
Nà hǎo ba! / Hǎo ba!
Okay then!

Structures

- 一點兒也不貴
- 該買新的了
- 要一個…
- 要/想買一個…
- 便宜的東西
- 要新的

B | 3.9 詞句聽說 cíjù tīngshuō　　FOCUS ON GRAMMAR

Aural-Oral Exercises: Do the online exercises to further familiarize yourself with the new vocabulary and grammar when it is used in sentences.

Main Features: To build on the previous lesson, we'll continue to work on adjectives. However, this time we'll look at their attributive use, that is, using <u>adjectives as modifiers</u> to describe people or things. An <u>Adj–的 phrase</u> can function as a noun phrase. When you observe differences between Chinese and your native language, you will discover similarities as well. Finally, you will master the forms for 要 and 想要 (*to want, would like to*). They are high-frequency words and have different usages.

1　Using adjectives as modifiers to specify a person or an object　　Adj + 的 + N

■■■ Adjectives can be divided into subcategories according to the grammar rules that govern them.

A) Adj + 的 + Noun: 貴的，便宜的，漂亮的，很小的…

1) 貴的筆，　很小的桌子，　漂亮的衣服，　很便宜的書包
　　guì de bǐ,　hěn xiǎo de zhuōzi,　piàoliang de yīfu,　hěn piányi de shūbāo

B) Adj + Noun: 大/小，新/舊，長/短，好/壞

■■■ These monosyllabic adjectives denoting general concepts can join a noun directly without 的.

1) 大書包，　小桌子，　新書，　舊衣服，　長褲
　　dà shūbāo,　xiǎo zhuōzi,　xīn shū,　jiù yīfu,　chángkù

C) Compare the following:

1) 新書，　很新的書；　舊衣服，　很舊的衣服；　小桌子，　很小的桌子
　　xīnshū,　hěn xīn de shū;　jiù yīfu,　hěn jiù de yīfu;　xiǎo zhuōzi,　hěn xiǎo de zhuōzi

2 Identifying people and things using a nominalized adjective phrase   Adj + 的

A) Adj + 的

▬ An Adj-的 phrase functions like a noun phrase. This avoids repetition of the noun.

1) 大的/小的，好的/壞的，新的/舊的，貴的/便宜的，高的/矮的，長的/短的
   dà de/xiǎo de,   hǎo de/huài de,   xīn de/jiù de,   guì de/piányi de,   gāo de/ǎi de, cháng de/duǎn de

2) 哪張桌子是你的：大的還是小的？   （＝大的桌子還是小的桌子？）
   Nǎ zhāng zhuōzi shì nǐ de: dà de háishi xiǎo de?

3) 那兩個女生哪個是王新的女朋友：高的還是矮的？
   Nà liǎng gè nǚsheng nǎge shì Wáng Xīn de nǚpéngyou: gāo de háishi ǎi de?

B) 是 + Adj + 的

▬ Some Adj-的 phrases are often used with 是 to identify items. Compare the following pairs.

1) 這張書桌是新的，那張是舊的。   (Identifying items)
   Zhè zhāng shūzhuō shì xīn de, nà zhāng shì jiù de.
   (This desk is a new one, and that one is an old one.)

2 – B) – 1)

   這張書桌很新，那張有點兒舊。   (Commenting on items)
   Zhè zhāng shūzhuō hěn xīn, nà zhāng yǒu diǎnr jiù.
   (This desk is pretty new, and that one is a little old.)

2) 這臺電腦是不是好的？   (Identifying)
   Zhè tái diànnǎo shì bú shì hǎo de?
   (Is this computer a good one /in good condition?)

   這臺電腦好不好？   (Commenting)
   Zhè tái diànnǎo hǎo bù hǎo?
   (Is this computer good [in quality, comparatively speaking]?)

3 Asking for prices   [item] (要) 多少錢?

▬ 元 is formal and 塊 is colloquial.

1) (￥2)兩塊/元，(￥20)二十塊/元，(￥200)兩百塊/元， or 二百塊/元，
   liǎng kuài/yuán,   èrshí kuài/yuán,   liǎngbǎi kuài/yuán   èrbǎi kuài/yuán,

   (￥2000)兩千塊/元
   liǎngqiān kuài/yuán

2) 這個書包(要)多少錢?　　　　　　→　　　這個書包(要)150塊(錢)。
   Zhège shūbāo (yào) duōshao qián?　　　　　　Zhège shūbāo (yào) yìbǎi wǔshí kuài (qián).

3) 請問，這套運動服多少錢?　　　→　　　這套運動服200元。　　(The verb is omitted.)
   Qǐngwèn, zhè tào yùndòngfú duōshao qián?　　　Zhè tào yùndòngfú liǎngbǎi yuán.

4　**Expressing someone's need or desire for an item　要/想要 + N**

■■■ Both 要 and 想要 convey the idea of "wanting" with different degrees of intensity.

A) 要

■■■ 要 conveys the certainty of a person's need or intention to have something.

1) 要一個新手機，　要一套運動服，　要一臺電腦
   yào yí gè xīn shǒujī,　　yào yí tào yùndòngfú,　　yào yì tái diànnǎo

2) 你要幾張桌子? 要大桌子　　　→　　　我要一張，不要大桌子，要小桌子。
   Nǐ yào jǐ zhāng zhuōzi? Yào dà zhuōzi　　　Wǒ yào yì zhāng, bú yào dà zhuōzi, yào xiǎo zhuōzi.
   還是小桌子?
   háishi xiǎo zhuōzi?

3) 你要不要這兩張(桌子)?　　　→　　　我不要這兩張，我要那兩張。
   Nǐ yào bú yào zhè liǎng zhāng (zhuōzi)?　　　Wǒ bú yào zhè liǎng zhāng, wǒ yào nà liǎng zhāng.

B) 想要

■■■ It expresses what someone wishes to have, which he/she may or may not get.

1) 想要一張大桌子，想要一個電腦，想要一件漂亮的衣服　(想一個… ✘)
   xiǎng yào yì zhāng dà zhuōzi, xiǎng yào yí gè diànnǎo, xiǎng yào yí jiàn piàoliang de yīfu.

2) 我的電腦太舊了，我想要一個新電腦，可是我沒有錢。
   Wǒ de diànnǎo tài jiù le, wǒ xiǎng yào yí gè xīn diànnǎo, kěshì wǒ méiyǒu qián.

3) 他想(要)不想要一個新電腦?　→　他不想要新電腦，他想要一個新手機。
   Tā xiǎng (yào) bù xiǎng yào yí gè xīn diànnǎo?　Tā bù xiǎng yào xīn diànnǎo, tā xiǎng yào yí gè xīn shǒujī.

4 – B) – 3)

A) 要 + Action VP

■ When used in this context, 要 is an auxiliary verb followed by an action verb and expresses a necessary or planned action. It expresses both *to need to* and *to be going to do something*.

1) 要學中文，要認識一個中國朋友，要買一個新手機
   yào xué Zhōngwén, yào rènshi yí gè Zhōngguó péngyou, yào mǎi yí gè xīn shǒujī

2) 你要買中文書還是英文書？ → 我要買英文書。
   Nǐ yào mǎi Zhōngwén shū háishi Yīngwén shū? Wǒ yào mǎi Yīngwén shū.

5 — A) — 2)

不 V; 不想 V

■ To negate a sentence, place 不 before the verb. To soften the tone of negation, use 不想 V.

3) 你要學中文嗎？ → 不，我不學中文。（我不想學中文。）
   Nǐ yào xué Zhōngwén ma?   Bù,   wǒ bù xué Zhōngwén.

B) 想(要) + Action VP

■ 想(要) (*to want to do something / would like to do something*) is different from 要 + VP in that it does not have the absolute certainty of action. Note 要 in this usage is habitually omitted. However, the action verb following 想 cannot be omitted.

1) 想買一個電腦，想買一套衣服，想學中文，想認識一個中國人
   xiǎng mǎi yí gè diànnǎo, xiǎng mǎi yí tào yīfu, xiǎng xué Zhōngwén, xiǎng rènshi yí gè Zhōngguórén

2) 因為我的衣服小了，所以我想買一件新衣服。
   Yīnwèi wǒ de yīfu xiǎo le,   suǒyǐ wǒ xiǎng mǎi yí jiàn xīn yīfu.

■ 很 can be added to emphasize the tone of voice.

3) 他很想買一個新手機，可是沒有錢。
   Tā hěn xiǎng mǎi yí gè xīn shǒujī, kěshì méiyǒu qián.

5 — B) — 3)

4) 她想不想買一個新電腦？ → 她不想買新電腦，她想買一個新手機。
   Tā xiǎng bù xiǎng mǎi yí gè xīn diànnǎo?   Tā bù xiǎng mǎi xīn diànnǎo, tā xiǎng mǎi yí gè xīn shǒujī.

6 Expressing the need for change

該 + [Action VP] 了
It's time to do something.

■ 該 is the short form for 應該 (*should, ought to*). In this case, 了 indicates a new state or situation.

1) 該買新衣服了，該學中文了，該認識幾個中國人了
   gāi mǎi xīn yīfu le,   gāi xué Zhōngwén le, gāi rènshi jǐ gè Zhōngguórén le

2) 我的電腦舊了，該買一臺新的了。
   Wǒ de diànnǎo jiù le,   gāi mǎi yì tái xīn de le.

3) 我的衣服小了，該買一件大的了。
   Wǒ de yīfu xiǎo le,   gāi mǎi yí jiàn dā de le.

7 Intensifying a negation

一點兒 + 也不/都不 + Adj
not at all . . .

■ 也 and 都 can be used interchangeably in this case.

1) 一點兒也不好，一點兒也不貴，一點兒都不漂亮
   yìdiǎnr yě bù hǎo,   yìdiǎnr yě bú guì,   yìdiǎnr dōu bú piàoliang

2) 這張書桌有點兒大。   ➔   大？我覺得一點兒也不大！
   Zhè zhāng shūzhuō yǒudiǎnr dà.   Dà?   Wǒ juéde yìdiǎnr yě bú dà!

3) 你覺得這件衣服怎麼樣？   ➔   很便宜，可是一點兒都不好！
   Nǐ juéde zhè jiàn yīfu zěnmeyàng?   Hěn piányi,   kěshì yìdiǎnr dōu bù hǎo!

8 Usage of 夠

不夠 X，不夠，夠了

■ Use only the three forms below.

1) **不夠 X**   這張桌子不夠大，也不夠新。(不夠 + Adj)
   (*not [good] enough*)   Zhè zhāng zhuōzi búgòu dà, yě búgòu xīn.

2) **不夠**   我的錢不夠。(NOT 我沒有夠錢; 不夠 cannot be followed by a noun.)
   (*X is not enough.*)   Wǒ de qián búgòu.

   我的筆和本子都不夠了 (*are running out*)，所以我要買一些。
   Wǒ de bǐ hé běnzi dōu búgòu le,   suǒyǐ wǒ yào mǎi yìxiē.

3) **夠了**   我的錢夠了。(了 is required. It is uncommon to say 我的錢夠.)
   (*X is enough.*)   Wǒ de qián gòu le.

   他們的學生不多，所以20本書夠了。
   Tāmen de xuésheng bù duō, suǒyǐ èrshí běn shū gòu le.

Before viewing . . .

1) In your culture, do parents normally buy things for their children when they ask for them?

2) Do you think Chinese parents tend to be indulgent or restrictive with regard to buying things for their children?

While viewing . . .

1) During your first viewing, focus on meaning.

2) During your second viewing, pay special attention to speech forms and tones.

3) Finally, practice saying the sentences by answering the questions below.

U3-B1

小南想要什麼?
Xiǎonán xiǎng yào shénme?

"媽，我要＿＿＿＿＿＿＿＿＿＿＿。"
Mā,　wǒ yào……

媽媽說什麼?
Māma shuō shénme?

"你的＿＿＿＿＿＿＿＿＿＿＿？
Nǐ de……

為什麼＿＿＿＿＿＿＿＿？"
Wèishénme……

小南說什麼?
Xiǎonán shuō shénme?

"因為＿＿＿＿＿＿＿＿＿＿＿，
Yīnwèi……

這個書包＿＿＿＿＿！而且這兒＿＿＿＿，
zhège shūbāo……　　　　Érqiě zhèr……

所以該＿＿＿＿＿＿＿。"
suǒyǐ gāi……

媽媽說什麼?
Māma shuō shénme?

"是有點兒＿＿＿＿＿。
Shì yǒudiǎnr……

那好吧，＿＿＿＿＿＿＿＿＿！"
Nà hǎo ba,

© Cengage Learning 2015

媽媽覺得這個書包怎麼樣？要多少錢？
Māma juéde zhège shūbāo zěnmeyàng? Yào duōshao qián?

"很＿＿＿＿＿！什麼？兩百塊！＿＿＿＿＿！"
Hěn……　　　Shénme? Liǎng bǎi kuài?

小南覺得貴不貴？她說什麼？
Xiǎonán juéde guì bú guì? Tā shuō shénme?

"我覺得＿＿＿＿＿＿＿＿＿＿＿＿＿。
Wǒ juéde……

看，＿＿＿＿＿＿＿＿＿＿＿＿＿！"
kàn

小南還想要一套新運動服，為什麼？
Xiǎonán hái xiǎng yào yí tào xīn yùndòngfú, wèishénme?

"因為＿＿＿＿＿＿＿＿＿＿＿！看，
Yīnwèi……　　　　　　　　　Kàn,

衣服＿＿＿＿＿，褲子＿＿＿＿＿。"
yīfu……　　　　　kùzi……

媽媽覺得怎麼樣？她說什麼？
Māma juéde zěnmeyàng?　Tā shuō shénme?

"是＿＿＿＿＿！＿＿＿＿＿＿＿＿！"
Shì……

小南高興嗎？她說什麼？
Xiǎonán gāoxìng ma? Tā shuō shénme?

"＿＿＿＿＿＿＿＿＿＿＿＿＿，

＿＿＿＿＿！"

1 **Forms and structures**
See 3.9 for more notes and examples.

Expressing need and intention

1) 我要一個新書包。
Wǒ yào yí gè xīn shūbāo.

要 + N
(to want an item)

2) 我還想要一套新運動服。
Wǒ hái xiǎng yào yí tào xīn yùndòngfú.

想要 + N
(to wish to have something)

Justifying

1) 因為……，而且這兒也壞了……
Yīnwèi……,　　érqiě zhèr yě huài le……

而且…也…
(而且…也… makes a statement more emphatic.
Do not use 和.)

2) 所以該買一個新的了。
Suǒyǐ gāi mǎi yí gè xīn de le.

該…了
(It's time to [buy] . . .)

3) 因為現在我高了！
Yīnwèi xiànzài wǒ gāo le,

因為……
(Here this statement responds to the question
"為什麼……?")

4) 衣服小了，褲子也不夠長了！
Yīfu xiǎo le,　　kùzi yě búgòu cháng le!

(The use of 了 here indicates a new situation in
present time.)

Accepting

1) (書包)是有點兒小了。/(你)是高了！
(Shūbāo) shì yǒudiǎnr xiǎo le.　　(Nǐ) shì gāo le!

(是 serves as an emphasis marker.)
(It [really] is . . . / You are tall!)

2) 那好吧，買新的、大的！
Nà hǎo ba,　　mǎi xīn de、dà de!

(新的 and 大的 here stand for the noun
phrases 新書包 and 大書包 respectively.)
(All right then. Buy a new and bigger one!)

Other forms and expressions

1) (有)什麼事?
(Yǒu) shénme shì?

(What's the matter?)

2) 這麼貴?！
Zhème guì?!

(In this context, 這麼 refers to a certain price.)
(It's this expensive?!)

3) 一點兒也不貴！
Yìdiǎnr yě bú guì!

(It's not expensive at all!)

Interrogative and negative forms 　　　　　　要，想要

Practice the following interrogative and negative sentences using the cues provided.

A) 要 / 想要 + N 　　　　　　　　　　Negative: 不要 X；不想要 X
want sth / want to have sth

1) 你<u>要不要</u>電腦？有新的，有舊的。　　我不要舊的，我要新的。
　　　　　　　　　　　　　　　　　　　　　　―――――――――――――――
　　　　　　　　　　　　　　　　　　　　　（不要 X，要 Y）

2) 你<u>要</u>運動服<u>嗎</u>？有貴的，也有便宜的。　―――――――――――――――
　　　　　　　　　　　　　　　　　　　　　（不要 X，也不要 Y）

3) 你<u>想不想要</u>一個大書桌？　　　　　　―――――――――――――――
　　　　　　　　　　　　　　　　　　　　　（不<u>想要</u> X 的）

B) 要 / 想 + Action Verb 　　　　　　Negative: 不買 X；不想買 X
be going to do / would like to do

1) 他<u>要</u>買手機嗎？　　　　　　　　　　他不買手機。
　　　　　　　　　　　　　　　　　　　　　（不買 X）

2) 他<u>要</u>賣電腦還是賣衣服？　　　　　　―――――――――――――――
　　　　　　　　　　　　　　　　　　　　　（不賣 X，也不賣 Y）

3) 他<u>想不想</u>賣手機？　　　　　　　　　―――――――――――――――
　　　　　　　　　　　　　　　　　　　　　（不想 V…）

3
Story narration

Pay special attention to the verb forms and the use of punctuation marks.

　　小南要一個新書包。媽媽覺得她的書包很好，為什麼要新的。小南
　　Xiǎonán yào mǎi yí ge xīn shūbāo. Māma juéde tā de shūbāo hěn hǎo, wèishénme yào mǎi xīn de. Xiǎonán

説因為她的東西太多，書包太小，而且書包也壞了，所以該買一個新的大
shuō yīnwèi tā de dōngxi tài duō, shūbāo tài xiǎo, érqiě shūbāo yě huài le, suǒyǐ gāi mǎi yí ge xīn de da

的了。媽媽覺得新書包很漂亮，可是200元有點兒貴。小南説還有300元、
de le. Māma juéde xīn shūbāo hěn piàoliang, kěshì liǎngbǎi yuán yǒudiǎnr guì. Xiǎonán shuō hái yǒu sānbǎi yuán、

400元的書包，所以200元一點兒也不貴。小南還想要一套新運動服，因為
sìbǎi yuán de shūbāo, suǒyǐ liǎngbǎi yuán yìdiǎnr yě bú guì. Xiǎonán hái xiǎng yào yí tào xīn yùndòngfú, yīnwèi

現在她高了，衣服小了，褲子也不夠長了。媽媽説："是高了！好吧好吧，
xiànzài tā gāo le, yīfu xiǎo le, kùzi yě búgòu cháng le. Māma shuō: "Shì gāo le! Hǎo ba hǎo ba,

買新的。"所以小南要買一個新書包和一套新運動服，她很高興！
mǎi xīn de." Suǒyǐ Xiǎonán yào mǎi yí ge xīn shūbāo hé yí tào xīn yùndòngfú, tā hěn gāoxìng!

1 **Pair Work**

First review the forms and the sample questions and answers on buying things. Then practice asking and answering these questions based on the following pictures.

Noun Phrases: 大的/小的，新的/舊的，貴的/便宜的，好的，漂亮的
dà de/xiǎo de, xīn de jiù de, guì de/ piányi de, hǎo de, piàoliang de

New State: 舊了，壞了，太小了，不夠好了
jiù le, huài le, tài xiǎo le, bú gòu hǎo le

Adverbs: 很＿，有點兒＿，不太＿，不夠＿，太＿了
hěn……, yǒudiǎnr……, bú tài……, bú gòu……, tài…… le

Questions:

你想買什麼？
Nǐ xiǎng mǎi shénme?

你的＿還很好，為什麼要買新的？
Nǐ de…hái hěn hǎo, wèishénme yào mǎi xīn de?

你想要＿的還是＿的？
Nǐ xiǎng yào…de háishi … de?

你覺得這個＿的怎麼樣？
Nǐ juéde zhè gè…de zěnmeyàng?

為什麼(不)想買/要這個＿的？
Wèi shénme (bù) xiǎng mǎi/yào zhège…de?

Answers:

→ 我想買一個……
Wo xiǎng mǎi yí gè……

→ 因為(舊了，壞了…)，該買新的了。
Yīnwèi (jiù le, huài le…), gāi mǎi xīn de le.

→ 我想要＿的，不想要＿的。
Wǒ xiǎng yào…de, bù xiǎng yào…de.

→ 這個[很/有點兒/太/不夠……]，
Zhège [hěn/yǒudiǎnr/ tài/ bú gòu……],

而且……
érqiě……

→ 因為……，所以……
Yīnwèi…, suǒyǐ……

2 Interview and report

1) **Interview:** Move around to interview classmates. Ask them what they want to buy and why. Have them specify whether what they want is big or small, new or used, expensive or inexpensive, etc.

2) **Report:** The teacher will ask students to report on their interviews.

3) **Quiz:** When the reports are finished, the teacher may quiz students on the information shared. Students are expected to confirm or correct the information given in the quiz and to practice affirmative and negative sentences.

B | 3.13 | 語法鞏固 yǔfǎ gǒnggù   REINFORCE THE GRAMMAR

These exercises are also available online with automatic feedback.

1 Give the Chinese equivalent for each dialogue

要/想要 + N，要 + Action V，想 + Action V

1) Q: Which desk do you want? The big one?   _____

   A: No, not the big one. I'd like to have the small one. _____

2) Q: Are you going to buy a computer?   _____

   A: No, I'm not.   _____

3) Q: Would you like to meet some Chinese students?   _____

   A: No, I don't think so.   _____

4) Q: Does she want to study Chinese?   _____

   A: No, she doesn't.   _____

2 Fill in the blank with the appropriate form

1) 我的衣服_____，我要買一件新的。 a. 舊的   b. 舊了

2) 我不要_____桌子，我要小的。   a. 大/大的   b. 很大

3) 我要買一個_____手機。   a. 好   b. 很好

4) 我不想買_____衣服。   a. 貴   b. 貴的

5) 這些書是_____。   a. 新的   b. 一點兒新

B | 3.14 | 聽答對話 tīngdá duìhuà   LET'S CHAT

In this listening-speaking activity you'll be asked to answer questions about the **video** segment as well as about **yourself.** You may be asked to record and submit your answers to the teacher.

COLLEGE
EXPENSES

Many western economists attribute China's wealth to its people's management of money; Chinese culture has traditionally emphasized saving more than it does spending. Penny-pinching and thrift are still highly valued in Chinese culture, but as China moves toward a more consumption-driven economy, today's consumers, especially those who live in metropolitan areas with comfortable incomes, are not that much different from their counterparts in the West in their shopping habits. Compared to thirty years ago, Chinese consumers certainly have much more purchasing power and thus spend considerably more on nonessentials, such as leisure travel, restaurant dining, and entertainment. Further, today's consumers, especially young urbanites, are more brand-name conscious and willing to pay premium prices for designer clothes or famous-brand electronic gadgets. The burgeoning sales of iPhones are a clear indication of this trend.

For most Chinese consumers, though, balancing of product quality and affordability is an important rule. Thus the expression, **xìngjiàbǐ** (性價比), or "cost-to-performance ratio," has become a new mantra for smart shoppers. Budget-conscious shoppers not only shop around, a

practice in a traditional Chinese society known as **huò bǐ sān jiā** (货比三家, literally, "comparing prices from three stores"), but also search beyond conventional retail channels. E-commerce sites, such as www.taobao.com (淘寶網), www.dangdang.com (當當網), and www.amazon.cn (Amazon China site, 亞馬遜), are flourishing today. Cybershopping has become quite popular not only for its convenience but also because online stores usually provide larger selections of competitively priced merchandise.

For most high school and university students, their biggest personal expenses are personal computers and electronic gadgets (mobile phones, MP3 players, digital cameras, etc.). Since governments at all levels subsidize housing and dining at most universities and some boarding high schools, living on campus is not expensive. Students are responsible for purchasing their textbooks, but they are considerably cheaper than those used at American universities. Some schools even include book fees in their tuition, which means they are subsidized by the government. But unlike most students at American universities, college students in China usually have to pay for their Internet usage, and WiFi is not widely available in student dormitories or classrooms. Another expense for many high school and college students is mobile phone usage. For many college students, the mobile phone has become an indispensable gadget that helps them connect outside of campus. Since texting is relative cheap in China (¥0.10 per outgoing text and free for incoming messages), it is the preferred means of communication among friends and peers. Those who have smartphones may also use them for instant messaging, social media networking, and even online gaming.

Here is a sample of the costs of a college education for an academic year (data gathered from a survey of a small group of students attending a university for science and technology in Shanghai):

1. Tuition: ¥5,000–5,500
2. Textbooks and other study materials: ¥400–800
3. Housing: ¥1,000
4. Food: ¥6,000–8,000
5. Phone service: ¥400–500
6. Internet service: ¥200–300
7. Local transportation: ¥300–800
8. Clothing: ¥2,000–4,000
9. Entertainment: ¥500–800
10. Extracurricular activities: ¥1,000–2,000

QUIZ

1. Traditionally, is China considered to have a "culture of spending" or a "culture of saving"? Why?
2. What is the traditional Chinese expression for budget-conscious shopping?

ACTIVITIES

1. If you have a friend from Hong Kong or Taiwan, ask him or her to help you get a sense of the cost of a college education where they come from, including tuition and living expenses.
2. Compare college expenses in China (based on the figures listed above) and those in the United States (based on your own expenses at college). Do your findings surprise you? Why or why not?

單元復習
Review and Integration

3.16 主課復習 zhǔkè fùxí **REVIEW THE STORY**

Read the following passages as fast as you can. Follow these steps:

1) Do not stop to check the meaning of words you don't recognize. Mark them and keep reading.
2) Read the passage again and guess the meaning of the marked words on a separate piece of paper.
3) Finally, look up the words in a dictionary or the vocabulary index and verify their meanings.

小南的書和本子都很多，她的書包太小了，而且也壞了。小南想買一個大的、漂亮的書包。新書包要200塊錢。媽媽說，200塊太貴了，可是小南覺得一點兒也不貴！

小南也想要一套新運動服。媽媽覺得她的運動服還很好，問她為什麼要買新的。小南說，因為她現在高了，所以她的衣服小了，褲子也不夠長了。媽媽覺得小南是高了，是該買新衣服了。媽媽說，好吧好吧，買新的！小南很高興！

Quickly provide the Chinese equivalents for the following phrases and sentences. Do not translate them word for word.

1 **Measure words:** 個，件，條，臺，塊，支，張，套，把

In English you say . . .   *In Chinese you say . . .*

1) three computers

2) a big desk and two chairs

3) several pens and sheets of paper

4) these two clothing items

5) that tracksuit

6) those things

2 **Adjectives and Nouns:**

1) This desk is an old one.

2) This desk is a little old.

3) This desk is too old!

4) This desk is old/worn now.

5) This desk is not big.

6) This desk is not big enough!

7) This desk is not very big.

8) This desk is not big at all!

3 **Expressions:**

1) This computer is a little expensive.

2) This computer is not expensive at all.

3) I have enough pens. / I don't have enough pens.

4) That backpack is not big enough.

5) Is ¥200 enough?

4 **Question Words and Question Forms:** 為什麼，怎麼樣，幾，多少，哪，X 不 X

1) How are these two books?

2) How many books do you want? (fewer than 10)

3) Is this book expensive? (use X不X)

4) <u>How much</u> (money) does this one cost? _____

5) <u>Which</u> book is more expensive? _____

6) <u>Which books</u> are in Chinese? (unspecified quantity) _____

7) <u>Why</u> do you want to buy this book? _____

3.18 語法小測驗 yǔfǎ xiǎo cèyàn   CHECK FOR ACCURACY

1 Correct the sentences

Identify the error(s) in each sentence and then rewrite the sentence correctly.

1) 這書是中文書。✗ _____

2) 我有200錢。✗ _____

3) 我有夠錢/我沒有夠錢。✗ _____

4) 這個書桌是新。✗ _____

5) 我想一個新電腦。✗ _____

6) 我要買一個很好手機。✗ _____

7) 多少錢是這個? ✗ _____

8) 那些本書是誰的? ✗ _____

9) 這個電腦一點兒貴。✗ _____

10) 這個電腦不新的。✗ _____

11) 因為我沒有錢，我不買新的。✗ _____

12) 我不買貴書。✗ _____

The following activities allow you to further practice your interpretive, interpersonal, and presentational communication skills in a meaningful, communicative context.

Interpretive

1 Listening

🔊 (U3.19_1_1: 你的手機很漂亮)

Take notes as you listen to each audio clip. Then tell whether each statement is true (T) or false (F).

True or False?

1) ☐ Xiaoxue bought a new cell phone because her old one did not look stylish.

2) ☐ It's time for Liu Ying to buy a new phone because her current one is broken.

3) ☐ Xiaoxue says a good cell phone can cost up to 7,000 *yuan*.

4) ☐ Liu Ying's roommate bought a very good cell phone at a low price.

5) ☐ Liu Ying thinks she can get a pretty good cell phone for about 1,000 *yuan*.

🔊 (U3.19_1_2: 我要買衣服)

True or False?

1) ☐ Ah Long intends to buy some new clothes because his T-shirts are all worn out.

2) ☐ Xiaodong agrees that Ah Long needs some new T-shirts.

3) ☐ Ah Long has grown, so his pants don't fit anymore.

4) ☐ Xiaodong needs to buy some books for his classes.

2 Reading

Read the passage and indicate if the following statements are true (T) or false (F).

王新想要一個新手機，爸爸說："新手機？你不是有手機嗎？為什麼要新的？"王新說他的手機太老了，不夠好，而且他的同學都有很漂亮的新手機了。爸爸說："中國的手機你覺得不夠好，可是外國的手機都太貴了！"王新說，以前很貴，可是現在不太貴了。爸爸說，不太貴了？要多少錢？王新說，3000塊，很便宜。爸爸說："3000塊？一點兒都不便宜！沒有錢，不買！"王新說，2000塊呢？爸爸說，2000塊也不買。王新問為什麼。爸爸說："家裡的電腦太舊了，也不夠好，該買新的了，所以沒錢買新手機了。"

True or False?

1) ☐ It can be inferred that Wang Xin currently has a cell phone made in China.

2) ☐ Wang Xin wants to have a fancier Chinese-made phone that costs 3,000 *yuan*.

3) ☐ Wang Xin thinks that cell phone prices used to be much higher.

4) ☐ Dad thinks 3,000 *yuan* is not too expensive. However, he can't afford it.

5) ☐ Dad wants to save the money needed to upgrade the home computer.

Interpersonal

3 Speaking

1) Review these expressions and forms before completing the following tasks.

Adjectives: 新/舊；好/壞，大/小，高/矮，長/短，貴/便宜，多/少，漂亮
Noun phrases: 一個新的，舊的，⋯⋯
Measure words: 個，件，條，臺，支，張，塊，套

Adjective phrases:	Key structures:	Question Words/Forms:
• 很＿	• 以前……，現在……了	• ……嗎？
• 太＿了	• 該……了	• V 什麼？
• 不太＿	• 要/想要……	• V 不 V？
• 有點兒＿	• 因為……，所以……	• A 還是 B？
• 不夠＿	• 可是……	• 怎麼樣？
• 一點兒也不＿	• 而且……也……	• 為什麼？

2) **Role Play:** You share a room with someone. The two of you discuss what items you want to buy. You have a budget limit.

Role A: Decide what items you need to buy and why. Explain your thoughts to your roommate.

Role B: Listen to your roommate's ideas and ask him/her to explain them. Then state your opinions.

Items shared:				Their current condition:
冰箱	bīngxiāng	fridge	→	in good condition, but a little small
微波爐	wēibōlú	microwave oven	→	usable but not in good condition
打印機	dǎyìnjī	printer	→	slow and sometimes jams
電視機	diànshìjī	TV set	→	an old model, in good condition
咖啡機	kāfēijī	coffee machine	→	worn, indicator light broken, still usable

Presentational

4 Writing

Fill out the following wish list with items you'd like for your next birthday. Include three items and explain your choices. Then make a slide presentation with images of your choices.

(You can use an online translator or other tools to find the Chinese equivalents for items we haven't covered in this unit. However, for other words and forms, try to use only vocabulary items taught in the unit.)

Items you'd like to have: *Reasons:*

1) _____   _____

2) _____   _____

3) _____   _____

5 Speaking

Present your wish list to the class using the slide presentation you have prepared.

Money and Shopping

The Story

Katie goes shopping with Xiaonan and has her first experience bargaining in China . . .

iStock/Thinkstock

FUNCTIONS & GLOBAL TASKS

- Making purchases
- Expressing preferences
- Negotiating prices

CORE VOCABULARY

- Basic clothing items
- Words for giving colors and sizes
- Money measure units

GRAMMAR

- Numerical expressions with 多
- Prepositions with action verbs
- 來/去 with action verb phrases
- Verb duplication
- This topic-comment structure

CULTURE

- The Chinese currency

© Cengage Learning 2015

© Cengage Learning 2015

iStock/Thinkstock

Communication

Interpretive

Understand listening and reading passages related to money and shopping.

Interpersonal

Negotiate with a salesclerk for a discount.

Presentational

Describe one item you plan to buy for someone and another item you want to sell.

UNIT 4

A 第一課

這個多少錢?
How much is this?

A 4.1 詞語預習 *cíyǔ yùxí* **PREVIEW THE VOCABULARY**

 Use the **online audio flashcards** to familiarize yourself with the new vocabulary in this section.

Nouns (N)   M

商場	shāngchǎng	mall, department store	個
商店	shāngdiàn	shop, store	個
書店	shūdiàn	bookstore	個
帽子	màozi	cap, hat	頂
鞋子	xiézi	shoes	雙
T恤衫	T-xùshān	T-shirt	件
外衣	wàiyī	coat, jacket, outerwear	件
毛衣	máoyī	sweater	件
價格	jiàgé	price	

Measure Words (M)

頂 dǐng	(used for hats, caps, etc.)	
雙 shuāng	pair (used for shoes)	
角 jiǎo	fractional unit of Chinese currency, equals 1/10 of a yuan	
毛 máo	spoken form for 角	
分 fēn	cent, fractional unit of Chinese currency, equals 1/100 of a yuan	

Numerals (Nu)

萬	wàn	ten thousand
零	líng	zero
多	duō	over a specified amount; and more

Adjectives (Adj)

有意思	yǒu yìsi	interesting, fun
好看	hǎokàn	good-looking

Adverb (Adv)

本來	běnlái	originally

Auxiliary Verbs (AV)

得	děi	need, have to, must
可以	kěyǐ	can, be allowed to

Verbs (V)

看	kàn	see, look at
來/去	lái/qù	come/go
賣	mài	sell
做	zuò	do, be engaged in
講價	jiǎng//jià	bargain, haggle over the price

Prepositions (Prep)/Coverbs (CV)

跟	gēn	together with, with
在	zài	at

Particle (P)

吧	(used at the end of a question)
ba	

Place Word (PW)

這邊/那邊	here, this side / there, that side
zhè biān/nà biān	

Structures

- 看(一)看/看一下
- 要去那邊看看
- 跟她去商場，跟她講價
- 在商場買東西
- 這裡有很多東西
- 便宜的、貴的都有
- 賣東西的人
- 很便宜吧?
- ……很有意思

A | 4.2) 詞句聽説 cíjù tīngshuō　　　FOCUS ON GRAMMAR

 Aural-Oral Exercises: Do the online exercises to further familiarize yourself with the new vocabulary and grammar when it is used in sentences.

> **Main Features:** This lesson focuses on shopping, so we'll introduce <u>money expressions</u> and forms and structures used to describe certain activities: You'll learn to say what you do, with whom, and at what place. <u>Prepositions</u> are needed to convey these meanings. The order of words in a Chinese sentence is very different from that in an English sentence. For instance, prepositional phrases generally appear <u>before</u> an action verb rather than after it: Instead of *He is studying Chinese in Beijing,* the Chinese say literally, *He in Beijing studies Chinese.* In fact, Chinese word order reflects natural or temporal sequence: You have to be at a location first before the action there can start! So keep this logic in mind as you experience sequencing features in Chinese.

1 | **Stating precise amounts of money**　　X元X角X分(錢)；X塊X毛X分(錢)

A) Chinese currency denominations: 元/塊, 角/毛, 分

▪ The primary unit of the Chinese currency is 元. One 元 is divided into 10 角, and one 角 is divided into 10 分. 塊 and 毛 are more commonly used in spoken Chinese. The last unit is often omitted when reading prices.

1) 兩元錢/兩塊錢，兩角錢/兩毛錢，兩分錢
   liǎng yuán qián/liǎng kuài qián, liǎng jiǎo qián/liǎng máo qián, liǎng fēn qián

2) ¥2.50/兩塊五(毛)，¥2.25/兩塊二毛五(分) or 兩塊兩毛五
   liǎng kuài wǔ (máo),　　liǎng kuài èr máo wǔ (fēn)　liǎng kuài liǎng máo wǔ

   ¥2.05/兩塊零五(分)
   liǎng kuài líng wǔ (fēn)

■ Arabic numerals are normally used for price tags. To express or read these prices in Chinese, the Chinese currency denominations 元/塊, 角/毛, or 分 need to be used.

3) ¥2.05/二元五角， ¥2.25/二元二角五分， ¥2.05/二元零五(分)
   èr yuán wǔ jiǎo,　　 èr yuán èr jiǎo wǔ fēn,　　 èr yuán líng wǔ (fēn)

B) 兩 and 二

■ 兩 is used only for cardinal numbers. The only exception is that if the final digit of a number is two, that digit should be expressed as "二" (because 兩 at the end of a number will be confused with another usage of 兩, which is a unit for measuring weights, i.e., one 兩 is equivalent to 50 grams).

1) 22: 二十二　　　　　　　（二十兩 ✘ ）
   èrshí'èr

2) 202: 兩百零二/二百零二　　（兩百零兩 ✘ ）
   liángbǎi líng èr / èrbǎi líng èr

2 Stating imprecise amounts of money with 多　　Nu-M-多；Nu-多-M

A) Nu-M-多

■ This pattern refers to an imprecise amount that is more than the number given but less than the next whole number. The decimal point stands for the measure word (e.g., 塊), and the numerals after the decimal point can be represented by 多.

1) ¥2.xx (e.g., ¥2.15, ¥2.70)　　　兩塊多　　（兩多塊! ✘ ）
   　　　　　　　　　　　　　　　　liǎng kuài duō

2) ¥20.xx (e.g., ¥20.30, ¥20.55)　二十塊多　（二十多塊! ✘ ）
   　　　　　　　　　　　　　　　　èrshí kuài duō

3) 這些東西多少錢?　　→　　這支筆5塊多，這個本子10塊多。
   Zhèxiē dōngxi duōshao qián?　　Zhè zhī bǐ wǔ kuài duō, zhè ge běnzi shí kuài duō.

2 — A) — 3)

B) Nu-多-M

▬ This pattern refers to a whole number that is more than the number given. 多 represents any number from 1 to 9. As part of a whole number, 多 goes before the measure word.

1) ¥2x.00 (¥21–29):   二十多塊（=21塊，24塊，……29塊）
                                           èrshí duō kuài

2) 50多塊 (¥51–59)，   250多塊 (¥251–259)，   200多塊 (over 200)
   wǔshí duō kài,   èrbǎi wǔshí duō kuài,   èrbǎi duō kuài

3) 桌子要多少錢？ ➡ 大的要100多塊，小的要50多塊。
   Zhuōzi yào duōshao qián?   Dà de yào yìbǎi duō kuài, xiǎo de yào wǔshí duō kuài.

   (要 here means "ask for," "require," or "cost.")

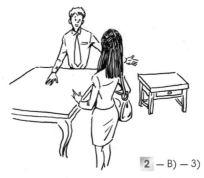

2 – B) – 3)

---

3 **Saying what is in a specific location**   **PW/Location + 有 + Sth**
                                              There is/are Sth + in/at + [location]

▬ Place Words: 這裡，那裡，學校，商場，商店，__ 裡. 裡 (inside) attached to a noun denotes an enclosed space, such as 商店裡，or a general space, such as 這裡/那裡.

1) 一個商場，一個書店，幾個小商店，很多東西
   yí gè shāngchǎng, yí gè shūdiàn, jǐ gè xiǎo shāngdiàn, hěn duō dōngxi

2) 那裡有一個商場，商場裡有很多小商店。
   Nàlǐ yǒu yí gè shāngchǎng, shāngchǎng li yǒu hěn duō xiǎo shāngdiàn.

3) 那個商場裡有沒有書店？ ➡ 有兩個。
   Nàge shāngchǎng li yǒu méiyǒu shūdiàn?   Yǒu liǎng gè.

3 – 2)

        A: How much is this?

4   Saying where someone is going to go or wants to go   要來/去 + PW; 想來/去 + PW

1) 去商店，去商場，來我們學校，來我的宿舍
qù shāngdiàn, qù shāngchǎng, lái wǒmen xuéxiào, lái wǒ de sùshè

2) to be going to or to need to go: 我要去書店，他要去商場，你要去哪裡？
Wǒ yào qù shūdiàn, tā yào qù shāngchǎng, nǐ yào qù nǎlǐ?

3) to want to or would like to go: 我想去書店，他想去商場，你想去哪裡？
Wǒ xiǎng qù shūdiàn, tā xiǎng qù shāngchǎng, nǐ xiǎng qù nǎlǐ?

4) 你們現在要去哪裡？ → 我們要去我朋友的家。
Nǐmen xiànzài yào qù nǎlǐ?   Wǒmen yào qù wǒ péngyou de jiā.

4 – 4)

5   Indicating the purpose of coming or going somewhere   來/去 + PW + Action VP

1) 去商店買東西，去5號樓看一個朋友，去那裡做什麼？
qù shāngdiàn mǎi dōngxi, qù wǔ hào lóu kàn yí ge péngyou, qù nàlǐ zuò shénme?

2) 我現在要去商場買東西，你呢？ → 我要去朋友家看朋友。
Wǒ xiànzài yào qù shāngchǎng mǎi dōngxi, nǐ ne?   Wǒ yào qù péngyou jiā kàn péngyou.

3) 那個人來你們宿舍做什麼？ → 他來看他的哥哥。
Nàge rén lái nǐmen sùshè zuò shénme?   Tā lái kàn tā de gēge.

6   Talking about someone's activities: where and what he/she does   Sb (不)在 Place + Action VP

■ Word order reflects the natural sequence of actions: you have to be at a location before an activity starts.

1) (不)在商店買東西，(不)在書店買書，(不)在北京學中文
(bú) zài shāngdiàn mǎi dōngxi, (bú) zài shūdiàn mǎi shū, (bú) zài Běijīng xué Zhōngwén

2) 你們現在在學校嗎？ → 不在學校，我們在商店買東西。
Nǐmen xiànzài zài xuéxiào ma?   Bú zài xuéxiào, wǒmen zài shāngdiàn mǎi dōngxi.

3) 他現在不在北京學中文。 (Negate the whole phrase.) （在北京不學中文 ✗）
Tā xiànzài bú zài Běijīng xué Zhōngwén.

Illustration © Cengage Learning 2015

7   Talking about an activity: doing something with someone   Sb 跟 Sb + Action VP

▭▭ The word order reflects the natural sequence: you are with another person before you start doing something together.

1) (不)跟室友去商店，   (不)跟室友説話，(不)跟他去5號樓
    (bù) gēn shìyǒu qù shāngdiàn, (bù) gēn shìyǒu shuōhuà, (bù) gēn tā qù wǔ hào lóu

2) 我想去商店，我想跟室友去商店，我想跟室友去商店買東西。
    Wǒ xiàng qù shāngdiàn, wǒ xiàng gēn shìyǒu qù shángdiàn, wǒ xiǎng gēn shìyǒu qù shāngdiàn mǎi dōngxi.

3) 你要跟我去商店買東西嗎？ ➡ 我不跟你去買東西，我要去學校。
    Nǐ yào gēn wǒ qù shāngdiàn mǎi dōngxi ma?   Wǒ bù gēn nǐ qù mǎi dōngxi, wǒ yào qù xuéxiào.

7 – 3)

8   Word usage examples

A) 得，可以

▭▭ The modal verbs 得 (must, need to) and 可以 (can, may) are used before other verbs.

1) 我的手機壞了，我得買一個新的；我得買書，我得去書店買一本書。
    Wǒ de shǒujī huài le, wǒ děi mǎi yí gè xīnde; Wǒ děi mǎi shū, wǒ děi qù shūdiàn mǎi yì běn shū.

2) 這個商店可以講價；我們可以現在去買東西；你可以跟我去。
    Zhège shāngdiàn kěyǐ jiǎngjià; Wǒmen kěyǐ xiànzài qù mǎi dōngxi; Nǐ kěyǐ gēn wǒ qù.

B) 吧

▭▭ The modal particle 吧 is used at the end of a statement to indicate agreement, or to form yes/no questions.

1) 好吧，你可以買新衣服；好吧，我們現在去商店。 (accepting)
    Hǎo ba, nǐ kěyǐ mǎi xīn yīfu; Hǎo ba, wǒmen xiànzài qù shāngdiàn.

2) 這件衣服很貴吧？ 這個是新的吧？   (yes/no question)
    Zhè jiàn yīfu hěn guì ba? Zhège shì xīnde ba?
    (I suppose..., isn't it?)   *(This is new, right?)*

Before viewing . . .

1) If you were in China, where would you like to shop: in a fancy store or in a local market? Why?

2) Which store do you visit most often for inexpensive things? Can you bargain and cut prices by half?

While viewing . . .

1) In the first viewing, focus on meaning.

2) In the second viewing, pay special attention to the speech forms and tones.

3) Then practice saying the sentences by answering the questions below.

 U4-A1

Katie 現在在哪兒？ 她在那兒做什麼？
····· xiànzài zài nǎr?　Tā zài nàr zuò shénme?

"現在我和小南＿＿＿＿＿＿＿＿＿＿＿＿。"
Xiànzài wǒ hé Xiǎonán·····

這裡有什麼東西？
Zhèlǐ yǒu shénme dōngxi?

"這裡有＿＿＿＿＿＿＿＿＿＿，
Zhèlǐ yǒu·····

＿＿＿＿＿＿＿＿＿＿＿＿。"

Katie 覺得什麼很有意思？
····· juéde shénme hěn yǒu yìsi?

"跟＿＿＿＿＿＿＿＿＿很有意思。"
Gēn·····　　　　　　　　hěn yǒu yìsi.

Katie 的帽子多少錢?
...... de màozi duōshao qián?

"本來＿＿＿＿＿＿＿＿＿＿＿＿＿＿＿＿＿＿＿,
Běnlái......

我說, ＿＿＿＿＿＿＿＿＿＿＿＿, 我不買,
wǒ shuō, ...   wǒ bù mǎi,

10塊＿＿＿＿＿＿＿＿＿＿＿?
shí kuài......

賣帽子的人說什麼?
Mài màozi de rén shuō shénme?

"10塊＿＿＿＿＿＿, ＿＿＿＿＿＿＿。"
Shí kuài......

Katie 覺得怎麼樣? 她說什麼?
...... juéde zěnmeyàng?   Tā shuō shénme?

"＿＿＿＿＿＿＿, ＿＿＿＿＿＿＿!"

  U4-A2

Katie 還要做什麼?
...... hái yào zuò shénme?

"現在我跟＿＿＿＿＿＿＿＿＿＿＿＿。
Xiànzài wǒ gēn......

小南要＿＿＿＿＿＿＿＿＿＿,
Xiǎonán yào......

我得＿＿＿＿＿＿＿＿＿＿......"
wǒ děi......

1 Forms and structures

See 4.2 for more notes and examples.

1) 現在我和小南在商店買東西。
Xiànzài wǒ hé Xiǎonán zài shāngdiàn mǎi dōngxi.

(在-Location comes first before the verb phrase. It is necessary to be at a location before performing an action there.)

2) 這裡/商場裡有很多東西。
Zhèlǐ/shāngchǎng li yǒu hěn duō dōngxi.

(The location word appears at the beginning of the sentence.)

3) 便宜的、貴的都有。
Piányide、guìde dōu yǒu.

(都 refers to all the items listed in front. Note that the form is 都 V, not 都 N.)

4) 跟賣東西的人講價……
Gēn mài dōngxi de rén jiǎngjià ……

(跟-person comes before the verb phrase. To engage in an activity with someone, that person must be present first.)

5) 賣東西的人，賣帽子的人
mài dōngxi de rén, mài màozi de rén

(V-的 phrases serve as noun modifiers.)
(*The person who sells . . .*)

6) ……去那邊看看。
…… qù nà biān kànkan.

(V V or V 一下 is a minimizer to soften the tone.)

▆▆ Topic-Comment Sentences:

1) 跟賣東西的人講價很有意思。
Gēn mài dōngxi de rén jiǎngjià hěn yǒu yìsi.

(It is wrong to place 很有意思 in front.)
(*Doing . . . is fun.*)

2) 這頂帽子多少錢？
Zhè dǐng màozi duōshao qián?

(It is wrong to place 多少錢 in front.)
(*How much is . . .?*)

3) 50塊我不買，10塊(你)賣不賣？
Wǔshí kuài wǒ bù mǎi, shí kuài (nǐ) mài búmài?

(Place the amount in front as the topic.)
(*I won't buy it for ¥50. Can I have it for ¥10?*)

▆▆ Auxiliary Verbs: 要，可以，得

1) 可以講價。
Kěyǐ jiǎngjià.

(可以：to allow. Negative: 不可以講價)
(*Prices are negotiable.*)

2) 現在我要跟小南去那邊看看。
Xiànzài wǒ yào gēn Xiǎonán qù nà biān kànkan.

(要 here means *I'm going to do . . .*)
(Compare: to *want to do*: 想 V)

3) 我得買一雙鞋。
Wǒ děi mǎi yì shuāng xié.

(得：must, have to; Negative: 不用 [búyòng].)
(*I have to buy . . .*)

吧 in question and non-question forms

1) 有意思吧?
Yǒu yìsi ba?

(When 吧 comes at the end of the sentence, it forms a yes-no question anticipating a positive response.)
(*It's fun, isn't it?*)

2) 好吧，我買。
Hǎo ba, wǒ mǎi.

(吧 conveys that you are yielding in a negotiation.)
(*OK, then . . .*)

2 Interrogative and negative forms

Practice these sentences. Pay special attention to the position of 不 in the negative form.

1) 那件衣服要<u>多少錢</u>? <u>要不要</u>100塊?

_____
(不要……，50多)

2) 她們<u>在不在</u>書店買書?

_____
(不在……)

3) 她<u>要跟誰</u>去買東西? <u>要跟同學</u>去嗎?

_____
(不跟……，室友)

4) 這個商店<u>可(以)不可以</u>講價?

_____
(不可以)

5) 這本書很貴吧?

_____
(一點兒也不)

6) 20塊你賣不賣?

_____
(……不賣，25塊)

3 Softening the tone of voice with VV or V 一下

The direct object should be placed at the end: VVO and V 一下 O. Do not use these "downtoners" / minimizers in negative sentences.

Direct:	*Tone softened:*
1) 你想不想<u>看</u>這本書?	→ 你想不想<u>看看</u>/<u>看一下</u>這本書?
2) 我要<u>認識</u>她的室友。	→ 我要<u>認識認識</u>/<u>認識一下</u>她的室友
3) 我想跟他<u>說</u>中文。	→ 我想跟他<u>說說</u>/<u>說一下</u>中文。
4) 你們想不想<u>看</u>我的新手機?	→ 你們想不想<u>看看</u>/<u>看一下</u>我的手機?

1 Pair work

First review the new vocabulary, then ask and answer questions based on the following pictures:

Place Words (PW) ：中國，美國，商場(裡)，書店(裡)

Auxiliary Verbs (AV) ：可以，得

Verb Phrases (VP) ：在Place + Action V，跟Person + Action V，去Place + Action V，
PW有(一個，很多⋯)，A和B都有

Mike 現在在美國學中文嗎？
　⋯ xiànzài zài Měiguó xué Zhōngwén ma?

他跟不跟中國人說英文？
Tā gēn bù gēn Zhōngguórén shuō Yīngwén?

Mike 現在去哪裡？跟誰去？去做什麼？
　⋯ xiànzài qù nǎlǐ? Gēn shéi qù? Qù zuò shénme?

這個書店有很多中文書嗎？
Zhège shūdiàn yǒu hěn duō Zhōngwénshū ma?

什麼人來買書？中國人還是外國人？
Shénme rén lái mǎi shū? Zhōngguórén háishi wàiguórén?

Mike 現在在哪裡？
　⋯ xiànzài zài nǎlǐ?

為什麼他得去那裡？
Wèishénme tā děi qù nàlǐ?

他的朋友想買什麼？
Tā de péngyou xiǎng mǎi shénme?

這裡的衣服賣多少錢？
Zhèlǐ de yīfu mài duōshao qián?

這裡的衣服可以講價嗎？ Mike 說什麼？
Zhèlǐ de yīfu kěyǐ jiǎngjià ma?　　　⋯ shuō shénme?

2 Role Play

1) Practice using the following dialogue as a model.

買東西的人：　　　　　　　　　　　　　賣東西的人：

這個[東西](要)多少錢？　　→　要¥50(一個/件……)

50塊太貴了！25塊賣不賣？　　→　不賣。35怎麼樣？

35我不買。30塊賣不賣？　　→　好吧，30塊。

2) Work in pairs, or move around the room to play the role of a buyer as well as a seller. Write on an index card and decide on the following: the item you want to sell, your asking price, and the lowest price you will accept. If you have a smartphone, you may use it to show images of your item.

3) **Report and Quiz:** Be prepared to report back to class about your buying and selling experiences. The teacher may also quiz students on the specific information shared in the reports by asking,

他賣什麼？ 誰賣……？ 要多少錢？ 你覺得[東西]怎麼樣？ 貴不貴？
你想不想買？

A 4.6 語法鞏固 yǔfǎ gǒnggù　　　REINFORCE THE GRAMMAR

These exercises are also available online with automatic feedback.

在 and 跟 as part of a Verb Phrase

1 Correct the sentences

Identify the errors and make corrections according to the rules explained earlier.

Intended meaning:	*Errors in word order:*	*Corrections:*
1) He is studying Chinese in China.	他學中文在中國。	_____
2) He isn't studying Chinese in China.	他不學中文在中國。	_____
3) He doesn't want to study Chinese in China.	他不想學中文在中國。	_____
4) I want to go to Beijing with him.	我想去北京跟他。	_____
5) I want to speak Chinese with a native speaker.	我想說中文跟中國人。	_____
6) She won't go to the mall with us.	她不去商場跟我們。	_____
7) I refuse to speak English with my roommate.	我不說英文跟我的室友。	_____
8) I don't want to speak English with my roommate.	我不想說英文跟我的室友。	_____

2 Give the Chinese equivalent for each sentence

Which word should be used? 可以，要，想，得

1) He <u>wants to</u> go to the bookstore now.　→　_____

2) He is <u>going to</u> go to the bookstore now.　→　_____

3) She <u>has to</u> go to the bookstore now.　→　_____

4) She <u>can go</u> to the bookstore now.　→　_____

A 4.7 聽答對話 tīngdá duìhuà　　　LET'S CHAT

In this listening-speaking activity you'll be asked to answer questions about the **video** segment as well as about **yourself**. You may be asked to record and submit your answers to your teacher.

UNIT 4

B | 第二課

你要什麼號的?

What size do you want?

B | 4.8 詞語預習 cíyǔ yùxí   PREVIEW THE VOCABULARY

 Use the **online audio flashcards** to familiarize yourself with the new vocabulary in this section.

Nouns (N)

顏色	yánsè	color
紅色	hóngsè	red
粉色	fěnsè	pink
黃色	huángsè	yellow
綠色	lǜsè	green
藍色	lánsè	blue
白色	báisè	white
黑色	hēisè	black
中號	zhōng hào	medium-sized
禮物	lǐwù	present, gift
售貨員	shòuhuòyuán	shop assistant, salesperson
牛仔褲	niúzǎikù	jeans
號碼	hàomǎ	number, code
電話	diànhuà	phone

Specifiers (Sp)

其他	qítā	other, else
別的	biéde	other, else

Adjective (Adj)/Stative Verb (SV)

合適	héshì	suitable, fit

Adverbs (Adv)

只	zhǐ	only
一共	yígòng	altogether, in all

Conjunction (Conj)

不過	búguò	but

Verbs (V)

給	gěi	give
試	shì	try
穿	chuān	wear
喜歡	xǐhuan	like
打折	dǎzhé	give a discount
付錢/款	fù//qián fù//kuǎn	pay
找錢	zhǎo//qián	give change

Expressions (Exp)

歡迎光臨！
Huānyíng guānglín!

Welcome to our store!

麻煩你……
máfan nǐ……

Could you please . . .

請稍等。
Qǐng shāo děng.

Just a moment, please.

打八折
dǎ bā zhé

give 20% off

好的。
Hǎo de.

Okay.

B 4.9 詞句聽說 cíjù tīngshuō   FOCUS ON GRAMMAR

🌐 **Aural-Oral Exercises:** Do the online exercises to further familiarize yourself with the new vocabulary and grammar when it is used in sentences.

Main Features: In this lesson we'll continue to introduce basic forms and phrases that are used in a daily shopping situations; for instance, asking a store clerk for help in selecting an item or specifying <u>sizes</u> and <u>color</u>. We'll introduce another basic word, 給, which functions both as a verb (to give) and a preposition (for [someone]). We'll revisit 都(all, both) and it'll be fun for you to see how it makes the object of the verb move from the end to the beginning of the sentence, which seldom happens in English. Now let's begin with colors.

1 Describing the color of items

▬ 色 is often attached to a color word (紅, 黃, 白, etc.) to form a color-色 pattern. This pattern can be used to describe the color of objects by placing it before the particle 的 and the noun.

1) 紅色的書包， 黃色的筆， 白色的紙， 綠色的衣服， 藍色的褲子，
   hóngsè de shūbāo, huángsè de bǐ, báisè de zhǐ, lùsè de yīfu, lánsè de kùzi,

   黑色的鞋
   hēisè de xié

▬ The common, monosyllabic color word can modify a noun without 色 and 的.

2) 一個紅書包， 一支黃筆， 一張白紙， 一件綠衣服， 一條藍褲子，
   yí gè hōng shūbāo, yì zhī huáng bǐ, yì zhāng bái zhǐ, yí jiàn lù yīfu, yì tiáo lán kùzi,

   一雙黑鞋
   yì shuāng hēi xié

■ Color + 的 can be used as a noun phrase. When 的 is used, 色 can be dropped in most cases.

3) 你想要什麼顏色的書包？ 紅(色)的還是藍(色)的？ → 我想要紅的。
Nǐ xiǎng yào shénme yánsè de shūbāo? Hóng(sè)de háishi lánú(sè)de?   Wǒ xiǎng yào hóng de.

4) 這件衣服有其他顏色的嗎？ → 有，還有黃的和藍的。
Zhè jiàn yīfu yǒu qítā yánsè de ma?   Yǒu, hái yǒu huáng de hé lán de.

1 — 4)

2 | Describing sizes

1) 大號，中號，小號， 8號，10號
dà hào,   zhōng hào, xiǎo hào, bā hào, shí hào

2) 你穿大號的還是中號的？ → 我穿小號的。
Nǐ chuān dà hào de háishi zhōng hào de?   Wǒ chuān xiǎo hào de.

3) 請問你們有沒有大號的？ → 沒有，只有中號和小號。
Qǐngwèn nǐmen yǒu méiyǒu dà hào de?   Méiyǒu, zhǐyǒu zhōng hào hé xiǎo hào.

2 — 3)

3 | Describing the act of giving someone something   給 + Sb + Object

1) 給我一本書，給我那本書，給他一個手機，給他我的電話號碼
gěi wǒ yì běn shū, gěi wǒ nà běn shū, gěi tā yí gè shǒujī,   gěi tā wǒ de diànhuà hàomǎ

2) 她給你什麼？ → 她給我一本書和一件衣服。
Tā gěi nǐ shénme?   Tā gěi wǒ yì běn shū hé yí jiàn yīfu.

3) 你要給他們什麼？ → 我要給他們我的電話號碼。
Nǐ yào gěi tāmen shénme?   Wǒ yào gěi tāmen wǒ de diànhuà hàomǎ.

4   **Describing the act of doing something for someone**   給 Sb + Action VP

▬ 給 is used as a preposition introducing the intended beneficiary or recipient of an action. Note the word order.

1) 給他買一件衣服，給她看一下那本書，給我看一下中號的衣服
     gěi tā mǎi yí jiàn yīfu,   gěi tā kàn yíxià nà běn shū,   gěi wǒ kàn yíxià zhōng hào de yīfu

2) 不給他買衣服，不給她看那本書
     bù gěi tā mǎi yīfu,   bú gěi tā kàn nà běn shū

3) 請給我看一下那件衣服，也給我看一下那條褲子。   (to show Sb an item)
     Qǐng gěi wǒ kàn yíxià nà jiàn yīfu,   yě gěi wǒ kàn yíxià nà tiáo kùzi

4) 我想給他買一個禮物。   →   你想給他買什麼？
     Wǒ xiǎng gěi tā mǎi yí gè lǐwù.   Nǐ xiǎng gěi tā mǎi shénme?

4 – 4)

5   **Emphasizing plural items**   A和B + 都V; A和B, Sb + 都V

A)   A和B + 都 V

▬ The adverb 都 (all, both) is used to sum up preceding elements that forms the main topic of the sentence.

1) 我和他都是大學生，我們都會說中文。
     Wǒ hé tā dōu shì dàxuéshēng, wǒmen dōu huì shuō Zhōngwén.

2) 這些東西都不貴，都不是她的。
     Zhèxiē dōngxi dōu bú guì, dōu bú shì tā de.

5 – A)– 1)

B) A和B，Sb + 都V

■■■ When 都 refers to the object of the verb, the object has to move to the front of the sentence to become the subject.

1) 你要手機還是電腦？
   Nǐ yào shǒujī háishi diànnǎo?
   →
   手機和電腦我都要。   ✓
   Shǒujī hé diànnǎo wǒ dōu yào.

   我都要手機和電腦。   ✗
   wǒ dōu yào shǒujī hé diànnǎo

2) 你想學中文還是日文？
   Nǐ xiǎng xué Zhōngwén háishi Rìwén?
   →
   中文(和)日文，我都想學。   ✓
   Zhōngwén (hé) Rìwén, wǒ dōu xiǎng xué.

   我都想學中文和日文。   ✗
   Wǒ dōu xiǎng xué Zhōngwén hé Rìwén.

3) 這些書你要買哪幾本？
   Zhèxiē shū nǐ yào mǎi nǎ jǐ běn?
   →
   這幾本我都不買。   ✓
   Zhè jǐ běn wǒ dōu bù mǎi.

   我都不買這幾本。   ✗
   Wǒ dōu bù mǎi zhè jǐ běn.

5 — B) — 1)

5 — B) — 2)

6 Softening the tone

V 一下(O) and VV (O)
do [Sth] briefly/a bit

▰▰▰ These two forms are "downtoners" frequently used with action verbs in spoken Chinese. Often interchangeable, they are typically used in expressing a wish or desire and offering suggestions.

1) 你想不想認識一下我的室友？　　(*Would you like to meet my roommate?*)
Nǐ xiǎng bù xiǎng rènshi yíxià wǒ de shìyǒu?

2) 我要看(一)看那個學校。　　(*I want to take a look at that school.*)
Wǒ yào kàn (yí) kàn nàge xuéxiào.

▰▰▰ Note that V一下/ VV forms are normally not used in negative forms.

3) 他不看看那個學校。　　✗

7 Asking for help

麻煩你⋯⋯
Could you please . . .

▰▰▰ 麻煩你 literally means "Trouble you . . ." It is routinely used as both a polite and an informal form for asking for help. It roughly corresponds to these English expressions, "Could you please . . .?" "Do me a favor, please . . ."

1) 麻煩你給我看一下那件衣服。
Máfan nǐ gěi wǒ kàn yíxià nà jiàn yīfu.

2) 麻煩你給我一張紙和一支筆。
Máfan nǐ gěi wǒ yì zhāng zhǐ hé yì zhī bǐ.

3) 麻煩你跟我去一下書店，好嗎？
Máfan nǐ gēn wǒ qù yíxià shūdiàn, hǎo ma?

4) 麻煩你給我你的電話號碼。
Máfan nǐ gěi wǒ nǐ de diànhuà hàomǎ.

7 — 2)

Before viewing . . .

1) In your culture, what does a salesclerk normally say to a customer when the customer walks in and leaves the store?

2) How do people ask for help in the store, e.g. ask a salesclerk to show them an item?

3) In your culture, what are the ways customers ask for discounts in stores?

While viewing . . .

1) In the first viewing, focus on meaning.

2) In the second viewing, pay special attention to the speech forms and tones.

3) Then practice saying the sentences by answering the questions below.

 U4-B1

售貨員説：
Shòuhuòyuán shuō:

"歡迎光臨！請問＿＿＿＿＿＿＿＿＿？"
Huānyíng guānglín! Qǐngwèn……

小南想看看那套紅色的運動服，
Xiǎonán xiǎng kànkan nà tào hóngsè de yùndòngfú,

售貨員説：
shòuhuòyuán shuō:

"你要＿＿＿＿＿＿＿？
Nǐ yào……

＿＿＿＿＿＿＿，没有＿＿＿＿＿＿＿。"
　　　　　　　　méiyǒu……

小南説：
Xiǎonán shuō:

"麻煩你＿＿＿＿＿＿＿＿＿＿＿＿。"
Máfan nǐ……

售貨員給小南中號的，小南説：
Shòuhuòyuán gěi Xiǎonán zhōnghào de, Xiǎonán shuō:

"我覺得＿＿＿＿＿＿＿＿＿＿＿。"
Wǒ juéde……

小南想看看其他顔色，她問：
Xiǎonán xiǎng kànkan qítā yánsè, tā wèn:

"請問＿＿＿＿＿＿＿＿＿＿＿＿＿＿＿？"
Qǐngwèn……

小南喜歡什麼顔色的？
Xiǎonán xǐhuan shénme yánsè de?

"這套紅的和 ＿＿＿＿＿＿＿＿＿！"
Zhè tào hóng de hé……

小南問可以不可以打折，售貨員說：
Xiǎonán wèn kěyǐ bù kěyì dǎzhé, shòuhuòyuán shuō:

"要兩套可以＿＿＿＿＿＿＿＿＿＿＿，
Yào liǎng tào kěyì……

一共是＿＿＿＿＿。"
yígòng shì……

小南有多少錢？ 夠不夠？
Xiǎonán yǒu duōshao qián? Gòu búgòu?

"我現在＿＿＿＿＿＿＿＿＿＿＿＿＿，
Wǒ xiànzài……

＿＿＿＿＿＿＿！"

小南要兩套，她給售貨員錢，說
Xiǎonán yào liǎng tào, tā gěi shòuhuòyuán qián, shuō:

"我要這套＿＿＿＿＿＿＿＿＿＿＿＿。
Wǒ yào zhè tào……

這是＿＿＿＿＿。"
Zhè shì……

售貨員說：
Shòuhuòyuán shuō:

"好的。＿＿＿＿＿。＿＿＿＿＿？"
Hǎo de.

1 Forms and structures

See 4.9 for more notes and examples.

▇▇▇ "Downtoning" to soften the tone with V-V or V 一下

1) 我想看看這套紅色的運動服。
Wǒ xiǎng kànkan zhèi tào hóngsè de yùndòngfú.

(看看, or 看一看: 一 is normally omitted.)

2) 麻煩你給我看一下中號的。
Máfan nǐ gěi wǒ kàn yíxià zhōng hào de.

(V一下 is often interchangeable with VV.)
(Could you please . . .?)

3) 你可以試試。
Nǐ kěyǐ shìshi.

(試試 can also be 試一下.)
(You may try it on.)

▇▇▇ Topicalizing with fronted elements

1) 大號中號都有。
Dà hào zhōng hào dōu yǒu.

(Large and medium sizes are both available, or, there are both large and medium sizes.)

2) 這套紅的和這套黃的我都喜歡。
Zhè tào hóng de hé zhè tào huáng de wǒ dōu xǐhuan.

(都 refers to items in front, not at the back.)
(The red one and the yellow one: I like them both, or I like both . . .)

3) 要兩套我可以給你打8折。
Yào liǎng tào wǒ kěyǐ gěi nǐ dǎ bā zhé.

([If you are] buying two sets, I can give you 20% off.)

▇▇▇ Question Forms:

1) 你要什麼號的? (你要幾號的?)
Nǐ yào shénme hào de? (Nǐ yào jǐ hào de?)

(什麼號 calls for 大號，中號, etc., 幾號 calls for numbered sizes.)

2) 請問有其他顏色嗎?
Qǐngwèn yǒu qítā yánsè ma?

(別的 [biéde] is another term for 其他 [qítā])
(Excuse me, do you have any . . .?)

3) 可以打折嗎?
Kěyǐ dǎzhé ma?

(可以 can be used in a sentence without a subject.)
(Excuse me, may I have a discount?)

4) 還要什麼嗎?
Hái yào shénme ma?

(Do you want anything else?)

▇▇▇ Uses of 給 (as a main verb or a preposition)

1) 給我兩套。
Gěi wǒ liǎng tào.

(給 as a main verb: Give me two sets.)

2) 給我看一下。
Gěi wǒ kàn yíxià.

(給 as a preposition means literally, give [it to] me to look at . . ., show me [the item].)

3) (我可以)給你打8折。
(Wǒ kěyǐ) gěi nǐ dǎ bā zhé.

(給 as a preposition.)
(I can take 20% off for you.)

2 Interrogative and negative forms

Answer all questions in the negative. Do not use VV or V 一下 in the negative form.

1) 她媽媽<u>給不給</u>她很多錢？ _____

2) 她想看看你的書，你<u>給不給她看</u>？ _____

3) 你<u>想試試/試一下</u>這件衣服嗎？ _____

4) 你<u>想不想看看</u>其他顏色？ _____

5) <u>這兩件衣服你都喜歡</u>嗎？ _____

6) <u>大號中號</u>你都要嗎？ _____

3 Story narration

Pay special attention to the verb forms and the use of punctuation marks.

小南和Katie在商店裡買東西。小南想看一下運動服，售貨員說
Xiǎonán hé ⋯ zài shāngdiàn li mǎi dōngxi. Xiǎonán xiǎng kàn yíxià yùndòngfú, shòuhuòyuán shuō

大號中號都有。小南覺得中號的很合適，可是她還想看看其他顏色。
dà hào zhōng hào dōu yǒu. Xiǎonán juéde zhōnghào de hěn héshì, kěshì tā hái xiǎng kànkan qítā yánsè.

售貨員給她一套黃色的和一套粉色的。Katie問小南喜歡哪一套，
Shòuhuòyuán gěi tā yí tào huáng sè de hé yí tào fěn sè de. ⋯ wèn Xiǎonán xǐhuan nǎ yí tào,

小南說，紅的和黃的她都喜歡。可是一套運動服要255元，
Xiǎonán shuō, hóng de hé huáng de tā dōu xǐhuan. Kěshì yí tào yùndǒngfú yào liǎngbǎi wǔshí wǔ yuán,

小南的錢不夠買兩套。售貨員說買兩套可以打8折，一共408元。
Xiǎonán de qián búgòu mǎi liǎng tào. Shòuhuòyuán shuō mǎi liǎng tào kěyǐ dǎ bā zhé, yígòng sìbǎi líng bā yuán.

小南現在正好還有400多塊錢，所以她要一套紅的，一套黃的。
Xiǎonán xiànzài zhènghǎo hái yǒu sìbǎi duō kuài qián, suǒyǐ tā yào yí tào hóng de, yí tào huáng de.

她很高興售貨員給她打折。
Tā hěn gāoxìng shòuhuòyuán gěi tā dǎzhé.

1 Pair work

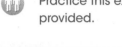

Practice this exchange between a salesclerk [S] and a customer [C], following the suggestions provided.

▰ Use 看一下/看看

S: [Greet the customer] _____

C: 麻煩你給我 _____
Máfan nǐ gěi wǒ……

S: 你想 _____
Nǐ xiǎng……

▰ A和B, Sb 都 V

S: 你想買衣服還是買鞋？   → C: _____
Nǐ xiǎng mǎi yīfu háishi mǎi xié?

S: 要什麼號的/幾號的？   → C: _____
Yào shénme hào de / jǐ hào de?

S: 想要什麼顏色的？   → C: _____
Xiǎng yào shénme yánsè de?

S: 想要哪一件/雙？   → C: _____
Xiǎng yào nǎ yí jiàn / shuāng?

▰ Use questions: 多少錢？ 可以打折嗎？ 怎麼樣？

C: 這件T-恤衫……？   → S: _____
Zhè jiàn T-xùshān…… ?

C: 買兩件 ……?   → S: _____
Mǎi liǎng jiàn……?

▰ Use 一共_____錢，找你_____

C: 請給我……，一共多少錢？ → S: _____
Qǐng gěi wǒ……, yígòng duōshao qián?

C: 好的。這是[100]元。 → S: 好的，請稍等。
Hǎo de. Zhè shì [yìbǎi] yuán.   Hǎo de, qǐng shāo děng.

S: 你給我_____元，
Nǐ gěi wǒ…… yuán,
找你_____元。
zhǎo nǐ…… yuán.

C: 謝謝！   → S: _____
Xièxie!

2 Role Play

1) **Selling-Buying activity:** With a partner, play the roles of seller and buyer, and switch the role with the same or a different partner. If you have a smartphone, you may use it to show items and prices.

2) **Report:** Be prepared to report back to class what happened in your role play.

3) **Quiz:** Be prepared to be quizzed on the information shared in the reports. You should confirm or correct the information given in the quiz to demonstrate positive and negative sentences. For instance, 不對，鞋和T-恤衫她都想買；對，賣東西的人不給她打5折⋯⋯

B 4.13 語法鞏固 yǔfǎ gǒnggù   REINFORCE THE GRAMMAR

These exercises are also available online with automatic feedback.

1 Give the Chinese equivalent for each sentence
Use appropriate forms and structures. You may use pinyin or Chinese characters.

給，給(Sb + V)，想，喜歡，都，可以，請問，麻煩你，吧

1) I'd like to give him a very good T-shirt. _____

2) I'd like to show him a very good T-shirt. _____

3) I like both the red and blue ones. _____

4) I don't like either of these colors. _____

5) Can you give me 10% off on this pair of shoes? _____

6) You can give a discount on this pair of shoes, I suppose? _____

7) Excuse me, how much is that blue cap? _____

8) Could you please show me that blue cap? _____

2 Convert each sentence into a 都-sentence

1) 小王會說英文，小李也會說英文。 → _____

2) 小王不想跟我們去，小李也不想跟我們去。 → _____

3) 小王喜歡她，小李也喜歡她。 → _____

4) 她喜歡小王，也喜歡小李。 → _____

5) 他想學中文，也想學日文。 → _____

6) 她得去書店，也得去商場。 → _____

B 4.14 聽答對話 tīngdá duìhuà   LET'S CHAT

In this listening-speaking activity you'll be asked to answer questions about the **video** segment as well as about **yourself.** You may be asked to record and submit your answers to the teacher.

THE CHINESE CURRENCY

The official currency of the People's Republic of China is known as **rénmínbì** (人民幣 or "the people's currency"), RMB for short. The *yuan* is the primary unit of Chinese currency. The word *yuan* (元, or 圓 in traditional form) literally means "circular" and refers to the round shape of traditional Chinese coins. Since Chinese coins were once made of silver, the Chinese currency during the Qing dynasty was also referred to as **yínyuán** (銀元, "silver money "). Even though silver is no longer used in minting currency, *yuan* remains the name for the standard monetary unit for modern Chinese currency as well as in other East Asian countries. In fact, the words *yen* in Japanese and *won* in Korean are both derived from Chinese *yuan*. The *yuan* is made up of 10 **jiǎo** (角) or 100 **fēn** (分). Thus, 1 *yuan* (元) = 10 **jiǎo** (角) and 1 **jiǎo** (角) = 10 **fēn** (分).

Renminbi

Since 1949, the central bank of the PRC, the People's Bank of China, has issued several different series of RMB banknotes, as well as coins with more than 60 different designs. The current bills show a portrait of the founding father of the PRC, Mao Zedong (1893–1976). Here is an example of a ¥100 note and a ¥1.00 coin. In many cities in China, ¥1.00 coins can be used as bus tokens. With the exception of the **fēn** (the smallest denomination of Chinese currency), the other two units of currency have alternate spoken forms. The **jiǎo** (¥0.10) is called the **máo** in spoken language and the *yuan* is often called the **kuài**.

The currency in Taiwan is called the New Taiwan Dollar (TWD), or **xīntáibì**, while the currency in Hong Kong is called the Hong Kong Dollar (HKD), or **gǎngyuán**. The exchange rates of these currencies against the RMB were 0.21 (TWD) and 0.80 (HKD) respectively as of March, 2013.

New Taiwan Dollar

Hong Kong Dollar

Cash payment is the primary and preferred payment method in a monetary transaction. In fact, prior to 1980, cash payments were the only way for the consumer to purchase anything, and even today China is still considered primarily a cash society. For various reasons, personal checking has never been widely used in Chinese transactions. However, since Chinese banks have begun to push noncash payment options to boost revenue, more and more stores and vendors now accept credit or debit cards. In the emerging B2B (business-to-business) market, several companies, such as Alipay (支付寶) and PayPal (貝寶), have stepped in to serve as third-party online payment platforms.

Kǎnjià (砍價), literally, to cut down a price, is the word for "bargain" in Chinese, but not everything is up for negotiation. For example, merchandise at state-owned shops, department stores, or corporate chain or franchise stores is sold at fixed or listed prices, known as míngjià (明價). Only street vendors, "mom-and-pop" stores, free markets, or farmers' markets allow bargaining. For most foreigners or even for Chinese who are traveling outside their hometown, bargaining is a tricky business as prices vary from one store to another and can be anywhere from 20 percent to 80 percent more or less than the listed price. It is often best to ask a tour guide or a local friend to negotiate prices on your behalf where bargaining is required.

QUIZ

1. What does RMB stand for?

2. Whose image is featured on the front of the RMB bills?

3. Which is the correct order of RMB denominations from high to low?
   a. yuan-fen-jiao (元-分-角)
   b. fen-jiao-yuan (分-角-元)
   c. jiao-yuan-fen (角-元-分)
   d. yuan-jiao-fen (元-角-分)

ACTIVITIES

1. Use online currency converters, such as oanda. com and Yahoo currency converter, to obtain real-time information on currency exchange rates between RMB (¥) and USD ($) or EUR (€).

2. Search online and find out what the RMB/USD exchange rate has been from the year 2000 to the present. What sort of a trend does this indicate?

單元復習
Review and Integration

 Read the following passages as fast as you can. Follow these steps:

1) Do not stop to check the meaning of words you don't recognize. Mark them and keep reading.

2) Read the passage again and guess the meaning of the marked words on a separate piece of paper.

3) Finally, look up the words in a dictionary or the vocabulary index and verify their meanings.

Katie跟小南去商場買東西。那裡有很多東西，便宜的、貴的都有，而且還可以講價。Katie覺得跟賣東西的人講價很有意思。看，她那頂帽子本來要50塊，她跟賣帽子的人說，50塊她不要。她問10塊賣不賣。賣帽子的說10塊不賣，15塊可以賣。Katie說15塊她買。

小南得買運動服，售貨員給她看一套紅色運動服，說大號中號都有。小南覺得中號很合適，可是她還想看看其他顏色。售貨員說還有一套粉色和一套黃色的。Katie問小南喜歡哪一套，小南說，紅的和黃的她都喜歡。可是一套運動服要255元，小南的錢不夠買兩套。售貨員說買兩套可以打8折，一共408元。小南現在還有400多塊錢，所以她要一套紅的，一套黃的。她很高興售貨員給她打折。

Quickly provide the Chinese equivalents for the following phrases and sentences. Do not translate them word for word.

1 **Measure words:** 雙，套，頂，件，條   *In Chinese you say...*

1) worn jeans; a worn pair of jeans   _____

2) new sneakers; a few pairs of new sneakers   _____

3) white tracksuit; three white tracksuits   _____

4) a few nice-looking caps   _____

2 **Actions/Activities:** Verb, Prep Phrase + V, and the Word Order

1) I'll go to the store with my roommate.   _____

2) I'll go to the store to buy things with my roommate.   _____

3) I won't go to the store with my roommate.   _____

4) We are not shopping in the bookstore now.   _____

5) She doesn't shop in this store.   _____

6) She doesn't like to shop in this store.   _____

7) I want to show him that book.   _____

8) He won't buy gifts for his friends.   _____

3 **Comparison of Words/Expressions:** 要，想，喜歡，可以，得，應該，麻煩你/請你

1) <u>I'm going to</u> look at that book.   _____

2) <u>I'd like to</u> look at that book.   _____

3) <u>May</u> I take a look at that book?   _____

4) You <u>have to</u> take a look at that book.   _____

5) You <u>can</u> take a look at that book.   _____

6) You <u>should</u> take a look at that book.   _____

7) <u>Could you please</u> show me that book?   _____

4 都-sentences

▬ 都不 means "none do", and 不都 means "not all do".

1) Neither Mr. Zhang nor Ms. Wang likes this color.   _____

2) None of them enjoys shopping here.   _____

3) I don't like some of these T-shirts (Out of the three, I like two of them).   _____

4) <u>We both</u> want to buy a cell phone.   _____

5) We want to buy <u>both a cell phone and a computer.</u>   _____

5 **Dialogue:** What gift should I buy?

A: I want to buy my sister a gift. What should I buy? _____

B: You can buy her a piece of clothing,
   or a pair of shoes. _____

A: She doesn't want clothes and shoes. _____

B: Does she want a cell phone or a computer? _____

A: Yes, but they are expensive. I don't have
   enough money. _____

B: How about giving her a book? _____

A: Right, I should buy her a book! _____

B: The school bookstore has many new books,
   and offers discounts on them. _____

A: Really? I should go and check it out. Want to go
   with me? _____

B: Okay, I'll go with you. I want to buy some books
   too. _____

4.18 語法小測驗 yǔfǎ xiǎo cèyàn   **CHECK FOR ACCURACY**

1 **Talking about amounts**

🌐 Where should 多 appear, before or after the measure word?

1) over ten pairs of shoes _____

2) more than a thousand T-shirts _____

3) thirty dollars and some change (e.g., $30.45) _____

4) over 30 dollars (e.g., 32, 36) _____

2 **Reading quantities: 2 and 0**

🌐 Have fun reading these amounts and numbers!

1) ¥22.20   二十二塊二(毛)

2) ¥22.02 _____

3) ¥220 _____

4) ¥202.02 _____

5) 2, 002 computers _____

The following activities allow you to further practice your interpretive, interpersonal, and presentational communication skills in a meaningful, communicative context.

Interpretive

1 Listening

(U4.19_1_1: 小東買什麼？)

Take notes as you listen to each audio clip. Then select the correct answer for each question.

1) What does Xiaodong want to buy?   a. school supplies   b. a pen and books

2) What colors does he want?   a. red and blue   b. black and red

3) For which item are stocks limited?   a. big notebooks   b. small notebooks

4) What's the total amount he spends?   a. ¥35.50   b. ¥35.05

5) How much change does the clerk give him? a. ¥4.05   b. ¥4.50

(U4.19_1_2: 阿龍買什麼？)

1) What does Ah Long want to buy?   a. T-shirts and jeans   b. a tracksuit

2) What size does he wear?   a. medium   b. large

3) What color does he prefer?   a. blue   b. white

4) Why doesn't he buy the T-shirts?   a. they aren't on sale   b. they are the wrong size or color

5) What else does he want to buy?   a. shorts   b. jeans

6) What is the sale price for the shorts? a. 10% off   b. less than ¥20

7) What does the clerk tell him to do? a. buy a few pairs of jeans   b. look for jeans elsewhere

2 Reading

Look at the poster, then say if each statement is true (T) or false (F).

大新鞋帽店

運動鞋	~~¥255~~ ¥55–¥85
男鞋	6折
女鞋	買一送一

True or False?

1) ☐ This store only sells shoes.

2) ☐ Sneakers are on sale.

3) ☐ There is a 60% discount on men's shoes.

4) ☐ For women's shoes, buy one pair and get one pair free.

3 Narrative reading

Read the story as fast as you can without stopping. Get the general idea and then try to answer the questions. Read it again for details and verify your answers.

李先生和太太想去商場買一些東西。看，家裡的書桌有點兒小，得買一張大的。電腦也太老了，該買一臺新的了。現在商場裡有很多電腦，便宜的、貴的都有，所以李先生和太太要去看看。他們的兒子李文是一個高中生，很喜歡玩電腦，所以他想跟爸爸媽媽去商場。他說，他想要一臺新的筆記本電腦。

李先生說："你的電腦不是還很新嗎，怎麼又要新的？"

李文說："爸，我想要一個最新的，我可以學很多新東西，不好嗎？"

李先生說："現在一個好的筆記本電腦要幾千塊錢，我們的錢不夠買兩個。"

太太對先生說："孩子的電腦給你，怎麼樣？那個電腦有點兒老了，可是給你很合適！而且，他的老師說他是一個好學生，你不是說要給他買一個好禮物嗎？"

Answer the questions:

1) 李先生和太太想去商場買什麼？
   a. 一張小書桌
   b. 一臺大電腦
   c. 書桌和電腦都買

2) 李文想跟爸爸媽媽去商場，因為……
   a. 他想要一個筆記本
   b. 他想給爸爸買一個禮物
   c. 他想要一個筆記本電腦

3) 李先生覺得李文現在的電腦怎麼樣？
   a. 還很新
   b. 很舊了
   c. 對李文不太合適

4) 李先生不想買兩個新電腦，因為……
   a. 新電腦對李文不合適
   b. 電腦很貴，錢不夠
   c. 李先生喜歡新電腦

5) 李太太説什麼？
   a. 可以買兩個電腦
   b. 可以給李文買新電腦
   c. 不給李文買電腦

True or False?

1) ☐ Mr. Li and his wife think it is time to buy their first computer.

2) ☐ Mr. Li knows that his son's computer is not new.

3) ☐ Their son is not a good student, according to his teacher.

4) ☐ The son wants to have a new laptop to learn new things.

5) ☐ Mr. Li can't afford two new computers.

6) ☐ Mr. Li had not planned to buy his son a gift.

7) ☐ Mrs. Li suggests that Mr. Li share the new computer with their son.

4 Speaking

1) Simulation: 買禮物 (Shopping for gifts)

Role A: You are the customer in a store and are shopping for gifts. Ask the salesclerk to show you a couple of items and try to negotiate a discount. Ask how much the total is and pay for the items.

Role B: You are the salesclerk in the store. Greet the customer and show him or her several items you think would make good gifts. Make comments on the items. Say, for example, that the item is pretty, affordable, suitable, of good quality, etc. Consider giving the customer a reasonable discount if the customer buys two or more items.

2) Pretend you are shopping in a Chinese store. Ask the clerk to show you several items. Ask for information about discounts or try to negotiate a reduced price on some items.

Useful phrases:

Review and familiarize yourself with the phrases that each of the two roles will need. Role play with a partner and switch roles so that you get to play both roles.

售貨員:

- 歡迎光臨! 請問你想買什麼?
- 要什麼號的? /要幾號的?
- 要什麼顏色的?
- 50元一件
- 你要幾件?
- 我可以給你打折/打9折
- 好的, 請稍等。
- 一共是X元X角。
- 請在那邊付款。
- 找你X元。謝謝光臨!

買東西的人:

- 我想看一下(那件……)
- 麻煩你給我看一下(大號的、紅色的……)
- 請問, 可以試試嗎?
- 請問有其他顏色嗎? /有沒有＿＿色的?
- 這件很合適/不合適。
- 請問, 多少錢一件/雙/頂/條?
- 請問, 可以打折嗎? /可以講價嗎?
- 那請你給我(一件白色的、中號的……)
- 請問在哪裡付款?
- 請問一共多少錢?

5 Speaking

What do you plan to buy for your holiday gifts this year? Share with the class one item you plan to buy for someone, your price range, and the reason you chose that item.

6 Writing

You want to sell one of your things (your cell phone, laptop, a piece of furniture, etc.). Create a flyer and post it online or make a hard copy and post it on the classroom bulletin board. Make it attractive and see how many responses you get.

City Highlights

Tianjin 天津

Tianjin:
Morning view of the city by the Haihe River

Tianjin Port

UNIT 5

第五單元

我的愛好

Hobbies and Activities

The Story

Ah Long and his roommates have different hobbies . . .

FUNCTIONS & GLOBAL TASKS

- Saying what you like to do
- Describing how well someone does something
- Making suggestions and requests
- Telling about when and where an event is taking place

CORE VOCABULARY

- Hobbies and pastimes
- Adverbs of frequency
- Action Verbs

GRAMMAR

- VO-phrases
- Prepositional phrases with 跟
- V-得 phrases
- Progressive verb forms
- 都/也-V phrases
- Negative imperative

CULTURE

- Extracurricular activities

iStock/Thinkstock

XiXinXing/Thinkstock

iStock/Thinkstock

Communication

Interpretive

Understand listening and reading passages related to someone's hobbies.

Interpersonal

Exchange information on your hobbies and favorite activities.

Presentational

Comment on leisure activities; describe your favorite pastimes.

A 第一課 你喜歡做什麼?

What do you like to do?

A 5.1 詞語預習 cíyǔ yùxí   PREVIEW THE VOCABULARY

 Use the **online audio flashcards** to familiarize yourself with the new vocabulary in this section.

Nouns (N)

愛好	àihào	hobby
運動	yùndòng	sports, exercise
音樂	yīnyuè	music
歌	gē	song
舞	wǔ	dance
球	qiú	ball
籃球	lánqiú	basketball
乒乓球	pīngpāngqiú	table tennis, ping-pong
網球	wǎngqiú	tennis
棒球	bàngqiú	baseball
拳	quán	fist, punch
功夫	gōngfu	kung fu
武術	wǔshù	martial arts
遊戲	yóuxì	game
電影	diànyǐng	movie
電視	diànshì	television
小說	xiǎoshuō	novel
一迷	–mí	fan of . . .

Adverbs (Adv)

有時候	yǒu shíhou	sometimes
經常	jīngcháng	often, frequently
不常	bù cháng	seldom
很少	hěn shǎo	rarely
一起	yìqǐ	together
最	zuì	most
非常	fēicháng	very, extremely

Preposition (Prep) / Coverb (CV)

跟	gēn	with, from

Verbs (AV)

看	kàn	watch, see
聽	tīng	listen, hear
寫	xiě	write
唱	chàng	sing
跳	tiào	jump, leap, dance
打	dǎ	hit, play
玩	wán	play (game), have fun

Verb-Object (VO) Compounds/Phrases

The "//" symbol means that the compound is separable.

看書	kàn//shū	read books
聽音樂	tīng//yīnyuè	listen to music
上網	shàng//wǎng	go online
唱歌	chàng//gē	sing (a song)
跳舞	tiào//wǔ	dance
打電話	dǎ//diànhuà	make a phone call
打球	dǎ//qiú	play a ball game
打拳	dǎ//quán	do/practice martial arts

Particle (P)

得 de	(used as a marker to introduce comments on an action or a performance)

Adjectives (Adj)/Stative Verbs (SV)

不同 bù tóng	different	
好聽 hǎotīng	pleasant to listen to	
好玩 hǎowán	fun, interesting	
好看 hǎokàn	(books, movies, etc.) interesting, intriguing; (person, thing) good-looking	

Structures

- 喜歡 + VO
- (打) 球打得很好
- VO1, VO2 他都喜歡
- 跟Sb一起V

 A | 5.2) 詞句聽説 cíjù tīngshuō　　　　FOCUS ON GRAMMAR

Aural-Oral Exercises: Do the online exercises to further familiarize yourself with the new vocabulary and grammar when it is used in sentences.

Main Features: When talking about hobbies and interests in Chinese, <u>Verb-Object (VO) compounds and phrases</u> are the main verb form used. They are also used to describe many other daily activities. What you may find interesting is that some Chinese <u>action verbs</u> (to read, to sing, to dance), unlike their English equivalents, must always be accompanied by a direct object (a book, a song, a dance). Sometimes, however, a VO compound is split. We'll also look at the <u>V得</u> commenting structure, which is used to tell how well or to what extent someone does something. Be sure to notice the word order used with this structure.

---

1 | **Talking about general activities** 　　　　(不)喜歡 + VO ; (不) 想 VO

A) 喜歡 + VO

■ A Verb-Object (VO) compound/phrase is used to talk about a general type of activity, such as reading, speaking, or dancing. In Chinese, these activities are expressed literally, such as read-book, speak-language, or sing-song.

1) 看書， 説話， 唱歌， 跳舞， 聽音樂， 打球， 看電視， 看電影
　 kàn shū,　shuōhuà,　chànggē,　tiàowǔ,　tīng yīnyuè,　dǎqiú,　kàn diànshì,　kàn diànyǐng

2) 我喜歡看書，你喜歡做什麼?　→　以前我喜歡跳舞，現在我喜歡唱歌了。
　 Wǒ xǐhuan kàn shū, nǐ xǐhuan zuò shénme?　　Yǐqián wǒ xǐhuan tiàowǔ, xiànzài wǒ xǐhuan chànggè le.

B) V 不 VO (Question form)

1) 你打不打球?
Nǐ dǎ bù dǎqiú?

→ 我不打籃球，我打乒乓球。
Wǒ bù dǎ lánqiú, wǒ dǎ pīngpāngqiú.

1 – B) – 1)

C) VVO/V一下O

▩ These two structures can be used to soften the tone. They are not used in negative sentences.

1) 你想不想聽聽音樂?
Nǐ xiǎng bù xiǎng tīngting yīnyuè?

→ 我現在不想聽音樂，我要看一下書。
Wǒ xiànzài bù xiǎng tīng yīnyuè, wǒ yào kàn yíxià shū.

---

2 **Specifying activities**   **V[Modifier]O; V + specific O**

▩ The object portion of a VO compound is usually general. To make the object more specific, a modifier can be inserted between the verb and the object, or the object can be replaced by a noun phrase.

A) V[Mod.]O

▩ Insert a modifier between a generic VO.

1) 看什麼書? 看中文書; 唱什麼歌? 唱英文歌; 打什麼球? 打籃球
kàn shénme shū? kàn Zhōngwén shū; chàng shénme gē? chàng Yīngwén gē; dǎ shénme qiú? dǎ lánqiú

2) 你喜歡看書，那你也看中文書嗎?
Nǐ xǐhuan kàn shū, nà nǐ yě kàn Zhōngwén shū ma?

→ 不看，我看英文書。
Bú kàn, wǒ kàn Yīngwén shū.

3) 他喜歡打球嗎? 他喜歡打什麼球?
Tā xǐhuan dǎqiú ma? Tā xǐhuan dǎ shénme qiú?

→ 他喜歡打籃球。
Tā xǐhuan dǎ lánqiú.

B) V + specific O

▩ Substitute a new noun phrase for the general "default" object.

1) 你喜歡看什麼書?
Nǐ xǐhuan kàn shénme shū?

→ 我喜歡看小說。
Wǒ xǐhuan kàn xiǎoshuō.

（看書小說；看小說書 **X**）

2) 她為什麼不喜歡說話?
Tā wèishénme bù xǐhuan shuōhuà?

→ 因為她不會說英文。
Yīnwèi tā bú huì shuō Yīngwén.

（說話英文；說英文話 **X**）

▆▆▆ This structure allows you to comment on how well and to what extent someone does something.

A) V 得 + positive or negative comment

Sb does Sth (well/poorly/a lot, etc.)

▆▆▆ This structure describes how well someone does something. Note that both positive and negative comments must appear after V 得.

1) 看得很多/很少，唱得很好/不好，打得很不錯/不太好
   kàn de hěn duō/hěn shǎo, chàng de hěn hǎo/bù hǎo, dǎ de hěn búcuò/bú tài hǎo

2) 她喜歡唱歌，而且唱得很好。   (唱歌得很好；唱歌很好 ✗)
   Tā xǐhuan chànggē, érqiě chàng de hěn hǎo.

3) 他喜歡跳舞，可是跳得不好。   (不跳舞得好 ✗)
   Tā xǐhuan tiàowǔ, kěshì tiào de bù hǎo.

4) 他打球打得怎麼樣?   →   他打得很不錯!
   Tā dǎqiú dǎ de zěnmeyàng?   Tā dǎ de hěn búcuò!

3 – A) – 4)

B) VO + V 得 …

As for [doing Sth], Sb does it (well/poorly/a lot, etc.)

▆▆▆ Sometimes the context in which V 得–phrases appear may be unclear, e.g., 她看得很多. Therefore, the VO phrase is often placed in front as the topic. In such cases, the verb is repeated, and 得 is always attached to the second verb instead of the first verb in the VO phrase.

1) 說中文說得很好/不好，唱歌唱得很好/不太好，
   shuō Zhōngwén shuō de hěn hǎo/bù hǎo, chànggē chàng de hěn hǎo/bú tài hǎo,

   打球打得不錯/很不好
   dǎqiú dǎ de búcuò/ hěn bù hǎo

2) 她唱歌唱得怎麼樣?   →   她唱得不錯。   (唱歌得怎麼樣? ✗)
   Tā chànggē chàng de zěnmeyàng?   Tā chàng de búcuò.

3) 他說英文說得好不好? → 他說得不太好。   (不說英文得好 ✗)
   Tā shuō Yīngwén shuō de hǎo bù hǎo?   Tā shuō de bú tài hǎo.

C) (V) O + V 得 …
As for [Sth], Sb does it (well/poorly/a lot, etc.)

■ This is a variation of the VO + V 得 structure and is typically used for emphasis or contrast.

1) 他電視看得很多，書看得很少。
   Tā diànshì kàn de hěn duō, shū kàn de hěn shǎo.

2) 她歌唱得很好，舞跳得不太好。
   Tā gē chàng de hěn hǎo, wǔ tiào de bú tài hǎo.

3 – C) – 1)

---

4   **Talking about activities**

一起 V；跟 Sb 一起 V
doing something together with someone

---

1) 一起唱歌跳舞，一起學中文，跟朋友一起打球，跟室友一起去看電影
   Yìqǐ chànggē tiàowǔ, yìqǐ xué Zhōngwén, gēn péngyou yìqǐ dǎqiú, gēn shìyǒu yìqǐ qù kàn diànyǐng

2) 我想跟他們(一起)打球。(一起 can be omitted without causing ambiguity.)
   Wǒ xiǎng gēn tā (yìqǐ) dǎqiú.

3) 我想跟他一起學中文。 (一起 is necessary for 學, meaning "learn Sth together with Sb.")
   Wǒ xiǎng gēn tā yìqǐ xué Zhōngwén.

4) 我想跟他學中文。 (跟 Sb 學… means "learn . . . from Sb.")
   Wǒ xiǎng gēn tā xué Zhōngwén.

4 – 2)

5   Describing the frequency of an activity   經常V, 不常V, 很少V, 有時候V

▬ Unlike English, Chinese adverbs of frequency only appear directly before action verbs.

1) 經常/常常看電影, 不常看電影
    jīngcháng/chángcháng kàn diànyǐng, bù cháng kàn diànyǐng

    有時候看電影, 很少看電影
    yǒu shíhou kàn diànyǐng, hěn shǎo kàn diànyǐng

2) 你經常看電視嗎? ➔ 我不常看, 有時候看。
    Nǐ jīngcháng kàn diànshì ma?   Wǒ bù cháng kàn, yǒu shíhou kàn.

3) 你經常聽音樂嗎? ➔ 我很少聽音樂, 可是我常常聽歌。
    Nǐ jīngcháng tīng yīnyuè ma?   Wǒ hěn shǎo tīng yīnyuè, kěshì wǒ chángcháng tīng gē.
                          (In this case, the opposite of 很少 is not 很多.)

▬ **Compare:** frequency vs. quantity

4) She reads *a lot*. (She reads *often/frequently*.)   她經常看書。   (她很多看書。 ✗)
                                            Tā jīngcháng kànshū.

5) She reads *a lot*. (She reads *a lot of books*.)   她看書看得很多。
                                             Tā kànshū kàn de hěn duō.

5 – 3)

Before viewing . . .

1) What are the five most popular recreational activities that students enjoy doing at your school?

2) What do you think Ah Long likes to do? How about his roommates?

While viewing . . .

3) During your first viewing, focus on meaning.

4) During your second viewing, pay special attention to speech forms and tones.

5) Finally, practice saying the sentences by answering the questions below.

 U5-A1

阿龍説:
Ā Lóng shuō:

"我有三個室友, _____
Wǒ yǒu sān gè shìyǒu, ……

_____。我們的_____。"
　　　　　　Wǒmen de……

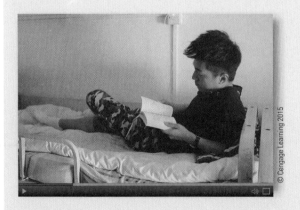

小東喜歡做什麼?
Xiǎodōng xǐhuan zuò shénme?

"小東喜歡_____,
Xiǎodōng xǐhuan……

也_____。"
yě……

大明有什麼愛好?
Dàmíng yǒu shénme àihào?

"大明＿＿＿＿＿＿＿＿＿＿,
Dàmíng……

籃球＿＿＿＿＿＿＿＿。"
lánqiu……

這是朱宇。他覺得什麼最有意思?
Zhè shì Zhū Yǔ. Tā juéde shénme zuì yǒu yìsi?

"朱宇呢，他覺得＿＿＿＿＿＿＿＿＿＿
Zhū Yǔ ne,　tā juéde……

＿＿＿＿＿＿，所以＿＿＿＿＿＿。"
　　　　　　　suǒyǐ……

 U5-A2

阿龍喜歡做什麼?
Ā Lóng xǐhuan zuò shénme?

"我最喜歡＿＿＿＿、＿＿＿＿!
Wǒ zuì xǐhuan……

我也非常喜歡＿＿＿＿＿＿。
Wǒ yě fēicháng xǐhuan……

這個電影＿＿＿＿＿＿!
Zhège diànyǐng……

我想＿＿＿＿＿＿,
Wǒ xiǎng……

可是＿＿＿＿＿＿＿＿＿＿? "
Kěshì……

1 Forms and structures

See 5.2 for more notes and examples.

1) 我們的愛好不同。
Wǒmen de àihào bù tóng.

xiāngtóng
(The opposite: 愛好相同)

2) 小東喜歡看書，也喜歡打乒乓球。
Xiǎodōng xǐhuan kàn shū, yě xǐhuan dǎ pīngpāngqiú.

(也 must be followed by a verb.)

3) 大明是個籃球迷。
Dàmíng shì gè lánqiúmí.

(迷 can be attached to other nouns as a suffix to refer to other types of fans, such as 影迷, 歌迷 and 電腦迷.)

4) 籃球打得不錯……
Lánqiú dǎ de búcuò……

(V)OV 得…
(打籃球打得... can also be used; 不錯 means 很好.)

5) 朱宇覺得在網上玩遊戲最有意思。
Zhū Yǔ juéde zài wǎngshàng wán yóuxì zuì yǒu yìsi.

(The opposite: 最沒意思)

6) 所以經常上網。
Suǒyǐ jīngcháng shàngwǎng.

(經常 always goes before the verb; the opposite: 不常V, 很少V)

7) (阿龍)想學武術。
(Ā Lóng) xiǎng xué wǔshù.

(Similar examples: 學籃球/學打籃球, 學中文歌/學唱中文歌)

8) 誰跟我一起學？
Shéi gēn wǒ yìqǐ xué?

(跟我一起學 is different from 跟我學: *learn together with me* vs. *learn from me*)

2 Interrogative and negative forms

Ask and answer the following questions. Use the information in parentheses in your answer.

A) Yes/no questions and alternative questions: V 不 V；A 還是 B

1) 小東喜歡打球嗎？他打不打籃球？   他喜歡打球，可是不打籃球，他打乒乓球。

2) 大明打不打乒乓球？ _____

3) 朱宇覺得打球有沒有意思？ _____

4) 他經常打球嗎？ _____
(不經常 / 很少)

5) 阿龍喜歡看書還是打球？ _____
(也不)

6) 阿龍想學唱歌還是學跳舞？ _____
(都不)

7) 阿龍的愛好是不是看書？ _____
(最喜歡…)

8) 你覺得小東想不想跟他一起學武術？ _____
(不)

B) Commenting on an action: **VO + V 得**…
Note that the negation comes after V 得.

1) 那個人打籃球打得怎麼樣？ 他打籃球打得不太好。_____
(不太好)

2) 他唱歌唱得好不好？ _____
(不好)

3) 他看書看得多不多？ _____
(很少)

4) 他學外語學得好不好？ _____
(不好)

C) Other words and forms: (不) 好聽，(不) 好看，(不) 好玩；經常 V，很少 V

1) 她唱歌歌唱得怎麼樣？ 她唱得很好聽，所以我經常聽她的歌。
(很好聽/經常)

2) 阿龍覺得功夫電影怎麼樣？ _____
(最好看/經常)

3) 他覺得打遊戲好玩不好玩？ _____
(不好玩/很少)

1 Pair work

Ask and answer questions based on the pictures using appropriate expressions and forms:

VO compounds : 唱歌，跳舞，打球，看電視，看電影
chànggē, tiàowǔ, dǎqiú, kàn diànshì, kàn diànyǐng

Adverbs : 最，經常/常常，不常，很少
zuì, jīngcháng/chángcháng, bù cháng, hěn shǎo

Adjectives : 好聽，好看，好玩，有意思
hǎotīng, hǎokàn, hǎowán, yǒu yìsi

Expressions
- 有什麼愛好？
- 喜歡V什麼O？
- 經常［VO］嗎？
- 跟誰一起［VO］？
- VOV得怎麼樣？
- 覺得VO有意思

這個男生有什麼愛好？（他喜歡…）
Zhège nánshēng yǒu shénme àihào? (Tā xǐhuan…)

他喜歡唱什麼歌？英文歌還是中文歌？
Tā xǐhuan chàng shénme gē? Yīngwén gē háishi Zhōngwén gē?

他唱歌唱得怎麼樣？（很好，很好聽，不太好…）
Tā chànggē chàng de zěnmeyàng? (hěn hǎo, hěn hǎotīng, bú tài hǎo…)

這個男孩跟誰一起打球？（爸爸、老師、同學…）
Zhège nánhái gēn shéi yìqǐ dǎqiú? (bàba, lǎoshī, tóngxué…)

他打得好不好？（不好，不夠好，不太好）
Tā dǎ de hǎo bù hǎo? (bù hǎo, búgòu hǎo, bú tài hǎo)

他覺得打球有沒有意思？
Tā juéde dǎqiú yǒu méiyǒu yìsi?

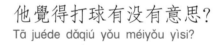

這個女生學什麼？（跳舞？武術？）
Zhège nǚshēng xué shénme? (tiàowǔ? wǔshù?)

她跟誰一起學？（一個男生、一個女生）
Tā gēn shéi yìqǐ xué? (yí gè nánshēng, yí gè nǚshēng)

誰學得不夠好？
Shéi xué de búgòu hǎo?

這個女生經常看什麼電視？（唱歌的，跳舞的？）
Zhège nǚshēng jīngcháng kàn shénme diànshì? (chànggē de, tiàowǔ de?)

她現在跟誰一起看電視？她們覺得好看不好看？
Tā xiànzài gēn shéi yìqǐ kàn diànshì? Tāmen juéde hǎokàn bù hǎokàn?

她跟她的室友說什麼？
Tā gēn tā de shìyǒu shuō shénme?

2 **Interview and report**

1) **Interview:** Move around the classroom and interview two classmates. Ask and answer questions about what they like to do or can do. Ask these five questions:

你有什麼愛好？ 你喜歡 V 什麼 O？ 你經常 [VO] 嗎？ 你跟誰一起 [VO]？
你/他 VO V 得怎麼樣？

2) **Report:** Be prepared to report back to the class about your interview results.

3) **Quiz:** The teacher may quiz students on the information shared in the reports.

A 5.6 語法鞏固 yǔfǎ gǒnggù   **REINFORCE THE GRAMMAR**

🌐 These exercises are also available online with automatic feedback.

1 **Give the Chinese equivalent for each sentence**
VO Compounds/Phrases:

1) He enjoys <u>reading</u>.   → _____

2) He enjoys <u>reading that book</u>.   → _____

3) She seldom <u>speaks</u>.   → _____

4) She seldom <u>speaks English</u>.   → _____

Question Form V 不 V:

5) <u>Does</u> your friend sing?   → _____

6) <u>Can</u> your friend sing?（會） → _____

7) <u>Can</u> you dance?（會） → _____

8) <u>Would you like</u> to dance with me?   → _____

2 **Change the sentences**
Change each sentence into first a question, then a negative statement.

V 得 + Adj-phrase

                                   Questions: Negative statement:

1) 她看書看得很多。 _____ _____

2) 他打球打得很好。 _____ _____

3) 小説他寫得很少。 _____ _____

4) 她學外語學得怎麼樣？ _____

A 5.7 聽答對話 tīngdá duìhuà   **LET'S CHAT**

🌐 In this listening-speaking activity you'll be asked to answer questions about the **video** segment as well as about **yourself.** You may be asked to record and submit your answers to the teacher.

UNIT 5
B 第二課

明天有晚會
There is a party tomorrow

 B 5.8 詞語預習 cíyǔ yùxí | **PREVIEW THE VOCABULARY**

🌐 Use the **online audio flashcards** to familiarize yourself with the new vocabulary in this section.

Nouns (N)

活動	huódòng	activity
比賽	bǐsài	competition
球賽	qiúsài	ball game, match
中心	zhōngxīn	center
事(情)	shì(qing)	matter
會	huì	meeting, gathering, party
晚會	wǎnhuì	evening party, soirée
舞會	wǔhuì	dance party, ball
音樂會	yīnyuèhuì	concert
卡拉OK	kǎlā-OK	karaoke
問題	wèntí	problem, question

Time Words (TW)/Expressions (Exp)

今天	jīntiān	today
明天	míngtiān	tomorrow
周末	zhōumò	weekend
的時候	de shíhou	when

Adverbs (Adv)

別	bié	don't
只	zhǐ	just, only

Question Word (QW)

什麼時候	shénme shíhou	when

Verbs (V)

運動	yùndòng	exercise
教	jiāo	teach
走	zǒu	walk, go, leave

Preposition (Prep)/Coverb (CV)

跟(Sb學)	gēn (…xué)	learn (from Sb)

Idiomatic Expressions (IE)

有事嗎?	Yǒu shì ma?	What can I do for you? / What's up?
沒問題。	Méi wèntí.	No problem.

那我走了。	Nà wǒ zǒu le.	I'll leave then.
好的。	Hǎo de.	Okay, all right.
明天見。	Míngtiān jiàn.	See you tomorrow.
你的意思是……	Nǐ de yìsi shì……	You are saying that . . . / You mean . . .

B 5.9 詞句聽説 cíjù tīngshuō FOCUS ON GRAMMAR

 Aural-Oral Exercises: Do the online exercises to further familiarize yourself with the new vocabulary and grammar when it is used in sentences.

Main Features: This lesson expands on previous topics and introduces the 在 VO structure, the counterpart of the English progressive tense. Unlike 在 PW-phrases that indicate location, 在 VO-phrases denote ongoing engagement in an action or activity. Note the difference and how the two 在 forms merge in one sentence. Also, we'll work on forms for telling about an event, that is, how to say <u>when, where, and what</u>, when talking about recreational activities. Another interesting sentence pattern we'll explore is <u>QW</u> (什麼, 誰…) used in a statement as an intensifier. So get ready!

1 Describing an ongoing action (正)在VO

■ 在 V (*in the process of doing* . . .) can be used to describe past or present time. 正 adds an emphasis to the person's active engagement, meaning "right in the middle of doing . . . ."

A) TW + (正)在 + VO

1) 現在在看書，在打球，現在正在聽音樂，正在打電話
   xiànzài zài kàn shū, zài dǎqiú, xiànzài zhèngzài tīng yīnyuè, zhèngzài dǎ diànhuà

2) 他現在在做什麼？ → 他在看書，他在看一本小説。
   Tā xiànzài zài zuò shénme? Tā zài kàn shū, tā zài kàn yì běn xiǎoshuō.

3) 你現在在看電視嗎？ → 我不在看電視，我正在看小説。
   Nǐ xiànzài zài kàn diànshì ma? Wǒ bú zài kàn diànshì, wǒ zhèngzài kàn xiǎoshuō.
   (Use 不在 VO for negation)

B) TW + (正)在 + PW + VO

▰ Add a place word (PW) to indicate a location. Note the position of the PW before the action verb.

1) 她現在在做什麼?
Tā xiànzài zài zuò shénme?

→ 她正在宿舍裡看電視。
Tā zhèngzài sùshè li kàn diànshì.

1 — B) — 1)

C) 在 VO

▰ The structure 在 VO is also used to describe an ongoing activity or engagement that lasts for a certain period of time:

1) 你現在在學日文還是在學中文? → 我在學中文,我在美國大學學中文。
Nǐ xiànzài zài xué Rìwén háishi zài xué Zhōngwén?   Wǒ zài xué Zhōngwén, wǒ zài Měiguó dàxué xué Zhōngwén.

---

2 **Telling about an event:** When, What, and Where   TW + PW + 有 Event

Event: 晚會, 舞會, 音樂會, 比賽, 球賽……
wǎnhuì, wǔhuì, yīnyuèhuì, bǐsài, qiúsài

A) When and What: TW + 有 Event

1) 什麼時候有活動?   明天有什麼活動?   周末有没有什麼活動?
Shénme shíhòu yǒu huódòng? Míngtiān yǒu shénme huódòng? Zhōumò yǒu méiyǒu shénme huódòng?

2) 這個周末有什麼活動?
Zhège zhōumò yǒu shénme huódòng?

→ 這個周末有籃球賽、乒乓球賽,
Zhège zhōumò yǒu lánqiú sài、pīngpāng qiúsài,

還有舞會。
hái yǒu wǔhuì.

2 — A) — 2)

B) When, Where, and What: TW + PW + 有 Event， **or** PW + TW + 有 Event

1) 今天我們學校有一個球賽，學生中心周末有一個舞會。
jīntiān wǒmen xuéxiào yǒu yí gè qiúsài, xuéshēng zhōngxīn zhòumò yǒu yí gè wǔhuì.

2) 這個周末學生中心有沒有　　→　學生中心沒有，可是我們
Zhège zhōumò xuéshēng zhōngxīn yǒu méiyǒu　　　Xuéshēng zhōngxīn méiyǒu, kěshì wǒmen

晚會？　　　　　　　　　　　　　宿舍樓有一個舞會。
wǎnhuì?　　　　　　　　　　　　sùshè lóu yǒu yí gè wǔhuì.

3) 明天有什麼活動？　　→　明天晚上在5號樓有一個晚會。
Míngtiān yǒu shénme huódòng?　　Míngtiān wǎnshang zài wǔ hào lóu yǒu yí gè wǎnhuì.

3　**Intensifying the tone**　　　　　QW + 都 (不) V / 也不 V

■ In this structure, 都 can be used positively or negatively, while 也 is only used in a negative sentence.

A) QW + 都 (不) V / 也不 V

1) 誰會唱這個歌？　　→　誰都會唱這個歌。　　*(Anyone can . . .)*
Shéi huì chàng zhège gē?　　Shéi dōu huì chàng zhège gē.

誰都不會唱這個歌。　*(No one can . . .)*
Shéi dōu bú huì chàng zhège gē.

2) 你喜歡什麼：唱歌、跳舞、打球？　→　我什麼都(不)喜歡。　*(I like all/none of*
Nǐ xǐhuan shénme: chànggē、tiàowǔ、dǎqiú?　　Wǒ shénme dōu (bù) xǐhuan.　*them.)*

我什麼也不喜歡。　*(I like none of*
Wǒ shénme ye bù xǐhuan.　*them.)*

B) QW + O 都 (不) V / 也不 V

Specifying the object:

3 – B) – 1)

1) 你喜歡打什麼球？　　→　我什麼球都不喜歡打。　✔
Nǐ xǐhuan dǎ shénme qiú?　　Wǒ shénme qiú dōu bù xǐhuan dǎ.

我什麼都不喜歡打球。　✗

4 Making a suggestion or request

[verb phrase] + 吧
Let's do . . . / Why don't you do . . .

■ Unlike the 吧 you learned previously (好吧 for accepting, and 有意思吧 for a yes/no question with a presupposition), this modal particle indicates a suggestion.

1) 你們去打球吧；我跟你去吧；你跟他學吧
   nǐmen qù dǎqiú ba;　　wǒ gēn nǐmen qù ba; nǐ gēn tā xué ba

2) 小李跳舞跳得很好，我們跟她學吧！
   Xiǎo Lǐ tiàowǔ tiào de hěn hǎo, wǒmen gēn tā xué ba!

3) 周末學校有球賽，你跟我們一起去看吧。
   Zhōumò xuéxiào yǒu qiúsài, nǐ gēn wǒmen yìqǐ qù kàn ba.

4 — 3)

■ Compare the usage of 吧 above with those in assumption-questions below:

4) 你會說中文吧？　　*(I suppose you can speak Chinese?)*
   Nǐ huì shuō Zhōngwén ba?

5) 你是美國人吧？　　*(I suppose you are an American?)*
   Nǐ shì Měiguórén ba?

4 — 4)

5 Telling someone not to do something

別 V / 不要 V
Don't . . .

■ 別 is spoken and 不要 can be either spoken or written. 別 V 了 means "Don't . . . " "Stop . . ."

1) 別說話(了)，　別去那兒，　別跟他去打球了，　別看那個電影
   bié shuōhuà (le),　　bié qù nàr,　　bié gēn tā qù dǎqiú le,　　bié kàn nàge diànyǐng

2) 我想跟小李學跳舞。　➜　小李跳舞跳得不好，(你)別跟她學。
   Wǒ xiǎng gēn Xiǎo Lǐ xué tiàowǔ.　　　Xiǎo Lǐ tiàowǔ tiào de bù hǎo, (nǐ) bié gēn tā xué.

   (不要跟她學 can also be used.)

3) 我想去打球，你想不想去？　➜　我現在正在學中文，(你)別跟我說話。
   Wǒ xiǎng qù dǎqiú, nǐ xiǎng bù xiǎng qù?　　Wǒ xiànzài zhèngzài xué Zhōngwén, (nǐ) bié gēn wǒ shuōhuà.

A)   Defining people: **VO 的那個人/人**
         the person who is/does . . .; those who are/do . . .

1) 唱歌的那個女孩， 唱中文歌的那個女孩， 喜歡唱歌的人
     chànggē de nàge nǚhái,   chàng Zhōngwén gē de nàge nǚhái, xǐhuan chànggē de rén

2) 唱歌的那個人是誰？   ➜   她是我的室友。
     Chànggē de nàge rén shì shéi?   Tā shì wǒ de shìyǒu.

3) 你認識打球的那幾個男生嗎？   ➜   我不認識。
     Nǐ rènshi dǎqiú de nà jǐ gè nánshēng ma?   Wǒ bú rènshi.

B)   Defining an object: **Sb + V 的 O**
        the O that Sb V

                                              6 — A) — 2)

1) 她唱的歌， 她唱的那個中文歌， 她喜歡唱的那幾個歌
     tā chàng de gē, tā chàng de nàge Zhōngwén gē, tā xǐhuan chàng de nà jǐ gè gē

     the song(s) she sang, the Chinese song she sang, those songs she likes to sing

2) 她唱的歌是什麼歌？   ➜   (她唱的歌)是一個美國歌。
     Tā chàng de gē shì shénme gē?   (Tā chàng de gē) shì yí gè Měiguó gē.

3) 你喜歡她唱的哪個歌？   ➜   她唱的歌我都喜歡。
     Nǐ xǐhuan tā chàng de nǎge gē?   Tā chàng de gē wǒ dōu xǐhuan.

                 6 — B) — 3)

Before viewing . . .

1) Is it more fun to learn something with someone or by yourself? Why?
2) What are your favorite activities to do by yourself?
3) What are some of the activities that are enjoyed by both male and female students?

While viewing . . .

1) During your first viewing, focus on meaning.
2) During your second viewing, pay special attention to speech forms and tones.
3) Finally, practice saying the sentences by answering the questions below.

U5-B1

阿龍問朱宇什麼？
Ā Lóng wèn Zhū Yǔ shénme?

"你＿＿＿＿＿？ ＿＿＿＿＿＿＿＿
Nǐ……

＿＿＿？"

朱宇說什麼？
Zhū Yǔ shuō shénme?

"別＿＿＿＿＿，我＿＿＿＿＿！"
Bié……   wǒ……

U5-B2

小東問阿龍想不想看書，
Xiǎodōng wèn Ā Lóng xiǎng bù xiǎng kànshū,

阿龍說什麼？
Ā Lóng shuō shénme?

"我＿＿＿＿＿，我想＿＿＿＿＿。"
Wǒ……   wǒ xiǎng……

小東問阿龍想不想打乒乓球，
Xiǎodōng wèn Ā Lóng xiǎng bù xiǎng dǎ pīngpāngqiú,

阿龍說什麼？
Ā Lóng shuō shénme?

"乒乓球＿＿＿＿＿，可是＿＿＿＿＿。"
Pīngpāngqiú……   kěshì……

小東說什麼？
Xiǎodōng shuō shénme?

"那沒問題，我＿＿＿＿＿。"
Nà méi wèntí,   wǒ……

大明説什麼？阿龍呢？
Dàmíng shuō shénme? Ā Lóng ne?

"阿龍，別_____，跟我_____。
Ā Lóng   bié……   gēn wǒ……

打籃球_____！"
dǎ lánqiú……

阿龍想打什麼球？他説：
Ā Lóng xiǎng dǎ shénme qiú? Tā shuō:

"我什麼球_____，我只想_____。"
Wǒ shénme qiú……   wǒ zhǐ xiǎng……

▶ U5-B3

阿龍和白曉雪在説什麼？
Ā Lóng hé Bái Xiǎoxuě zài shuō shénme?

"周末_____？明天_____？"
Zhōumò……   míngtiān……

明天有什麼活動？
Míngtiān yǒu shénme huódòng?

"明天_____，
Míngtiān……

_____、_____。
"

咱們一起去吧，很好玩！"
Zánmen yìqǐ qù ba, hěn hǎowán!

小東為什麼覺得沒意思？
Xiǎodōng wèishénme juéde méi yìsi?

"唱歌_____，跳舞_____！"
Chànggē……   tiàowǔ……

阿龍説他可以教小東跳舞，大明和
Ā Lóng shuō tā kěyǐ jiāo Xiǎodōng tiàowǔ, Dàmíng hé

朱宇説什麼？
Zhū Yǔ shuō shénme?

"對，_____。"
Duì,……

"你的意思是，_____？"
Nǐ de yìsi shì,……

1 Forms and structures

See 5.9 for more notes and examples.

1) 別跟我説話。/別打乒乓球。
Bié gēn wǒ shuōhuà. /Bié dǎ pīngpāngqiú.

(不要跟我説話 can also be used.)

2) 我正在打遊戲呢！
Wǒ zhèngzài dǎ yóuxì ne!

(呢 here helps soften the tone in 在-VO sentences.)

3) 你在做什麼？ → 我在看英文小説。
Nǐ zài zuò shénme? Wǒ zài kàn Yīngwén xiǎoshuō.

(在VO: *Someone is doing / is in the middle of doing something.*)

4) 我不想看書，我想運動運動。
Wǒ bù xiǎng kàn shū, wǒ xiǎng yùndòng yùndòng.

(As a "downtoner", the VV form for disyllabic verbs: ABAB; also, AB 一下)

5) 那没問題，我可以教你。
Nà méi wèntí, wǒ kěyǐ jiāo nǐ.

(可以 [*can*] should not be confused with 會 [*can or know how to do*].)

6) 跟我打籃球吧。
Gēn wǒ dǎ lánqiú ba.

(Giving suggestions using 吧: *Come play ...with me.*)

7) 跟我一起學吧。/咱們一起去吧。
Gēn wǒ yìqǐ xué ba.   /Zánmen yìqǐ qù ba.

(This usage is different from using 吧 to form assumption-questions: 你要去打籃球吧？)

8) 周末有活動。
Zhōumò yǒu huódòng.

TW + 有 Event (TW as topic of the sentence)

9) 明天在學生中心有一個新生晚會。
Míngtiān zàixuéshēng zhōngxīn yǒu yí gè xīnshēng wǎnhuì.

TW + PW + 有 Event (在 zai is optional)

▬ Making a VO or O the topic of a sentence

1) 乒乓球我會打，可是我打得不好。
Pīngpāngqiú wǒ huì dǎ, kěshì wǒ dǎ de bù hǎo.

([*As for*] <u>Ping pong</u>, *I know how to play it, but ...*)

2) 打籃球最好玩！
Dǎ lánqiú zuì hǎowán!

(<u>Playing basketball</u> *is the most fun./ It is the most fun to . . .*)

3) 我什麼球都不想打。
Wǒ shénme qiú dōu bù xiǎng dǎ.

(<u>Whatever ball game</u> *it is, I don't want to play it.*)

4) 唱歌我唱得不好，跳舞我也不會！
Chànggē wǒ chàng de bù hǎo, tiàowǔ wǒ yě bú huì!

(*I'm not good at* <u>singing</u>. *I don't know how to* <u>dance</u> *either.*)

2 Interrogative and negative forms　　QW (O) + 都/也不 V

Practice these questions and respond with negative answers.

1) 那個男生喜歡打什麼球?　　他什麼球也不喜歡打。

2) 他看什麼電視?

3) 他會說什麼外語?

4) 誰想跟那個女生跳舞?

5) 誰要跟她學跳舞?

6) 周末學生中心有什麼活動?

7) 周末他們要去哪裡?

3 Story narration

Pay special attention to the verb forms and the use of punctuation marks.

阿龍想學武術，他問室友想不想跟他一起學。朱宇正在網上玩
Ā Lóng xiǎng xué wǔshù,　tā wèn shìyǒu xiǎng bù xiǎng gēn tā yìqǐ xué.　Zhū Yǔ zhèngzài wǎngshàng wán

遊戲，小東在看英文小說，大明想去打籃球，他們誰都不想學武術。
yóuxì,　Xiǎodōng zài kàn Yīngwén xiǎoshuō, Dàmíng xiǎng qù dǎ lánqiú, tāmen shéi dōu bù xiǎng xué wǔshù.

小東問阿龍想不想打乒乓球。大明說，別打乒乓球，打籃球最有意思。
Xiǎodōng wèn Ā Lóng xiǎng bù xiǎng dǎ pīngpāngqiú. Dàmíng shuō, bié dǎ pīngpāngqiú, dǎ lánqiú zuì yǒu yìsi.

可是阿龍什麼球都不想打，他只想打拳。
Kěshì Ā Lóng shénme qiú dōu bù xiǎng dǎ,　tā zhǐ xiǎng dǎquán.

白曉雪給阿龍打電話，她說明天學生中心有一個新生晚會，
Bái Xiǎoxuě gěi Ā Lóng dǎ diànhuà,　　tā shuō míngtiān xuéshēng zhōngxīn yǒu yí gè xīnshēng wǎnhuì,

可以跳舞，唱卡拉OK。阿龍覺得很好玩，問室友想不想一起去。小東說
kěyǐ tiàowǔ,　　chàng kǎlā OK.　Ā Lóng juéde hěn hǎowán, wèn shìyǒu xiǎng bù xiǎng yìqǐ qù. Xiǎodōng shuō

他唱歌唱得不好，跳舞也不會。阿龍說他可以教小東跳舞。可是小東
tā chànggē chàng de bù hǎo, tiàowǔ yě bú huì.　Ā Lóng shuō tā kěyǐ jiāo Xiǎodōng tiàowǔ.　Kěshì Xiǎodōng

不想去，他說："你去跳你的舞吧，我看我的書。"
bù xiǎng qù, tā shuō:　"Nǐ qù tiào nǐ de wǔ ba,　wǒ kàn wǒ de shū."

1 Pair work

Ask and answer questions based on the images. Decide what structure should be used in each case.

- 喜歡 + VO
- 在 VO，正在 VO
- V 得⋯
- QW + 都(不)V
- 跟 Sb 一起 V
- 跟 Sb V

這個男孩喜歡做什麼？
Zhège nánhái xǐhuan zuò shénme?

他在跟誰一起打？
Tā zài gēn shéi yìqǐ dǎ?

他打得怎麼樣？
Tā dǎ de zěnmeyàng?

這個學生喜歡做什麼？
Zhège xuésheng xǐhuan zuò shénme?

他在看英文書還是中文書？
Tā zài kàn Yīngwén shū háishi Zhōngwén shū?

他看得多不多？
Tā kàn de duō bù duō?

學生中心有什麼活動？ (dance, concert, Karaoke)
Xuéshēng zhōngxīn yǒu shénme huódòng?

什麼時候在哪裡有這些活動？ (today, tomorrow, weekend)
Shénme shíhou zài nǎlǐ yǒu zhèxiē huódòng?

這個學生喜歡什麼活動？   (all)
Zhège xuésheng xǐhuan shénme huódòng?

這兩個女生在跟誰學跳舞？ (a teacher)
Zhè liǎng gè nǚshēng zài gēn shéi xué tiàowǔ?

誰學得好？ (neither: QW 都 V 得⋯)
Shéi xué de hǎo?

老師教得很高興嗎？
Lǎoshī jiāo de hěn gāoxìng ma?

2 Interview and report

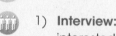

1) **Interview:** Before interviewing a classmate, identify two or three activities you might be interested in trying. Next, ask a classmate if he/she has the same interest in these activities, and if he/she would like to try them sometime in the future. Take turns asking and answering questions about each other's interests. You may use the sample questions below.

2) **Report:** Report back to the class about the plans you and your classmate have on trying those activities both of you are interested in.

CHINESE STUDENTS' CLUB WEEKEND ACTIVITIES

中國學生會
周末活動

Chinese Films 中國電影
Chinese Taichi 中國太極拳
Table Tennis 乒乓球
Chinese Calligraphy 中國書法
Chinese Music 中國音樂

Location: Building #2 (2號樓)

A: Interviewer
• Ask if B likes activity X or Y. (喜歡，有意思)
• Ask if B often does one of the activities he/she likes. (經常V)
• Tell B there's . . . on the weekend. (周末...有X and Y)
• Ask if B wants to learn about activity X or Y with you over the weekend. (我想…，你跟我一起V吧)

B: Interviewee
Respond to A's questions and improvise with these:
• 我覺得 X and Y [很有意思，沒有意思，很好玩…]
• X 和 Y 我都(不)V(會，喜歡，想學…)
• 別V [X]，我們一起V [Y] 吧
• 好吧，我跟你一起V吧；對不起，周末我有別的活動。

B 5.13 語法鞏固 yǔfǎ gǒnggù   REINFORCE THE GRAMMAR

These exercises are also available online with automatic feedback.

1 Give the Chinese equivalent for each sentence
Pay attention to the Chinese structures and avoid word-for-word translation. Pinyin may be used.

1) Currently she is studying Chinese in Beijing.　→ _____

2) Now she's watching a movie with her friend.　→ _____

3) There is a concert this weekend.　→ _____

4) There is a concert this weekend at the Student Center.　→ _____

5) He is going to teach me how to dance tomorrow.　→ _____

6) I suppose you can't play ping-pong?　→ _____

7) Why don't we learn ping-pong from him? (suggestion)　→ _____

8) Don't watch that movie.　→ _____

9) Don't watch that movie with him.　→ _____

10) What is he teaching? How well does he do it?　→ _____

2 Answer the questions
Create an intensified tone using QW + 都 (不) V. Note that some sentences require moving the noun object to the beginning of the sentence (before or after the subject).

1) 誰想看這個電影？　(no one)　_____
2) 誰會唱這個歌？　(everyone)　_____
3) 他喜歡看什麼書？　(all)　_____
4) 她想去哪兒？　(nowhere)　_____
5) 這個商店有什麼？　(everything)　_____
6) 這個周末有什麼活動？　(none)　_____

B 5.14 聽答對話 tīngdá duìhuà   LET'S CHAT

In this listening-speaking activity you'll be asked to answer questions about the **video** segment as well as about **yourself**. You may be asked to record and submit your answers to the teacher.

Eternity in an Instant/Taxi/Getty Images

EXTRACURRICULAR
ACTIVITIES

To say that Chinese parents are often obsessed with intervention in their children's early education would be an understatement. Many Chinese parents believe that cultivating talent should start young, sometimes even at the toddler stage. Often, at a family gathering or friend's party, a recitation of a Tang poem by a three-year-old boy or a piano performance by a five-year-old girl starts an impromptu talent show.

The belief that intelligence alone does not guarantee success has long been held in Chinese culture. In fact, many Chinese would say that good students do well because they get started earlier and work harder than others, not because they are smarter. A Chinese proverb, 笨鳥先飛 (bèn niǎo xiān fēi, A slow sparrow should make an early start), exemplifies the importance in Chinese culture of beginning education and training young. It is similar in spirit to the old English saying, "The early bird catches the worm."

iStock/Thinkstock

David Cooper Toronto Star/Getty Images

Thinkstock

Fuse/Thinkstock

To ensure a good "early start," families and certain institutions work together to create a vast social network for fostering young talent. Among the most important institutions geared toward training and developing young talent is the grade certificate examinations system, which is a standardized testing system for evaluating progress and determining if students are meeting qualifications in a given field. Similar systems exist in Taiwan, Hong Kong, and in overseas Chinese communities worldwide. Every year, tens of thousands of children flock to local testing centers to take the grade certificate examinations in various fields, including violin, piano, the pipa lute, the zheng zither, ballet, foreign languages, and Chinese calligraphy. Students earn a grade based on their performance as well as the level of difficulty of the pieces selected from the required repertoire. Piano prodigies, such as Lang Lang, Wang Yujia, and Li Yundi, have all gone through the grade certificate examination system before making it into prestigious conservatories.

Lang Lang   Wang Yujia   Li Yundi

For many students, this system has tangible benefits. In some cases, attaining a certain grade in a given field (such as a woodwind or brass instrument) would mean having an advantage in applying to a prestigious high school that happens to have an excellent marching band program. The same can be said for college applications, where a grade-certified softball player could be boosted by as many as 30 bonus points toward his/her goal of college admission. This is part of the motivation that drives parents and children to enroll in the grade certificate examination system. But given the competitive college market and the high pressure placed on particularly an only child, it is not surprising that many view it as an incentive for college opportunity as well as a kind of lifelong learning enhancement.

Once enrolled in college, some students continue to participate in the fine arts activities of their choice, while others pursue newly found passions through various extracurricular activities. One notable trend is that more and more students are interested in service learning and community service. Various volunteer teaching projects have sprung up in the country in recent years aimed at providing volunteer and service opportunities in poor rural areas.

QUIZ

1. State one benefit of the grade certificate examinations system.

2. In light of your understanding of extracurricular activities in China, which of the following is NOT among the most popular activities:
   a. Music
   b. Drama
   c. Dance
   d. Foreign languages

3. The pipa lute and zheng zither (mentioned above) are among the most popular traditional instruments in China. One of them does not have a Chinese origin. Which one? Where did it originate from?

ACTIVITIES

1. Investigate online the three musicians mentioned here and find out where they are originally from, where they studied (either in China and elsewhere), and which one performed at the 2008 Beijing Olympic Games Opening Ceremony.

2. Many believe that early childhood education in certain fields, such as music, is essential to developing critical skills essential for long term professional development. Do you agree with this statement? Why or why not?

單元復習
Review and Integration

 Read the following passages as fast as you can. Follow these steps:

1) Do not stop to check the meaning of words you don't recognize. Mark them and keep reading.
2) Read the passage again and guess the meaning of the marked words on a separate piece of paper.
3) Finally, look up the words in a dictionary or the vocabulary index and verify their meanings.

阿龍和三個室友都有不同的愛好。小東喜歡看書，也喜歡打乒乓球。大明是個球迷，經常看電視上的籃球比賽，他打籃球也打得不錯。朱宇覺得打遊戲最有意思，所以經常上網打遊戲。阿龍喜歡什麼呢？他喜歡中國武術，也叫"功夫"！他最喜歡看功夫電影，也想學武術。誰想跟他一起學呢？

阿龍想問問室友，看誰想跟他一起學武術。朱宇正在打遊戲，小東正在看一本英文小說，大明要去打籃球。小東說他可以教阿龍打乒乓球，大明說打籃球最有意思，他說阿龍應該跟他一起去打籃球。阿龍什麼球都不想打，他只想學武術，可是他的室友誰都不想跟他一起學。

白曉雪給阿龍打電話，她跟阿龍說，明天在學生中心有一個新生晚會，可以跳舞、唱卡拉OK。阿龍覺得很有意思，他跟小東說："我們一起去吧。"小東覺得沒有意思，因為他唱歌唱得不好，跳舞也不會。阿龍說他可以教小東跳舞。可是小東不想跟他學。他說："你去跳你的舞吧，我看我的書！"

Quickly provide the Chinese equivalents for the following phrases and sentences. Do not translate them word for word.

1 VO compounds

In English you say . . .   *In Chinese you say . . .*

1) to read, to sing, to dance   _____

2) to read novels, to sing Chinese songs, and to   _____
   dance that dance

3) to speak, to speak English   _____

4) to sing well (to be good at singing)   _____

2 Ongoing activities, performances, frequency

1) I am watching a movie right now.   _____

2) I'm watching a movie with my friend at his house   _____
   right now.

3) I watch a lot of movies. (quantity)   _____

4) I watch movies a lot/frequently. (frequency)   _____

5) I seldom watch foreign films. (frequency)   _____

6) I don't watch many foreign films. (quantity)   _____

3 Telling about events and plans

1) There will be a vocal contest tomorrow.   _____

2) There will be a vocal contest at school tomorrow.   _____

3) I want to go to a concert with my friend this weekend.   _____

4) I want to go to the movies tomorrow.   _____

5) I'm going to watch TV with my roommate on weekends.   _____

4 Describing people and things (不)好聽， (不)好看， (不)好玩， (没)有意思

1) That song is pretty; she sings it well too.   _____

2) Don't watch that movie. It's really boring!   _____

3) The activities at the Student Center are a lot of fun!   _____

4) Your singing contest was really interesting!   _____

5 Imperatives: Making suggestions/requests

1) Let's watch TV.   _____

2) Let's have some music. (V一下 O to soften your tone)   _____

3) He doesn't teach well. Don't learn from him.   _____

4) I'm making a call right now. Don't talk to me.   _____

6 **Comparing words and forms:** 會/可以，跟Sb V/跟Sb一起V，打/玩，想/喜歡

What is the Chinese equivalent for the underlined word in each sentence?

1) She studies Chinese, so she <u>can speak Chinese.</u> _____

2) She is Chinese, so she <u>can speak Chinese with us.</u> _____

3) He is good at kungfu, so I want to <u>learn it from him.</u> _____

4) He also wants to learn Chinese, so you can
   <u>learn it with him.</u> _____

5) They often <u>play ball together</u> on weekends. _____

6) They often <u>get together</u> on weekends. _____

7) I <u>like</u> reading novels. _____

8) I'<u>d like to </u>read novels. _____

7 **Intensifying the tone** QW(O)都V；QW(O)都/也不V

1) <u>Nobody</u> wants to go. _____

2) <u>Everyone</u> likes that song. _____

3) She likes to watch <u>all kinds of movies.</u> _____

4) Whom does he like? → He likes <u>everyone.</u> _____

5) There are <u>no events whatsoever</u> this weekend. _____

8 **Idiomatic expressions**

1) What's up? _____

2) [after a suggestion] What do you think/say? _____

3) No problem/Not a problem. _____

4) It's a lot of fun! _____

5) See you tomorrow! _____

6) OK/All right! _____

9 **Dialogue:** What do you like to do?

A: What do you like to do? _____

B: I like to watch movies. _____

A: What movies do you like? _____

B: All kinds of movies. _____

A: Do you often watch movies with your roommate? _____

B: Sometimes. _____

A: What does she like to do? _____

B: She likes singing, and she sings really well! _____

A: Oh, there's a party at the Student Center tomorrow. _____

B: It's no fun. Don't go. Let's watch a movie! _____

1 **Correct the sentences**

Identify the error(s) in each sentence and then rewrite the sentence correctly.

1) 我經常打球在<u>學校周末</u>。 ✗ _____

2) 我現在不學中文<u>在北京</u>。 ✗ _____

3) 我現在不在看電視<u>跟室友</u>。 ✗ _____

4) 我看書<u>得</u>很多。 ✗ _____

5) 我<u>不</u>看電視看得多。 ✗ _____

6) 我想跟你<u>說話一下</u>。 ✗ _____

7) 誰<u>也</u>喜歡這本書。 ✗ _____

8) 我<u>打得</u>不好。 ✗ _____

9) 我什麼都喜歡<u>看書</u>。 ✗ _____

10) 我明天<u>喜歡</u>跟你去打球。 ✗ _____

11) 她教得不好，你<u>不</u>跟她學。 ✗ _____

12) 我想學跳舞，你們想不想<u>跟我學</u>? ✗ _____

2 **Fun translation:** Verb phrase or clause as premodifier   V 的 N; Sb V 的 N

The girl likes to read. (Sentence w/o modifier)   那個女孩喜歡看書。

1) the girl who likes to read   喜歡看書的那個女孩

2) books the girl likes   _____

3) books the girl likes to read   _____

4) I have the books the girl likes.   _____

5) I know the girl who likes to read.   _____

The following activities allow you to further practice your interpretive, interpersonal, and presentational communication skills in a meaningful, communicative context.

Interpretive

1 Listening

🔊 (U5.19_1：你喜歡做什麼？）

Take notes below as you listen to the audio clip.

小南喜歡什麼？她有時候做什麼？　_____

她可以教Katie什麼？跟Katie學什麼？　_____

她喜歡什麼運動？　_____

她經常跟哥哥做什麼？　_____

Katie想不想跟小南去唱歌？　_____

她會不會唱中文歌？　_____

她會打什麼球？　_____

她覺得做什麼很有意思？　_____

Select the correct answer for each question.

1)	What does Xiaonan like to do?	a. dance	b. sing
2)	What does she offer to teach Katie?	a. how to sing karaoke	b. Chinese songs
3)	What is her favorite sport?	a. tennis	b. ping-pong
4)	Who is her sports partner?	a. her brother	b. her friend
5)	What does she want to learn from Katie?	a. English	b. English songs
6)	What can't Katie do?	a. play ball games	b. sing
7)	What is fun for Katie to do?	a. watch a ball game	b. compete in a game
8)	What does "laladuiyuan" mean?	a. cheer leaders	b. name of a sport

2 Reading

Read the flyer and tell whether the statements are true (T) or false (F).

中國學生會新年晚會

時間　：12月31日晚7:30
地點　：學生中心305室
門票　：5元
聯系人：李新文
　　　　lixinwen@gmail.com

★ 節目表演
★ 卡拉OK演唱
★ 舞會

1) ☐ This event is an evening party for Chinese students.

2) ☐ The party is for incoming Chinese students.

3) ☐ The party is going to be held at the Student Center.

4) ☐ There will be singing and dancing.

5) ☐ The party is free.

3 Narrative reading

Read the passage and answer the questions that follow.

© Cengage Learning 2015

王家有兩個孩子，他們的愛好很不同。老大是女孩，在上高一。她的愛好很多，什麼她都喜歡。有時候她跟女生一起跳舞、唱卡拉OK，有時候她跟男生一起玩兒，打球、看球賽。老二是男孩，是初中二年級的學生。他跟姐姐不同的是，他什麼學校的活動都不喜歡，也不太喜歡跟同學一起玩兒。他喜歡做什麼呢？他只喜歡上網打遊戲，所以周末常常在家裡上網打遊戲，哪裡也不去。

爸爸媽媽覺得常常打遊戲不好，所以跟老二說："經常打遊戲不好，別打了。周末跟姐姐去打打球吧。"

老二說："跟姐姐打球？我不會打球。"

媽媽說："那沒問題，姐姐打得不錯，可以教你。"

爸爸說：“對，爸爸也喜歡打球，我們可以一起打，一家人一起打球應該很好玩兒！”

老二想，打球沒意思，他不想學打球，也不想跟家人一起玩兒，他只想打遊戲。“我不喜歡打球。你們去打你們的球，我要打我的遊戲。”

可是媽媽說：“不行！你的老師說，以前你是個好學生，現在不是了。所以周末你得看書，不可以打遊戲了！”

1) What is this story about?
   a. Wang's family's hobbies
   b. The Wang's two children and their hobbies

2) Which best describes the older child?
   a. a girl, big in size, who loves everything
   b. a high school girl who hangs around with boys

3) Which best describes the younger child?
   a. a boy who plays at home alone
   b. a computer lover who plays with classmates

4) What point are the parents trying to make when they talk to the boy?
   a. The boy's hobby is not healthy.
   b. It's fun for the family to play ball together.

5) What does the boy think after his parents talk to him?
   a. He is interested in trying their idea.
   b. He rejects their idea.

6) Why does the mom demand that the boy stop doing his hobby on weekends?
   a. The boy has been doing poorly in school lately.
   b. The boy is a good student, but could be better.

7) What is your best guess for the meaning of each item below?

   1. 老大   a. the oldest kid   b. the taller kid
   2. 初中   a. middle school   b. elementary school
   3. 別打了。   a. Don't play it.   b. Don't play it anymore.
   4. 不行！   a. No!   b. Not now!

Interpersonal

4 Speaking

1) Your new roommate has just arrived. Have a conversation with him/her:

   a) Find out about his/her hobbies and favorite activities.

   b) Ask him/her to teach you some Chinese things that you are interested in, and offer to teach something in return.

   c) Invite him/her to join you for some extracurricular activities or weekend events.

2) Visit a Chinese Students Association. Introduce yourself, including what you like to do. Find out if there is an event for the upcoming weekend and any details about the event.

5 Writing

An introductory letter: To get ready for a Chinese student who is to share a room with you, write a letter introducing yourself to better prepare the new roommate. Provide basic information about yourself, including your hobbies, favorite pastimes, and weekend events that you plan to attend. Ask the Chinese roommate what he/she likes to do and invite him/her to join you.

Presentational

6 Speaking

The Chinese Students Association is inviting students who are studying Chinese to join them for their weekly Chinese conversation hour. They also offer lectures and lessons on Chinese culture, Taichi, Kungfu, music, and calligraphy on weekends. As a member of the Association, you want to share this information with your classmates.

1) Give specific information on the activities. Tell when, where, and what is being offered.

2) Comment on activities. Say which ones you would find most interesting.

3) Give your contact information (or the contact information of the Association).

7 Writing

A personal profile: Write a description of yourself accompanied by a photo for your personal blog or a class blog. Include your hobbies and preference for pastimes.

UNIT 6

第六單元

時間和活動

Time and Activity Schedule

The Story

Liu Ying has a busy schedule every day. What does she normally do? Meanwhile, Ah Long talks to Xiaoxue about . . .

FUNCTIONS & GLOBAL TASKS

- Telling time
- Describing a daily schedule
- Talking about activities at school

CORE VOCABULARY

- Calendar
- Time expressions
- Daily routine
- School facilities

GRAMMAR

- Sequence of time
- Time-when phrases
- Time duration
- Conjunctions 除了……還 and 除了……都
- Adverbs: 就，才

CULTURE

- School schedules

	星期二	星期三	星期
英語閱讀	英語語法	英語聽力	英語閱讀
美國文學	詞匯學	英國文學	英語寫作
政治經濟學	哲學	電腦	法律基礎
英語聽力		英語口語	第二外語
		中西文化	

Communication

Interpretive

Understand listening and reading passages related to someone's daily schedule.

Interpersonal

Share with someone your hobbies and the activities you are interested in.

Presentational

Talk about college activities.

UNIT 6

A 第一課

這個星期做些什麼？
My activities for this week

A 6.1 詞語預習 cíyǔ yùxí — PREVIEW THE VOCABULARY

 Use the **online audio flashcards** to familiarize yourself with the new vocabulary in this section.

Nouns (N)

時間	shíjiān	time
歲	suì	year (referring to age)
日期	rìqī	date
年	nián	year
日	rì	day (formal)
天	tiān	day
月	yuè	month
星期/周	xīngqī/zhōu	week

Time Words (TW)

今年	jīnnián	this year
去年	qùnián	last year
明年	míngnián	next year
昨天	zuótiān	yesterday
一月	yīyuè	January
二月	èryuè	February
星期一	xīngqīyī	Monday
星期二	xīngqī'èr	Tuesday
星期天/日	xīngqītiān/rì	Sunday
上/下個月	shàng/xià gè yuè	last/next month

上/下個星期	shàng/xià gè xīngqī	last/next week
早上	zǎoshang	(early) morning
上午	shàngwǔ	morning
中午	zhōngwǔ	noon, midday
下午	xiàwǔ	afternoon
晚上	wǎnshang	evening, night

Others

生日	shēngrì	birthday
課	kè	class, lesson
課外	kèwài	extracurricular, outside class, after school
教室/_室	jiàoshì/_shì	classroom /_room
圖書館	túshūguǎn	library
考試	kǎoshì	examination
時間表	shíjiānbiǎo	timetable

Verbs: VO compounds

上學	shàng//xué	go to school
上大學(中學/小學)	shàng dàxué (zhōngxué/xiǎoxué)	go to college (high school / elementary school)
上課	shàng//kè	go to class

下課	xià//kè	finish/leave class
有空	yǒu kòng	have free time
考試	kǎo//shì	take an examination
做作業	zuò zuòyè	do homework
打電話	dǎ diànhuà	make a phone call

Adjectives (Adj)/Stative Verbs (SV)

忙	máng	busy
累	lèi	tired

Measure Word (M)

節	jié	(used for class periods)

Specifier (Sp)

每	měi	each, every, per

Conjunction (Conj)

除了……以外	chúle……yǐwài	in addition to; apart from

Question Forms (QF)/Expressions (Exp)

星期幾	xīngqī jǐ	which day (of the week)
幾月/幾號	jǐ yuè/jǐ hào	which month / which date
哪年/哪天	nǎ nián/nǎ tiān	which year / which day
多大	duō dà	how old

Structures

- X年X月X日，星期X
- 今天星期幾/幾號
- 每X都……
- 除了X以外，還/也

 Aural-Oral Exercises: Follow the online exercises to further familiarize yourself with the new vocabulary and grammar when it is used in sentences.

Main Features: In this lesson we focus on <u>time-when expressions</u>, words or phrases denoting a point of time. In modern Chinese, time expressions are easy to remember, as they use numbers instead of unique names! On the other hand, the <u>measure words</u> and <u>sequencing rules</u> for telling the date can make your learning tasks challenging. In addition, simple words like 上個 (last) and 下個 (next) also deserve your attention. So let's get ready for more time expressions and some fun with the word order difference in Chinese!

■ Expressing the year (年) and day (天) share similar rules. Note also the different word for "years" when referring to age.

A) 年 (*Year*): 去年，今年，明年，2020年
               qùnián,   jīnnián, míngnián, èr-líng-èr-líng nián

1) 哪年？去年，今年，明年；1900年，2014年   (這年 for "current year" ✗)
   nǎ nián? qùnián,   jīnnián,   míngnián; yī-jiǔ-líng-líng nián, èr-líng-yī-sì nián

2) 去年我(有)18歲，今年我(有)19歲，明年我(有)20歲。 (我是18歲。✗)
   Qùnián wǒ (yǒu) shíbā suì, jīnnián wǒ (yǒu) shíjiǔ suì, míngnián wǒ (yǒu) èrshí suì.

3) 去年我是高中生，今年我是大學生(了)。   (Use 了 only if the change is emphasized.)
   Qùnián wǒ shì gāozhōngshēng, jīnnián wǒ shì dàxuéshēng (le).

1 – A) – 3)

B) 天 (*Day*): 昨天，今天，明天
              zuótiān, jīntiān, míngtiān

1) 哪天？昨天，今天，明天
   nǎ tiān? zuótiān,   jīntiān,   míngtiān

2) 今天是我的生日，昨天我18歲，今天我19歲了！   (Denoting a change of status:
   Jīntiān shì wǒ de shēngrì, zuótiān wǒ shíbā suì, jīntiān wǒ shíjiǔ suì le!   "Today I turn 19!")

1 – B) – 2)

Illustrations © Cengage Learning 2015

Indicating a time frame or a point of time: Month and week　　　X月，X星期

■■■ Expressing the month (月) and week (星期) share similar rules. When used with 月 and 星期, 上 (up) refers to the past and 下 (down) refers to the future - just like what you see on a calendar!

A) 月 (*Month*): 上個月，這個月，下個月；一月，二月
shàng gè yuè, zhège yuè, xià gè yuè; yīyuè, èryuè

1) 哪個月？ 上個月，這個月，下個月　　　　　　(Use 個 with specifiers.)
　 nǎge yuè?　 shàng gè yuè, zhège yuè, xià gè yuè

2) 幾月？ 一月(1月)，二月(2月)，三月(3月)……　　(Don't use 個 with names.)
　 jǐ yuè?　 yīyuè,　　　èryuè,　　　sānyuè……

3) 你的生日是下個月嗎？　　➡　　不是，我的生日是上個月。
　 Nǐ de shēngrì shì xià gè yuè ma?　　Bú shì, wǒ de shēngrì shì shàng gè yuè.

4) 這個月你們有很多活動嗎？　➡　　這個月沒有很多，12月和1月的活動
　 Zhège yuè nǐmen yǒu hěn duō huódòng ma?　　Zhège yuè méiyǒu hěn duō, shí'èryuè hé yīyuè de huódòng
　　　　　　　　　　　　　　　　　　　　很多。
　　　　　　　　　　　　　　　　　　　　hěn duō.

2 — A) — 4)

B) 星期 (*Week*): 上個星期，這個星期，下個星期
shàng gè xīngqī, zhège xīngqī, xià gè xīngqī

■■■ The week in Chinese starts with Monday (星期一) and ends on Sunday (星期天/日).

1) 哪個星期？ 上個星期，這個星期，下個星期
　 nǎge xīngqī?　 shàng gè xīngqī, zhège xīngqī,　 xià gè xīngqī
　 which week?　 *last week,*　　*this week,*　　*next week*

2) 星期幾？ 星期二，星期六，星期天(日)
　 xīngqī jǐ?　 xīngqī'èr,　 xīngqī liù,　 xīngqī tiān (rì)

3) 你的生日是這個星期嗎？　➡　　不是，是上個星期。
　 Nǐ de shēngrì shì zhège xīngqī ma?　　Bú shì, shì shàng gè xīngqī.

3 Giving the date X年X月X日，星期X

■■■ Important rule: The sequence for dates is *the whole before the part*, so the bigger unit comes before the smaller one: year-month-day.

A) **Day of the month:** X日，X號

1) 日 (formal)：幾月幾日？ 7月4日，2月2日；新年是1月1日。
    rì: jǐ yuè jǐ rì?   qīyuè sì rì, èryuè èr rì; Xīnnián shì yīyuè yī rì.

2) 號 (spoken)：今天(是)幾號？ ➔ 今天(是)2號。
    hào: Jīntiān (shì) jǐ hào?   Jīntiān (shì) èr hào.

B) **Day of the week:** 星期X

1) 今天(是)星期幾？ ➔ 今天(是)星期天。
    Jīntiān (shì) xīngqī jǐ?   Jīntiān (shì) xīngqī tiān.

2) 你星期幾去書店？ ➔ 我下個星期天去。
    Nǐ xīngqī jǐ qù shūdiàn?   Wǒ xià gè xīngqī tiān qù.

3 — B) — 2)

C) **Date in full:** X年X月X日，星期X

1) Formal/Written：2012年2月12日，星期日。
        èr-líng-yī-èr nián èryuè shí'èr rì, xīngqī rì

2) Informal/Spoken：12年2月12號，星期天
        yī-èr nián èryuè shí'èr hào, xīngqī tiān

4 Parts of the Day 早上，上午，中午，下午，晚上

1) 昨天早上，今天中午，明天晚上，星期一下午，下個星期六晚上
    zuótiān zǎoshang, jīntiān zhōngwǔ, míngtiān wǎnshang, xīngqīyī xiàwǔ, xià gè xīngqī liù wǎnshang

2) 我們星期五下午去還是晚上去？ ➔ 我們星期五晚上去吧。
    Wǒmen xīngqīwǔ xiàwǔ qù háishi wǎnshang qù?   Wǒmen xīngqīwǔ wǎnshang qù ba.

⬛ Phrases indicating the time an activity takes place are normally placed before the main action verb, either before or after the personal pronoun.

1) 上學: 你的朋友今年上高中 　→　他今年上高四，明年上大學。
   shàngxué: Nǐ de péngyou jīnnián shàng gāozhōng　　Tā jīnnián shàng gāosì, míngnián shàng dàxué.
   還是上大學？
   háishi shàng dàxué?

2) 上課: 你現在要去上課嗎？ 　→　我要去上中文課。
   shàngkè: Nǐ xiànzài yào qù shàngkè ma?　　Wǒ yào qù shàng Zhōngwén kè.
   上什麼課？
   Shàng shénme kè?

3) 有課: 明天你有沒有課？ 　→　有，明天上午有四節課，
   yǒu kè: Míngtiān nǐ yǒu méiyǒu kè?　　Yǒu, míngtiān shàngwǔ yǒu sì jié kè,
   下午有兩節課。
   xiàwǔ yǒu liǎng jié kè.

4) 有考試: 我們明天有沒有考試？ →　有，明天有中文考試。
   yǒu kǎoshì: Wǒmen míngtiān yǒu méiyǒu kǎoshì?　　Yǒu, míngtiān yǒu Zhōngwén kǎoshì.

5) 考試: 你們明天考什麼(試)？ →　我們要考中文。
   kǎoshì: Nǐmen míngtiān kǎo shénme (shì)?　　Wǒmen yào kǎo Zhōngwén.

6) 有空: 今天你有沒有空？ 　→　我今天很忙，沒空。
   yǒukòng: Jīntiān nǐ yǒu méiyǒu kòng?　　Wǒ jīntiān hěn máng, méi kòng.
   我明天有空。
   Wǒ míngtiān yǒukòng.

7) 做作業: 你什麼時候做作業？ →　我今天晚上做中文作業。
   zuò zuòyè: Nǐ shénme shíhou zuò zuòyè?　　Wǒ jīntiān wǎnshang zuò Zhōngwén zuòyè.

6 **Expressing additions**
　　　　　　　　　　　　　　　　除了 X 以外，Sb 還/也……
　　　　　　　　　　　　　　　　Besides X, Sb also . . .

⬛ Use 還/也 to include an additional item or information. (還 is limited to positive forms only.)

1) 除了上課以外，她還有很多活動。 *(Besides attending classes, she has many*
   Chúle shàngkè yǐwài,　tā hái yǒu hěn duō huódòng. *other activities.)*

2) 除了上午以外，她下午也(沒)有課。 *(In addition to mornings, she also has (no)*
   Chúle shàngwǔ yǐwài,　tā xiàwǔ yě (méi)yǒu kè. *classes in afternoons.)*

Before viewing . . .

1) At your college, do students go to more than four classes per day?

2) Do you know what activites college students in China normally do after class?

While viewing . . .

1) During your first viewing, focus on meaning.

2) During your second viewing, pay special attention to speech forms and tones.

3) Finally, practice saying the sentences by answering the questions below.

 U6-A1

這個女生是誰？
Zhège nǚshēng shì shéi?

"我叫劉英，是_____,
Wǒ jiào Liú Yīng, shì……

現在_____。"
xiànzài……

她現在在哪裡？ 她在那裡做什麼？
Tā xiànzài zài nǎlǐ?   Tā zài nàlǐ zuò shénme?

"這個是_____,
Zhège shì……

今天_____。"
jīntiān……

	星期一	星期二	星期三	星期四	星期五
上午	英語閱讀	英語語法	英語聽力	英語閱讀	語言學
	美國文學	詞匯學	英國文學	英語寫作	翻譯
下午	政治經濟學	哲學	電腦	法律基礎	(考試)
	英語聽力		英語口語	第二外語	
晚上			中西文化		

© Cengage Learning 2015

她哪天最忙？哪天課不多？
Tā nǎ tiān zuì máng? Nǎ tiān kè bù duō?

"星期三＿＿＿＿＿＿＿＿＿＿＿＿＿＿＿＿，
Xīngqīsān……

＿＿＿＿＿＿＿＿＿＿＿＿＿＿＿＿！

星期五＿＿＿＿＿＿＿，＿＿＿＿＿＿，
Xīngqīwǔ……

可是＿＿＿＿＿＿＿＿＿。"
kěshì……

U6-A2

© Cengage Learning 2015

為什麼她每天都很忙？
Wèishénme tā měi tiān dōu hěn máng?

"除了上課以外，
Chúle shàngkè yǐwài,

＿＿＿＿＿＿＿＿＿＿＿＿＿＿＿，

所以＿＿＿＿＿＿＿＿。"
suǒyǐ……

© Cengage Learning 2015

劉英今年有多大了？星期五她要
Liú Yīng jīnnián yǒu duō dà le? Xīngqī wǔ tā yào

做什麼？
zuò shénme?

"這個星期五＿＿＿＿＿，今年＿＿＿＿＿。"
Zhège xīngqī wǔ……　　　　　jīnnián……

"星期五下午＿＿＿＿＿，在＿＿＿＿＿＿。
Xīngqī wǔ xiàwǔ……　　　　zài……

晚上＿＿＿＿＿＿＿＿＿＿。"
Wǎnshang……

1 Forms and structures
See 6.2 for more notes and examples.

1) 我是外語學院的學生，現在上大二。
Wǒ shì wàiyǔ xuéyuàn de xuésheng, xiànzài shàng dà èr.

(…… 是大二的學生 can also be used.)

2) 今天上英國文學課。
Jīntiān shàng Yīngguó wénxué kè.

(上x課: 有x課 can also be used.)

3) 星期三是我每周最忙的一天。
Xīngqīsān shì wǒ měi zhōu zuì máng de yì tiān.

(The whole before the part: 每周 appears before 一天.)

4) [我]上午、下午、晚上都有課！
[Wǒ] shàngwǔ, xiàwǔ, wǎnshang dōu yǒu kè!

(都 sums up the items before it, not after.)

5) 星期五的課最少，只上兩節課，
Xīngqīwǔ de kè zuì shǎo, zhǐ shàng liǎng jié kè,

可是有時候有考試。
kěshì yǒu shíhou yǒu kǎoshì.

(有時候 is a time word and appears before a verb.)

6) 除了上課以外，我還有很多課外活動……
Chúle shàngkè yǐwài, wǒ hái yǒu hěn duō kèwàihuódòng……

(也 can also be used instead of 還.)

7) 所以每天都很忙。
Suǒyǐ měi tiān dōu hěn máng.

(每+都 emphasizes totality: every, all …)

8) 這個星期五是我的生日，今年我(有)20歲了！
Zhège xīngqīwǔ shì wǒ de shēngrì, jīnnián wǒ (yǒu) èrshí suì le!

(Use 了 for a change of status. It should be 有20歲, not 是.)

9) 星期五下午見！
Xīngqīwǔ xiàwǔ jiàn!

(The time word appears before the action verb.)

2 Interrogative and negative forms

Ask and answer the questions based on the video segment A.

1) 她是不是文學院的學生？　　　　　　　_____

2) 她現在上大學一年級/大一嗎？　　　_____

3) 她現在在不在宿舍裡？　　　　　　　　_____

4) 她星期六和星期天也上課嗎？　　　　_____

5) 她周三有沒有空？　　　　　　　　　　　_____

6) 她周五的課多不多？　　　　　　　　　　_____

7) 她周五下午的活動是不是在宿舍樓？　_____

8) 她的生日晚會在中午嗎？　　　　　　　_____

9) 她今年有多大了？ 有22歲了嗎？　　_____

3 Time expressions　　什麼時候，幾號，幾月幾號，星期幾，哪天，哪年

Ask questions about the underlined information.

1) 小王的生日是(在)下個月。
_____
(什麼/哪)

2) 她的生日是2月。
_____
(幾)

3) 她的生日是2月5號。
_____
(幾)

4) 她的生日是星期二。
_____
(幾)

5) 那個球賽是(在)明天。
_____
(哪)

6) 那個電影是(在)明天晚上。
_____
(哪)

7) 星期天有活動。
_____
(什麼/哪)

8) 他要明年去中國。
_____
(哪)

9) 我們每個星期都有考試。
_____
(哪)

10) 我每天都有空。
_____
(哪)

1 **Pair work**

Ask and answer questions based on the class schedule below using appropriate expressions and forms::

Question hints:

- 哪天/星期幾……?
- 上什麼課? 上幾節課?
- 什麼時候v……?
- 在哪裡v……?
- TW 忙不忙/有沒有空?

Statement forms:

- TW 有課(有x課，有x節課)
- TW [他]很忙/不忙，沒空/有空
- TW1，TW2 [他]都……
- [他]每天/每個星期x都……
- 除了x以外，[他]還/也……

王新的時間表

	一	二	三	四	五
上午	英語		英語		
	英語		英語		考試
中午			課外活動		
下午	文學	英語	英語	文學	課外活動 (3號樓)
	文學	英語	英語	文學	課外活動 (3號樓)
晚上	圖書館	課外活動 (學生中心)	圖書館	課外活動 (學生中心)	電影

Answer these questions:

1) 王新每天都有課嗎? _____
2) 他周二上午沒有課吧? (X和Y都) _____
3) 他中午有沒有空? _____
4) 星期一他有幾節課? _____
5) 哪天他有考試? 是什麼時候考? _____
6) 他星期幾最忙? 為什麼? (除了X以外，還) _____
7) 他星期幾不太忙? 上午還是下午? _____
8) 他什麼時候去圖書館? _____
9) 星期二、四晚上他有空嗎? _____
10) 他的課外活動都在學生中心嗎? _____

2 **Interview and report**

1) **Interview:** Move around the classroom and speak to at least two classmates. Ask and answer questions about each other's weekly schedules for classes, tests, and recreational activities. Also ask about when the other classmates have free time to join you for recreational activities. Use the forms listed above as a guide.

2) **Report:** Share with the class what you learned from interviewing your classmates.

3) **Quiz:** Your teacher may choose to quiz the class on the information that is shared. Be prepared to correct the information if it is wrong.

A **6.6** 語法鞏固 yǔfǎ gǒnggù   REINFORCE THE GRAMMAR

🌐 These exercises are also available online with automatic feedback.

1 **Give the Chinese equivalent for each item or sentence**

    A) Word order

    Take note of the Chinese structure rules as you translate the following.

      1) May 5, 2012 _____

      2) There will be a ball game on Saturday, May 5. _____

      3) I don't have classes on Fridays. _____

      4) He doesn't have classes on Fridays. In addition, he doesn't have classes on Mondays. _____

      5) He has club activities every afternoon. _____

      6) She often goes to the library to study in the evening. _____

      7) She often goes to the library on Tuesday evenings. _____

      8) She goes to the library on Thursdays as well as on Tuesdays. _____

    B) Question words and forms

    Tips: Use the word order for statements to form questions. Time words appear before an action verb.

      1) <u>What day of the wee</u>k is it today? _____

      2) <u>What day of the month</u> is it today? _____

      3) <u>How old</u> is your friend? _____

      4) <u>What date</u> is his birthday? _____

      5) <u>When</u> is his birthday party? _____

      6) <u>What</u> day do we have a test? _____

      7) <u>When</u> do you have a class today? _____

      8) <u>What year</u> is he going to go to college? _____

      9) <u>Which week</u> do you have free time? _____

A **6.7** 聽答對話 tīngdá duìhuà   LET'S CHAT

🌐 In this listening-speaking activity you'll be asked to answer questions about the **video** segment as well as about **yourself**. You may be asked to record and submit your answers to your teacher.

B | 第二課

你周末有空嗎？
Are you free this weekend?

B | 6.8 詞語預習 cíyǔ yùxí — **PREVIEW THE VOCABULARY**

 Use the **online audio flashcards** to familiarize yourself with the new vocabulary in this section.

Time Expressions (TE)

鐘	zhōng	clock
表	biǎo	watch
點鐘	diǎn zhōng	o'clock
小時	xiǎoshí	hour
鐘頭	zhōngtóu	hour (spoken)
刻	kè	quarter (of an hour)
分鐘	fēnzhōng	minute
秒鐘	miǎozhōng	second
差	chà	short of
半	bàn	half

Nouns (N)

早點	zǎodiǎn	(light) breakfast
飯(早飯，午飯，晚飯) fàn (zǎofàn, wǔfàn, wǎnfàn)		meal (breakfast, lunch, dinner)
餐館	cānguǎn	restaurant
社團	shètuán	club, organization
口試	kǒushì	oral test
筆試	bǐshì	written test
票	piào	ticket

Adjectives (Adj)/Stative Verbs (SV)

早	zǎo	early
晚	wǎn	late
快	kuài	fast
慢	màn	slow

Adverbs (Adv)

平常	píngcháng	normally, usually
就	jiù	already, as early as
才	cái	only, only then

Verbs (V)

參加	cānjiā	join, participate in
學習	xuéxí	study, learn
請	qǐng	ask, invite, treat

Verb-Object (VO) Compounds

起床	qǐ//chuáng	get up, get out of bed
吃飯	chī//fàn	have a meal
睡覺	shuì//jiào	sleep
寫字	xiě//zì	write (a character)

Prepositions (Prep)/Coverbs (CV)			Expression (Exp)	
從	cóng	from	早! / 早上好!	Good morning!
到	dào	to, until	Zǎo! / Zǎoshang hǎo!	

Question Words (QW)

幾點(鐘)	jǐ diǎn zhōng	what time (i.e., clock time)
什麼時間	shénme shíjiān	what time (i.e., time of the day)
多長時間	duōcháng shíjiān	how long (i.e.,length of time)

Structures

- TW 就V了/才V
- T+B 我一個人去沒意思
- V多長時間的O; VOV多長時間
- 除了X以外，都……
- 請Sb+V

 B | 6.9 | 詞句聽説 cíjù tīngshuō   **FOCUS ON GRAMMAR**

Aural-Oral Exercises: Follow the online exercises to further familiarize yourself with the new vocabulary and grammar when it is used in sentences.

Main Features: This lesson introduces <u>clock time</u> and how it is associated with daily activities. Two adverbs, <u>就</u> and <u>才</u>, are often used to convey how early or late an action is, based on the speaker's presupposition. While considering the time an action or activity takes place, we will also introduce how to express the <u>duration of an action</u> or activity. Note that expressing "when" and duration in Chinese require opposite word orders: the when-phrase precedes the action verb while the duration phrase follows the action verb. This is consistent with the Temporal Sequence Principle, where the word order is determined by the logical sequence of events. Let's see how these two types of time concepts work in sentences!

1   **Telling clock time**   X點X分， 上午X點，下午X點， 從X點到Y點

A) Clock time

1) 幾點鐘? 3點鐘，3點05分，3點10分，3點15分/一刻，
   jǐ diǎn zhōng? sān diǎn zhōng, sān diǎn líng wǔ fēn, sān diǎn shí fēn, sān diǎn shíwǔ fēn/yí kè,

   3點半，3點45/4點差一刻
   sāndiǎn bàn, sān diǎn sìshíwǔ fēn/sì diǎn chà yí kè

2) 早上6點， 上午9點， 中午12點， 下午3點， 晚上7點 (Do not put the clock time first.)
   zǎoshang liù diǎn, shàngwǔ jiǔ diǎn, zhōngwǔ shí'èr diǎn, xiàwǔ sān diǎn, wǎnshang qī diǎn

3) (現在)幾點了? → 10:05 (10點零5分)了。   (了 indicates a change in time here.)
   (Xiànzài) jǐ diǎn le?   Shí diǎn líng wǔ fēn le.

B) (從) [starting point] 到 [ending point]

■ This structure is used to indicate a specific time period. 從 (from) is often omitted.

1) 從早上6點到中午12點
cóng zǎoshang liù diǎn dào zhōngwǔ shí'èr diǎn

上午9點10分到11點40
shàngwǔ jiǔ diǎn shí fēn dào shíyī diǎn sìshí

晚上7點半到9點半
wǎnshang qī diǎn bàn dào jiǔ diǎn bàn

1 – B) – 2)

2) 你們的晚會是什麼時候? → 是星期六晚上7:30到9:00 (7點半到9點)。
Nǐmen de wǎnhuì shí shénme shíhou?   Shì xīngqīliù wǎnshang qī diǎn bàn dào jiǔ diǎn.

---

2 | **Telling about one's daily schedule**   **Clock Time + Action Verb**

1) 起床: 你平常幾點(鐘)起床? → 我平常8點一刻(8:15)起床。
qǐchuáng: Nǐ píngcháng jǐ diǎn (zhōng) qǐchuáng?   Wǒ píngcháng bā diǎn yí kè qǐchuáng

2) 吃飯: 你每天幾點吃飯? → 我8點半吃早飯,兩點吃午飯,
chīfàn: Nǐ měitiān jǐ diǎn chīfàn?   Wǒ bā diǎn bàn chī zǎofàn, liǎng diǎn chī wǔfàn,

晚上7、8點吃晚飯。
wǎnshang qī、bā diǎn chī wǎnfàn.

你在哪裡吃午飯? → 我在餐館吃午飯。
Nǐ zài nǎlǐ chī wǔfàn?   Wǒ zài cānguǎn chī wǔfàn.

3) 睡覺: 你晚上幾點睡覺? → 我平常晚上11點睡(覺),
shuìjiào: Nǐ wǎnshang jǐ diǎn shuìjiào?   Wǒ píngcháng wǎnshang shíyī diǎn shuì(jiào),

周末12點睡。
zhōumò shí'èr diǎn shuì.

4) 上課: 你平常幾點去上課? → 我每天都10點去上課。
shàngkè: Nǐ píngcháng jǐ diǎn shàngkè?   Wǒ měi tiān dōu shí diǎn qù shàngkè.

2 – 4)

■■ 就 (already, as early as) and 才 (only, not until) indicate earliness or lateness respectively, which is in relative terms based on the speaker's presumption or expectation.

A) TW 就 V 了
do . . . as early as [time]; have already . . . by [time]

1) 我平常8點半起床，可是今天我有考試，所以起得很早，
   Wǒ píngchǎng bā diǎn bàn qǐ chuáng, kěshì wǒ jīntiān yǒu kǎoshì, suǒyǐ qǐ de hěn zǎo,

   7點就起(床)了。
   qī diǎn jiù qǐ (chuáng) le.

2) 你每天12點睡覺，怎麼今天睡得這麼早，11點就睡了?
   Nǐ měi tiān shíèr diǎn shuìjiào, zěnme jīntiān shuì de zhème zǎo, shíyī diǎn jiù shuì le?

B) TW 才 V
not do… until [time]; do… only at [time]…

1) 我平常6點起床，可是今天我沒課，所以起得晚，我7點才起(床)。
   Wǒ píngcháng liù diǎn qǐchuáng, kěshì jīntiān wǒ méi kè, suǒyǐ qǐ de wǎn, wǒ qī diǎn cái qǐ(chuáng).

2) 我們10點上課，可是他來得很晚，10點半才來。
   Wǒmen shí diǎn shàngkè, kěshì tā lái de hěn wǎn, shí diǎn bàn cái lái.

---

4   Talking about quantities of time   When to use 個

A) 年，天，周，分鐘

■■ 個 should not be placed between the numeral and the noun because these terms are measure units.

1) 兩年，20年，兩天，20天，兩周，20分鐘
   liǎng nián, èrshí nián, liǎng tiān, èrshí tiān, liǎng zhōu, èrshí fēnzhōng

B) 月

■■ 個 must be placed between the numeral and the noun. Without 個, the meanings would be different.

1) 一個月，3個月，12個月 vs. 一月，三月，12月
   yí gè yuè,   sān gè yuè,   shí'èr gè yuè   yīyuè,   sānyuè,   shí'èryuè
   one month   3 months   12 months   January   March   December

C) 星期，小時/鐘頭

■■ 個 is normally used in this case, especially when fractions are included.

1) 3(個)星期，3個多星期；10(個)小時，10個多小時
   sān (gè) xīngqī, sān gè duō xīngqī; shí (gè) xiǎoshí,   shí gè duō xiǎoshí

5 Telling the amount of time spent on activity [Dur] 的 N；V + [Dur] + (的)O

■ This structure is often used to indicate duration of an action or activity. Note the word order difference in expressing duration and when an action or activity takes place.

A) [Dur] 的 N

1) 半個小時的考試，兩年的中文課，幾個小時的社團活動 (duration of N)
   bàn ge xiǎoshí de kǎoshì, liǎng nián de Zhōngwén kè, jǐ ge xiǎoshí de shètuán huódòng

B) V + [Dur] + (的)N

■ For VO compounds/phrases, the duration comes between V and O.

個 should not be used:

5 – B) – 1)

1) 學兩年(的)中文，看3天(的)書，聽幾分鐘(的)音樂 (幾 means a few.)
   xué liǎng nián (de) Zhōngwén, kàn sān tiān (de) shū, tīng jǐ fēnzhōng (de) yīnyuè

個 should be used:

2) 學兩個月(的)中文，看1個多星期(的)書，上幾個鐘頭(的)課 (個 must be used.)
   xué liǎng ge yuè (de) Zhōngwén, kàn yí ge duō xīngqī (de) shū, shàng jǐ ge zhōngtóu (de) kè

3) 你每天上幾個小時的課？   →   我上3、4個小時的課。
   Nǐ měi tiān shàng jǐ ge xiǎoshí de kè?   Wǒ shàng sān、sì ge xiǎoshí de kè.

4) 你每周有幾個小時的社團活動？ →   我每周有3個多小時的社團
   Nǐ měi zhōu yǒu jǐ ge xiǎoshí de shètuán huódòng?   活動。
                                                        Wǒ měi zhōu yǒu sān ge duō xiǎoshí de shètuán
                                                        huódòng.

C) VOV + [Dur]

■ Use this structure to specify the activity up front.

1) 你每周打球打多長時間？   → 我打10多個小時。
   Nǐ měi zhōu dǎqiú dǎ duō cháng shíjiān?   Wǒ dǎ shí duō ge xiǎoshí.
   (多長時間 can refer to any length of time.)

5 – B) – 3)

Illustrations © Cengage Learning 2015

6 Expressing exceptions 　　　　　除了X以外，都⋯⋯
⋯ except X.

■ The item introduced by 除了 is an exception to the 都-part of the sentence.

1) 除了星期六星期天以外，她每天都有課。　　*(She has classes every day but*
　　Chúle xīngqīliù xīngqītiān yǐwài,　　　tā měi tiān dōu yǒu kè. 　*Saturday and Sunday.)*

2) 除了星期五以外，她這個星期都沒有考試。　*(She doesn't have any tests this*
　　Chúle xīngqīwǔ yǐwài,　　tā zhège xīngqī dōu měiyǒu kǎoshì. 　*week except on Friday.)*

■ Compare the above structure with this 除了 X 以外，還/也 *(besides X, apart from X, other than X)*

3) 除了星期六以外，她星期天也沒有課。　　*(In addition to Saturday, she doesn't*
　　Chúle xīngqīliù yǐwài,　　tā xīngqītiān yě měiyǒu kè. 　*have any classes on Sunday either.)*

4) 除了我以外，她今天也很忙。　　　　　　*(Other than I, she is another person*
　　Chúle wǒ yǐwài, tā jīntiān yě hěn máng. 　*who is busy today.)*

5) 除了上課以外，他還有很多課外活動。　　*(Besides attending classes, he also*
　　Chúle shàngkè yǐwài, tā hái yǒu hěn duō kèwài huódòng. 　*has many other activities.)*

7 Giving someone a treat or inviting someone to do something 　請[Sb]⋯⋯

A) 請 [Sb] + [treat]
treat somebody to [a dinner, movie . . .]

1) 你明天有空嗎？我想請你吃晚飯。　　　*(I'd like to treat you to dinner.)*
　　Nǐ míngtiān yǒu kòng ma? Wǒ xiǎng qǐng nǐ chī wǎnfàn.

7 — A) — 1)

B) 請 [Sb] + Action Verb
invite somebody to do something; ask somebody to do something

1) 你明天有空嗎？我想請你去我家玩。　　*(I'd like to invite you to come over to*
　　Nǐ míngtiān yǒu kòng ma? Wǒ xiǎng qǐng nǐ qù wǒ jiā wán. 　*my house.)*

2) 你明天有空嗎？我想請你教我跳舞。　　*(I'd like to ask you to teach me how*
　　Nǐ míngtiān yǒu kòng ma? Wǒ xiǎng qǐng nǐ jiāo wǒ tiàowǔ. 　*to dance.)*

Before viewing . . .

1) Name some things that college students tend to do when they go out. What is your favorite?

2) Do young people go out more in groups or as couples?

3) When young people go out as couples, who pays? The person who does the inviting? Or are costs split?

While viewing . . .

1) During your first viewing, focus on meaning.

2) During your second viewing, pay special attention to speech forms and tones.

3) Finally, practice saying the sentences by answering the questions below.

▶ U6-B1

阿龍說他現在去做什麼？
Ā Lóng shuō tā xiànzài qù zuò shénme?

"我＿＿＿＿＿＿＿＿，
Wǒ……

＿＿＿＿＿＿＿＿。"

曉雪說什麼？
Xiǎoxuě shuō shénme?

"4點半＿＿＿＿＿？＿＿＿＿＿？"
Sì diǎn bàn……

阿龍說他有哪兩個社團？
Ā Lóng shuō tā yǒu nǎ liǎng gè shètuán?

"一個是＿＿＿＿，一個是＿＿＿＿，
Yí gè shì……　　　　yí gè shì……

每天＿＿＿＿＿＿＿。"
měitiān……

曉雪說她在哪個社團？
Xiǎoxuě shuō tā zài nǎge shètuán?

"我在＿＿＿＿＿＿，
Wǒ zài……

我們＿＿＿＿＿＿＿＿＿＿＿。
wǒmen……

我有時候 ＿＿＿＿＿＿。"
Wǒ yǒu shíhou……

U6-B2

阿龍問曉雪什麼？曉雪說什麼？
Ā Lóng wèn Xiǎoxuě shénme? Xiǎoxuě shuō shénme?

"對了，我們電影學社＿＿＿＿＿＿＿
Duì le, wǒmen diànyǐng xuéshè……

＿＿＿＿＿＿。想不想＿＿＿＿＿？"
　　　　　　　　Xiǎng bù xiǎng……

"我星期五＿＿＿＿＿，要考＿＿＿＿
Wǒ xīngqī wǔ……　　　　yào kǎo……

＿＿＿＿＿，＿＿＿＿＿＿＿。
所以我＿＿＿＿＿，12點＿＿＿＿。"
Suǒyǐ wǒ……　　　　shí'èr diǎn……

U6-B3

阿龍說周末請曉雪看電影。為什麼？
Ā Lóng shuō zhōumò qǐng Xiǎoxuě kàn diànyǐng? Wèishénme?

"我覺得＿＿＿＿＿＿＿＿＿，
Wǒ juéde……

所以＿＿＿＿＿＿＿＿＿＿＿。"
suǒyǐ……

曉雪去不去？
Xiǎoxuě qù bú qù?

"謝謝你！可是我＿＿＿＿＿＿。"
Xièxie nǐ!　Kěshì wǒ……

1   Forms and structures

See 6.9 for more notes and examples.

■ Forms and Structures

1) 我去參加社團活動。
Wǒ qù cānjiā shètuán huódòng.

(參加活動/晚會, not 去活動/晚會)

2) 每天都有1個半小時的活動。
Měi tiān dōu yǒu yí gè bàn xiǎoshí de huódòng.

([Dur]的N indicates the duration of an action.)
(1 1/2 hours' worth of . . .)

3) 4點半就有活動了?
Sì diǎn bàn jiù yǒu huódòng le?

(TW 就V了 indicates earliness.)
(. . . already V at 4:30)

4) 我們星期一、三、五晚上8點才有活動。
Wǒmen xīngqī yī、sān、wǔ wǎnshang bā diǎn cái yǒu huódòng.

(TW 才V indicates lateness.)
(. . . only at 8:00 p.m. do we . . .)

5) 我有時候去參加。
Wǒ yǒu shíhou qù cānjiā.

(有時候, meaning sometimes, always goes before the verb.)

6) 要考15分鐘的口試，(考)1個小時的筆試。
Yào kǎo shíwǔ fēnzhōng de kǒushì, (kǎo) yí gè xiǎoshí de bǐshì.

(Alternative expression: (考)口試要考15分鐘，筆試考1個小時。)

7) 你每天都睡得這麼晚嗎?
Nǐ měi tiān dōu shuì de zhème wǎn ma?

(這麼晚 means that late. 這麼 refers to what has been mentioned.)

8) 除了周末以外，我每天都有課……。
Chúle zhōumò yǐwài, wǒ měi tiān dōu yǒu kè……

(Compare: 除了周末以外，我每天也有很多活動。)

9) 我想請你看電影……
Wǒ xiǎng qǐng nǐ qù kàn diànyǐng, ……

請[Sb] + 看電影 / 吃飯
(invite someone to . . . [as a treat])

10) 我想請你跟我一起去。
Wǒ xiǎng qǐng nǐ gēn wǒ yìqǐ qù.

請[Sb] + verb
(ask/invite Sb to do . . .)

2   Interrogative forms: When vs. Duration

The Temporal Sequence: While the time phrase indicating when an action takes place appears before the verb, the phrase indicating duration appears after the verb. VO phrases can be split to insert amount of time (duration of action).

TW + V	V + Duration + O (or: VOV + Duration)
1) 上課：你每天什麼時候上課?	你上多長時間的課(你上課上多長時間)?
2) 吃飯：你每天幾點吃午飯?	你吃多長時間的午飯(你吃午飯吃多長時間)?

3) 睡覺：你平常幾點睡覺？　　你睡幾個小時的覺(你睡覺睡幾個小時)？

4) 寫字：他什麼時候寫漢字？　　他每天寫多長時間的漢字(寫漢字寫多長時間)？

Disyllabic verbs: The two syllables should not be separated.

1) 學習：你幾點學習？　　你得學習多長時間？ (學習 must not be split.)

你什麼時候學習中文？　你得學習多長時間的中文？ (中文 is the object of 學習。)

3　Sequencing rule

When there are multiple elements in a sentence, the sequencing rule follows the Temporal Sequence Principle (see Appendix 3 for details.).

Translate the following into Chinese by following this sequencing rule:

TW - Accompaniment - PW - Action - Duration

1) watch a movie with a friend at 8 tonight

2) watch a movie with a friend at the Student Center at 8 tonight

3) watch a movie for 3 hours with a friend at the Student Center at 8 tonight

4　Story narration

Pay special attention to the verb forms and the use of punctuation marks.

現在4點多，阿龍要去參加社團活動。他每天都有1個半小時
Xiànzài sì diǎn duō, Ā Lóng yào qù cānjiā shètuán huódòng. Tā měi tiān dōu yǒu yí gè bàn xiǎoshí

的活動：武術社的活動是下午4:30到6:00，電影社是晚上7:30
de huódòng: wǔshù shè de huódòng shì xiàwǔ sì diǎn bàn dào liù diǎn, diànyǐng shè shì wǎnshang qī diǎn bàn

到9:00。曉雪在外語學社，她每星期一、三、五晚上8點才有活動。
dào jiǔ diǎn. Xiǎoxuě zài wàiyǔ xuéshè,　tā měi xīngqī yī、sān、wǔ wǎnshang bā diǎn cái yǒu huódòng.

阿龍問曉雪明天想不想跟他去電影社看電影，曉雪說她星期五
Ā Lóng wèn Xiǎoxuě míngtiān xiǎng bù xiǎng gēn tā qù diànyǐng shè kàn diànyǐng, Xiǎoxuě shuō tā xīngqí wǔ

上午有考試，要考15分鐘的口試，還要考1個小時的筆試，所以她
shàngwǔ yǒu kǎoshì, yào kǎo shíwǔ fēnzhōng de kǒushì, hái yào kǎo yí gè xiǎoshí de bǐshì, suǒyǐ tā

明天晚上要學習，12點才睡覺。除了周末以外，她每天都有課，所以
míngtiān wǎnshang yào xuéxí, shí'èr diǎn cái shuìjiào. Chúle zhōumò yǐwài, tā měi tiān dōu yǒu kè, suǒyǐ

很忙，每天都睡得很晚。阿龍說，那周末他想請曉雪去看電影。
hěn máng, měi tiān dōu shuì de hěn wǎn. Ā Lóng shuō, nà zhōumò tā xiǎng qǐng Xiǎoxuě qù kàn diànyǐng.

曉雪說，周末兩天她都有事。
Xiǎoxuě shuō, zhōumò liǎng tiān tā dōu yǒu shì.

1 **Pair work**

Ask and answer questions based on the images, using appropriate forms and structures.

- 什麼時候 V，幾點 V
- V 多長時間的 O
- VO V 得很早/晚
- 幾點就 V 了/才 V
- 除了 X 以外，也/還……
- 除了 X 以外，都……

Ask/answer questions:

1) What time does Jack ...?
   What does he do at [time]?　　→　（幾點 V，什麼時間 V）

2) Does he do ... early or late?　　→　（VOV 得很早/晚，TW 就/才 V）

3) Does he do ... by himself or with others?　　→　（一個人 V）

4) Does he do ... it quickly or slowly?　　→　（VOV 得快/慢）

5) How long does he do ...?　　→　（V 多長時間的 O，VOV 多長時間）

6) Other than X, what does he do at [time]?　　→　（除了 X 以外，還/也……）

7) What does he do at [time] except X?　　→　（除了 X 以外，都……）

2 Interview and report

1) **Interview:** Find out from a classmate about his/her daily schedule. Ask when and where he/she does various things, and for how long. Be sure to say what he/she does early or late. Find out if his/her daily routine is fast or slow.

你每天幾點VO？ 你VOV得很快/慢/早/晚 嗎？ 你VOV多長時間？

除了X以外，你還V什麼？ 什麼時間V？ V多長時間？

2) **Report:** Be prepared to report back to the class about your interview results.

3) **Quiz:** Your teacher may choose to quiz the class on the information that is shared. Be prepared to correct the information if it is wrong.

B 6.13 語法鞏固 yǔfǎ gǒnggù　　　　REINFORCE THE GRAMMAR

These exercises are also available online with automatic feedback.

1 Give the Chinese equivalent for each sentence

Pay attention to word order when expressing the time of action and the duration. Pinyin may be used.

1) He will study Chinese <u>for a year</u>. → _____

2) He will study Chinese <u>this year</u>. → _____

3) She has classes <u>at 2:00 p.m.</u> every Monday. → _____

4) She has classes <u>for 2 hours</u> every Monday. → _____

5) I am usually <u>already up at 6:00 a.m.</u>　(TW就V了) → _____

6) I don't get up <u>until 11:00 a.m.</u> on weekends. (TW才V) → _____

7) I read books <u>for 2 hours</u> in the library every day. → _____

8) I go to the library to read <u>at 2 p.m.</u> every day. → _____

2 Fill in the blanks with appropriate words

1) 她起床起得很晚，9:30____起來。　　a. 才　　b. 就

2) 除了周末以外，她每天____沒空。　　a. 還/也　　b. 都

3) 他吃飯吃得很____，要吃1個多小時。　　a. 快　　b. 慢

4) 她今天睡覺睡得很早，11:30____睡了。　　a. 才　　b. 就

5) 除了考口試以外，她____要考筆試。　　a. 還/也　　b. 都

B 6.14 聽答對話 tīngdá duìhuà　　　　LET'S CHAT

In this listening-speaking activity you'll be asked to answer questions about the **video** segment as well as about **yourself**. You may be asked to record and submit your answers to the teacher.

SCHOOL SCHEDULES

In China, **zìxí** (self-study) is widespread throughout secondary and universities systems. Students typically spend a couple of hours in the classroom on their studies before their very first and/or after their last class. Some schools, mostly high schools, even institutionalize a designated period of time for *zixi* (typically in the late afternoons) to ensure that students get extra time to study. In some cases, these *zixi* periods are monitored or supervised by instructors.

In most universities, the school library remains one of the most popular places for *zixi*, as it provides ample space with vast resources. Some university libraries have designated areas that are open 24 hours a day. Still, many students prefer classrooms as their "default" *zixi* area for various reasons, including their convenience for group study. Classrooms are used extensively for early-morning and evening studying. Sometimes classrooms get very crowded, especially during examination periods. A popular Internet song, 大學自習室 (Dàxué Zìxí Shì, literally, *College Classroom for Self-Studying*), captures the intensity of the fight for classroom space during the *zixi* hours.

Before morning *zixi* hours, many college students start their day with physical exercises at 6:30 or 7:00 a.m. Morning physical exercises are popular on college campuses. In some colleges, morning physical exercises are voluntary, but in others they are programmed into the curriculum. For example, students at one of the major universities in Shanghai are required to do morning jogging at least ten times every month during

their freshman year as part of the physical education requirement. The university also requires students to pass a swimming test as part of students' basic survival skills.

Chinese college students usually start their classes at 8:00 a.m. A typical class session lasts 50 minutes, but 75-minute sessions are also common in most universities.

Depending on majors and academic programs, students attend between four and six 50-minute classes each day, and some also take evening classes, which usually end by 9:30 p.m. Besides academic studies and recreational activities, students spend much of their spare time on the Internet, watching movies, listening to music, and chatting online.

Here is a sample of a college sophomore's schedule from a major university in the South.

6:30	Get up
6:50–7:20	Morning physical exercises
8:00-11:30	Classes
11:30-12:10	Lunch
12:30-2:00	Free/nap time
2:00-6:00	Classes
6:00-6:30	Dinner
6:30-8:30	Attending public lectures
9:00-11:00	Student association/club-related activities, homework
11:00-11:30	Online chatting, watching online videos, or listening to music
12:00 a.m.	Bedtime

QUIZ

1. Many college students in China use their classrooms as a place for *zixi* (self-study), because
   a. they are conveniently located.
   b. students taking the same class can easily form a study group.
   c. many classrooms are open late.
   d. all of the above.
2. Chinese universities do not offer evening courses for undergraduate students.
   a. true
   b. false

ACTIVITIES

1. Talk to a Chinese friend and find out how much time he or she spends when in China on the morning or evening *zixi* (self-study) on a regular basis. Also find out how he or she spend his/her spare time.
2. Compare your own schedule with that of the typical Chinese student. How does your schedule differ from that of the Chinese student in terms of intensity of academic studies, and the time spent on extra-curricular activities?

單元復習
Review and Integration

Read the following passages as fast as you can. Follow these steps:

1) Do not stop to check the meaning of words you don't recognize. Mark them and keep reading.

2) Read the passage again and guess the meaning of the marked words on a separate piece of paper.

3) Finally, look up the words in a dictionary or the vocabulary index and verify their meanings.

劉英是外語學院的學生，現在在上大二。除了星期六和星期天以外，她每天都有課。星期三是劉英每周最忙的一天，上午、下午、晚上都有課！星期五只有兩節課，可是有時候有考試。除了上課以外，她也有很多課外活動。這個星期五是她的生日，她今年20歲了。她星期五下午去學生中心參加活動，晚上她有一個生日晚會。

阿龍每天都有1個半小時的社團活動。他參加兩個社團的活動：武術社的活動是下午4:30到6:00，電影社是晚上7:30到9:00。阿龍有兩張電影票，想請曉雪去看電影，他說他覺得一個人去沒意思。

曉雪在外語學社，她每星期一、三、五晚上8點才有社團活動。這個星期曉雪很忙，她星期五上午有考試，要考15分鐘的口試，還要考1個小時的筆試。所以她明天晚上要學習，沒有時間跟阿龍去電影社看外國電影。阿龍有兩張電影票，問曉雪周末有沒有空，可是曉雪說，周末她也有事。

Quickly provide the Chinese equivalents for the following phrases and sentences. Do not translate them word for word.

1 When, Where, What, for How Long, with Whom

In Chinese you say . . .

1) I have classes Monday through Friday.

2) I have club activities for 1 1/2 hours on Wednesday evenings.

3) I have a 20-minute oral test tomorrow.

4) I read in the library for two hours every day.

5) Sometimes I have lunch with my friends in a restaurant at 1:00 p.m.

2 Sequencing of time expressions

1) That event is on Monday, December 12.

2) That event is from 7 to 9 p.m., Monday, December 12.

3) I have classes from 10:00 a.m. to 3:30 p.m. on Tuesdays.

4) We are going to that event at 7:00 p.m. on November 2.

5) I am usually already in bed at 10:00 p.m. (就 or 才?)

6) I won't go to bed until 11 p.m. tonight. (就 or 才?)

3 Using 除了⋯⋯以外

1) I have classes every day except Saturday and Sunday.

2) In addition to Mondays, I don't have any classes on Fridays either.

3) Besides Chinese, I also study Japanese.

4) She doesn't like any activities except dancing.

4 Commenting on activities and people V得, Topic + Comment

1) A: Is it fun to learn Chinese characters?
   B: Sometimes.

2) A: How is he doing at learning Chinese?
   B: He's doing well. He learns fast!

3) A: Is it fun to join a club?
   B: I really think so.

4) A: She is usually early; she gets here by 7:30.
   B: But she came late today; she got here only at 8:30.

5 Question words and forms 幾, 哪, 多長時間, 什麼時候

1) What days do you have Chinese class?

2) What day of the month is it today?
   What's the date of that event?

3) What time is your Chinese class today?

4) How long is your Chinese class?

5) Which days don't you have Chinese class?

6) When do you want to study Chinese?

7) How long do you want to study Chinese?

6 **Dialogue:** Do you want to go to movies with me?

A: Wang Xin, do you have classes on Tuesday afternoon? _____

B: Yes, I have two periods of literature. _____

A: How long will you be in the class? _____

B: I'll be in the class for an hour and a half, from 2:30 to 4:00. _____

A: Do you want to go to the movies with me? _____

B: I'm busy this week. I have two exams.
   Besides the exams, I also have other activities. _____

A: I suppose you are free over the weekend? _____

B: I'll be watching a basketball match. Why don't you
   go with me? _____

6.18 語法小測驗 yǔfǎ xiǎo cèyàn CHECK FOR ACCURACY

1 **Correct the time expressions**

Identify the error(s) in the Chinese translations and then rewrite them correctly.

1)	last year	上年 ✘ _____
2)	next week	上個星期 ✘ _____
3)	two days	2個天 ✘ _____
4)	two months	2月 ✘ _____
5)	this year	這年/這個年 ✘ _____
6)	last February	上個二月 ✘ _____
7)	23-27 days	20天多 ✘ _____
8)	2.5 years	2個半年 ✘ _____
9)	Friday, October 16, 1999	星期五，10月16日，1999年 ✘ _____
10)	8:30 p.m.	8點半下午 ✘ _____
11)	2 hours and 5 minutes	2小時5分 ✘ _____
12)	2:05 p.m.	2點5分鐘下午 ✘ _____

2 Choose the correct word or phrase

1) 你＿＿有社團活動？   a. 幾個星期   b. 星期幾

2) 你明天2:00＿＿5:00有空嗎？   a. 從   b. 到

3) 你今天要看＿＿的書？   a. 什麼時候   b. 多長時間

4) 她＿＿都去圖書館。   a. 每天   b. 有時候

5) 我很忙，所以很晚＿＿睡覺。   a. 就   b. 才

6) 你明天想＿＿哪個社團活動？   a. 參加   b. 去

7) 除了社團活動以外，你＿＿做什麼？   a. 都   b. 還

8) 今天她＿＿你打電話，想＿＿你吃飯。   a. 跟/給   b. 給/請

6.19 交際任務 jiāojì rènwù — COMMUNICATIVE TASKS

The following activities allow you to further practice your interpretive, interpersonal, and presentational communication skills in a meaningful, communicative context.

Interpretive

1 Listening

(U6.19_1：Katie 今天做什麼？)

Listen to the dialogue and tell whether the statements are true (T) or false (F).

1) ☐ Katie normally gets up pretty late.

2) ☐ She is getting up early today because she has a test in her Chinese class.

3) ☐ Her test is at 1:00 p.m.

4) ☐ The test's written part is hard for Katie, as she doesn't write Chinese characters well.

5) ☐ She doesn't have Chinese calligraphy lessons except on Friday.

6) ☐ She enjoys Chinese calligraphy lessons because it helps improve her general Chinese skills.

2 Reading

Quickly browse the weekly planners of 王東 and 林紅 and then answer the questions.

王東的時間表	林紅的時間表
11月22日 （星期一） 　　晚上6點–7點，學生中心，中文電影	11月22日 （星期一） 　　下午2點–3點，英語考試
11月23日 （星期二） 　　下午1點，林紅，乒乓球	11月23日 （星期二） 　　下午1點，王東，乒乓球
11月24日 （星期三） 　　上午9點，英語口試 　　上午10點，英語筆試 　　下午4點，籃球	11月24日 （星期三）
11月25日 （星期四） 　　下午4點，李小明家，吃飯	11月25日 （星期四） 　　下午4點–5點，跳舞
11月26日 （星期五） 　　下午5點，跟王平、林紅去買衣服 　　晚上9點，學生中心活動室，跳舞	11月26日 （星期五） 　　下午5點，跟王東、王平去買衣服 　　晚上7點–9點，生日晚會

Who has the following planned activities for this week?

1) Chinese film   a. 王東   b. 林紅   c. both   d. neither

2) English test   a. 王東   b. 林紅   c. both   d. neither

3) Birthday party   a. 王東   b. 林紅   c. both   d. neither

4) Shopping for clothing   a. 王東   b. 林紅   C. both   d. neither

5) Singing   a. 王東   b. 林紅   c. both   d. neither

6) Having a meal with friends   a. 王東   b. 林紅   c. both   d. neither

7) Dancing   a. 王東   b. 林紅   c. both   d. neither

8) Playing a ball game   a. 王東   b. 林紅   c. both   d. neither

3 Narrative reading

📖 Read the passage and indicate if the following statements are true (T) or false (F).

© Cengage Learning 2015

王東是大學新生，他哥哥是大學三年級學生。王東這兩個星期考試考得不太好。

哥哥問他每天做什麼。王東説，他每天除了上課以外，還有很多課外活動：籃球、乒乓球、武術，每天2、3個小時。他有三個社團，每天都參加社團活動，最少兩個小時。

哥哥覺得他運動的時間太多了，社團活動也太多了。可是王東説："我不是不喜歡學習，可是一個人學習沒意思。跟朋友在一起很好玩，所以我參加很多社團活動。而且，我的朋友很多，我們每天都一起運動。我覺得每天5、6個小時一點兒也不多！"哥哥説："可是你學習的時間不夠。你應該每天在圖書館看5、6個小時的書，運動1個小時就夠了，也別每天都參加社團活動。"王東説："我試試看吧。今天我只打籃球，也只參加了一個社團活動。"

True or False?

1) ☐ Wang Dong doesn't care about his studies or his academic performance.

2) ☐ Wang Dong doesn't like to do things alone.

3) ☐ His brother thinks he should stop hanging out with his friends.

4) ☐ His brother suggests that he spend equal time on his club activities and on his workout.

5) ☐ His brother suggests that he reduce his workout time by one hour a day.

6) ☐ Wang Dong is not willing to follow his brother's advice.

4 Speaking

1) **Find a partner:** Choose two activities that you are interested in from the flyer. Talk to your classmates about them and find at least one classmate who wants to join you for these activities. Use the following guide for your preparation.

> ## Panda中文學社活動時間表
> ### 歡迎參加我們的每周活動!
>
> 學生中心505號活動室
> 下午—晚上
>
> | | | |
> |---|---|---|
> | 中國音樂
Chinese Music | 周一 | 7:30–8:30 |
> | 中國電影
Chinese Films | 周二 | 8:30–10:30 |
> | 中國功夫
Chinese Kungfu | 周三 | 5:00–7:00 |
> | 中國書法
Chinese Calligraphy | 周四 | 5:00–7:00 |
> | 中國畫
Chinese Art | 周五 | 7:00–9:00 |

Role A: Ask B these questions or give information.

- Find out whether B likes X or Y.
- Ask whether B does . . . often.
- Express your interest in going to X or Y.
- Invite B to go to the activity with you and give him/her the schedule information.

Role B: Improvise with the following.

- VO很有意思/没有意思
- 經常/很少/有時候VO
- 什麼時間都可以
- 除了……以外，都(可以)
- 對我最好/合適

- TW就V了/才V
- 是什麼時候? 幾點鐘?
- 還有誰參加?
- 多長時間 (how long)?
- 還有別的活動嗎?

2) **Meet a Chinese friend:** Meet a Chinese person and find out his or her interests and hobbies. Look for anything you have in common, so that you can arrange to do something with each other.

3) **Simulated phone/video chatting:** Imagine you and your Chinese friend have an online video chat. He/she is very interested in your college life (大學生活). Listen carefully and then respond to his/her questions. Complete this task online.

5 Speaking

Imagine you work for the admissions office of your university as a volunteer and are giving an information session for a student group from China. Get ready to talk about college students' typical weekdays and weekends, as well as providing information on classes, student groups, and cultural activities.

6 Writing

Write a blog entry to share your ideas on weekly activities in which Chinese international students in your school might be interested in participating. Specify the time and location for your favorite events/activities, and give your contact information.

City Highlights

Chongqing 重慶

A river view

People's Square

UNIT 7

第七單元

旅行計劃

Making Travel Plans

The Story

The winter break is around the corner. What does everyone plan to do during the winter break?

FUNCTIONS & GLOBAL TASKS	CORE VOCABULARY	GRAMMAR	CULTURE
• Talking about things to do • Making plans for a vacation • Discussing travel itineraries	• Means of transport • Vacations • Activities	• Future activities • The 要 V 了 structure • Event sequence • Embedded questions	• New Year's Gala

Communication

Interpretive

Understand listening and reading passages related to travel and planning for a vacation.

Interpersonal

Exchange information about travel plans.

Presentational

Describe program itineraries for a visiting student group.

A 第一課

寒假快到了

Winter break is almost here

A 7.1 詞語預習 cíyǔ yùxí — PREVIEW THE VOCABULARY

 Use the **online audio flashcards** to familiarize yourself with the new vocabulary in this section.

Nouns (N)

假期	jiàqī	vacation, break
寒假	hánjià	winter break
春假	chūnjià	spring break
暑假	shǔjià	summer break
節日	jiérì	festival, holiday
新年	xīnnián	New Year
春節	Chūn Jié	Spring Festival, Lunar New Year
計劃	jìhuà	plan
打算	dǎsuàn	plan (spoken)

Pronouns (Pron)

大家	dàjiā	everybody
有的	yǒude	some

Time Words (TW)

以前	yǐqián	before, ago
以後	yǐhòu	after, later

Adverbs (Adv)

已經	yǐjīng	already
真	zhēn	so, indeed
還	hái	still
可能	kěnéng	perhaps, maybe, possibly

Auxiliary Verbs (AV)

會	huì	would, will

Verbs (V)

到	dào	arrive
開始	kāishǐ	start, begin, commence
打算	dǎsuàn	plan, intend
計劃	jìhuà	plan
做計劃	zuò jìhuà	make a plan
旅遊	lǚyóu	travel, tour (for pleasure)
旅行	lǚxíng	travel
打工	dǎ//gōng	do a temporary job

知道	zhīdào	know, realize, understand
回來/去	huílai/qu	come back / go back
回家	huíjiā	come/go home
出去	chūqu	go out
過(年/節)	guò (nián/jié)	celebrate (the New Year / a festival)

Structures

- 快要V了 / 就要V了
- X以前 / 以後
- 打算V
- 不知道 + embedded question
- 有的⋯，有的⋯
- 還不V呢

A | 7.2) 詞句聽說 cíjù tīngshuō   **FOCUS ON GRAMMAR**

 Aural-Oral Exercises: Do the online exercises to further familiarize yourself with the new vocabulary and grammar when it is used in sentences.

Main Features: In this lesson we'll introduce some basic forms for expressing <u>future activities</u>. You'll learn how to talk about imminent happenings using a relatively simple structure, 要V了. Along with these future-oriented structures, we'll practice some <u>new action verbs</u> used to discuss activity planning. In addition, we'll learn another important feature of 會 for expressing future actions. First, we'll introduce a few new terms for expressing relative time, including when doing . . . (V的時候) and before/after a time or an activity (. . .以前/以後). Again, note that word order in Chinese differs from that used in English.

1   **Expressing a specific time**   __的時候；　__以前/以後

▬ In Chinese, the modifier or reference appears in front.

A) __的時候

when . . . , at [the time of] . . . , during . . .

1) 吃飯的時候，上課的時候，新年的時候，我給你打電話的時候
     chīfàn de shíhou,   shàngkè de shíhou,   xīnnián de shíhou,   wǒ gěi nǐ dǎ diànhuà de shíhou

2) 你平常什麽時候看電視?   →   我吃飯的時候看。
     Nǐ píngcháng shénme shíhou kàn diànshì?   Wǒ chīfàn de shíhou kàn.

1 — A) — 2)

B) __ 以前 / 以後

before / after . . . , [amount of time] ago / later

1) 下午3點以前, 上課以前, 新年以後, 一個月以前/以後
xiàwǔ sān diǎn yǐqián, shàngkè yǐqián, xīnnián yǐhòu, yí gè yuè yǐqián/yǐhòu

2) 你什麼時候給我打電話? → 我今天晚上9點以後打。
Nǐ shénme shíhou gěi wǒ dǎ diànhuà?   Wǒ jīntiān wǎnshang jiǔ diǎn yǐhòu dǎ.

3) 她什麼時候去北京? → 她一個月以後去。
Tā shénme shíhou qù Běijīng?   Tā yí gè yuè yǐhòu qù.

1 — B) — 3)

2 **Telling what will be happening soon** 快 V 了, 要 V 了, 快要 V 了

■ Just as 了 functions as an updater for changes and new events, forms with 快 and 要 indicate that an event is upcoming or an action or change is imminent.

1) 新年快到了, 寒假快要到了, 快要上課了
xīnnián kuài dào le, hánjià kuài yào dào le, kuài yào shàngkè le

2) 他快回來了, 她要去臺北了, 她妹妹快要上大學了
tā kuài huílai le, tā yào qù Táiběi le, tā mèimei kuài yào shàng dàxué le

2 — 3)

3) 你今天為什麼這麼高興? → 因為我爸爸媽媽快要來了。
Nǐ jīntiān wèishénme zhème gāoxìng?   Yīnwèi wǒ bàba māma kuài yào lái le.

Negation: 還不 V (呢)

4) 你要上課了嗎? → 我還不上課呢, 我3點以後才上課。
Nǐ yào shàngkè le ma?   Wǒ hái bù shàngkè ne, wǒ sān diǎn yǐhòu cái shàngkè.

Compare with 要 V *(to be going to do something)*:

5) 你今天要去哪裡? → 我要去書店買幾本書。
Nǐ jīntiān yào qù nǎlǐ?   Wǒ yào qù shūdiàn mǎi jǐ běn shū.

1) 開_會：   開晚會，開舞會；下周我們要開一個春節晚會。
   kāi...huì: kāi wǎnhuì,   kāi wǔhuì;   xià zhōu wǒmen yào kāi yí gè Chūn Jié wǎnhuì.

2) 開始：   中文課兩點開始，我們兩點開始上中文課，
   kāishǐ: Zhōngwén kè liǎng diǎn kāishǐ, wǒmen liǎng diǎn kāishǐ shàng Zhōngwén kè,
   我們的寒假下周就開始了。
   wǒmen de hánjià xià zhōu jiù kāishǐ le.

3) 打算：   打算做什麼？這個假期我打算出去玩幾天，你不打算出去嗎？
   dǎsuàn: Dǎsuàn zuò shénme? Zhège jiàqī wǒ dǎsuàn chūqu wán jǐ tiān, nǐ bù dǎsuàn chūqu ma?

4) 計劃：   做新年計劃，做學習計劃；你這個假期有什麼計劃？
   jìhuà: zuò xīnnián jìhuà,   zuò xuéxí jìhuà; nǐ zhège jiàqī yǒu shénme jìhuà?

5) 回來/去：   我晚上9點回來，她明天回中國去   (split 回去 to insert the destination)
   huílai/qu: wǒ wǎnshang jiǔ diǎn huílai, tā míngtiān huí Zhōngguó qù

6) 回家：   我快回家了，他這個假期不回家(去)
   huíjiā: wǒ kuài huíjiā le,   tā zhège jiàqī bù huíjiā (qù)

7) 過：   過年，過節，過生日，過假期；你打算在哪裡過春假？
   guò: guònián,   guòjié,   guò shēngrì,   guō jiàqī;   Nǐ dǎsuàn zài nǎlǐ guò chūnjià?
   我今年要在學校過春節。
   Wǒ jīnnián yào zài xuéxiào guò Chūn Jié.

8) 旅行/遊：   出去旅行/旅遊，去外國旅行；我打算假期出去旅遊，
   lǚxíng/yóu: chūqu lǚxíng/lǚyóu,   qù wàiguó lǚxǐng;   wǒ dǎsuàn jiàqī chūqu lǚyóu,
   你想去哪裡旅遊？
   nǐ xiǎng qù nǎlǐ lǚyóu?

3 — 1)

3 — 7)

A: Winter break is almost here

4   Expressing probability and likelihood
會 + Action Verb
will, would, likely to, tend to

■ 會 as a modal auxiliary verb can express probability, tendency, or likelihood in the present or future.

1) 會下午回來，　會去參加晚會，　會在家裡過新年，　會出去旅行/旅遊
   huì xiàwǔ huílai,　　huì qù cānjiā wǎnhuì,　huì zài jiā li guò xīnnián,　huì chūqu lǚxíng/lǚyóu

2) 他今天會什麼時候來？　➔　他說他會下午來。
   Tā jīntiān huì shénme shíhou lái?　　Tā shuō tā huì xiàwǔ lái.

3) 你假期會不會回家？　➔　我不會回家，我會出去旅遊。
   Nǐ jiàqī huì bú huì huíjiā?　　Wǒ bú huì huíjiā,　wǒ huì chūqu lǚyóu.

4 — 3)

Compare with 要 V:

■ 要 denotes someone's definite and scheduled plan or someone's own volition.

4) 我假期不回家，我要出去旅遊。
   Wǒ jiàqī bù huíjiā,　wǒ yào chūqu lǚyóu.

5   Emphasizing with an emotive tone
真 + Adj/Modal Verb

■ As a tonal intensifier (*so, truly, really, indeed*), this adverb is typically used with an adjective or a modal verb to express feelings. It usually ends with an exclamation.

1) 我真高興！我真想去！我真喜歡過春節！
   Wǒ zhēn gāoxìng! Wǒ zhēn xiǎng qù! Wǒ zhēn xǐhuan guò Chūn Jié!

2) 春假快到了，我真高興！　　　　　　　　(. . . I'm <u>so</u> happy!)
   Chūnjià kuài dào le, wǒ zhēn gāoxìng!

3) 我真高興你明天會來參加我的生日晚會！　(I'm <u>so</u> glad you will come to my . . . !)
   Wǒ zhēn gāoxìng nǐ míngtiān huì lái cānjiā wǒ de shēngrì wǎnhuì!

4) 他們假期要出去旅遊，我真想跟他們一起去！(. . . I <u>really</u> want to go with them!)
   Tāmen jiàqī yào chūqu lǚyóu,　wǒ zhēn xiǎng gēn tāmen yìqǐ qù!

The original question form should remain unchanged in the embedded forms. 知道不知道 is usually shortened to 知不知道 in conversations.

Original questions: Question embedded in a question or a statement:

1) 他新年要去哪兒？
Tā xīnnián yào qù nǎr?

你知不知道他新年要去哪兒？
Nǐ zhī bù zhīdào tā xīnnián yào qù nǎr?

→ 我知道他新年要去哪兒。
Wǒ zhīdào tā xīnnián yào qù nǎr.

2) 他是誰？
Tā shì shéi?

你知不知道他是誰？
Nǐ zhī bù zhīdào tā shì shéi?

→ 我不知道他是誰。
Wǒ bù zhīdào tā shì shéi.

3) 他哪天回來？
Tā nǎ tiān huílai?

你知道他哪天回來嗎？
Nǐ zhīdào tā nǎ tiān huílai ma?

→ 我不知道他哪天回來。
Wǒ bù zhīdào tā nǎ tiān huílai.

4) 假期從幾號開始？
Jiàqī cóng jǐ hào kāishǐ?

你知道假期從幾號開始嗎？
Nǐ zhīdào jiàqī cóng jǐ hào kāishǐ ma?

→ 我知道假期從幾號開始。
Wǒ zhīdào jiàqī cóng jǐhào káishǐ.

Note that for 嗎–questions, the V不V form needs to be used in the embedded question/statement.

5) 他想去旅遊嗎？
Tā xiǎng qù lǚyóu ma?

→ 你知不知道他想不想去旅遊？
Nǐ zhī bù zhīdào tā xiǎng bù xiǎng qù lǚyóu?

→ 我不知道他想不想去旅遊。
Wǒ bù zhīdào tā xiǎng bù xiǎng qù lǚyóu.

6 – 1)

6 – 3)

Before viewing . . .

1) At your school, in which month does winter break fall and how long does it normally last?

2) During which month do you think Chinese universities take their winter break? Make a guess and explain why.

3) How do you spend your winter or spring break? Do you normally go home or travel?

While viewing . . .

1) During your first viewing, focus on meaning.

2) During your second viewing, pay special attention to speech forms and tones.

3) Finally, practice saying the sentences by answering the questions below.

▶ U7-A1

Katie説什麼？
··· shuō shénme?

"寒假＿＿＿＿＿＿，
　Hánjià······

我也＿＿＿＿＿＿＿！"
wǒ yě······

Katie有什麼計劃？
··· yǒu shénme jìhuà?

"回美國以前，＿＿＿＿＿＿＿＿＿＿，
　Huí Měiguó yǐqián,······

所以＿＿＿＿＿＿＿＿＿＿。
suǒyǐ······

＿＿＿＿＿＿＿！"

阿龍有什麼計劃？
Ā Lóng yǒu shénme jìhuà?

"寒假快到了，＿＿＿＿＿＿＿＿＿＿＿。
Hánjià kuài dào le, ……

可是，＿＿＿＿＿＿＿＿＿＿＿！
kěshì……

U7-A2

劉英有什麼計劃？
Liú Yīng yǒu shénme jìhuà?

"今年寒假＿＿＿＿＿＿＿＿＿，
Jīnnián hánjià……

我＿＿＿＿＿＿＿＿＿。"
wǒ……

小東說什麼？
Xiǎodōng shuō shénme?

"現在＿＿＿＿＿＿＿＿＿：
Xiànzài……

有的＿＿＿＿＿＿＿＿＿，
yǒu de……

有的＿＿＿＿＿＿。
yǒu de……

可是＿＿＿＿＿＿＿＿＿。"
Kěshì……

1 Forms and structures

See 7.2 for more notes and examples.

Telling what will be happening soon

1) 寒假快到了，我也快要回美國了！
Hánjià kuài dào le,　wǒ yě kuài yào huí Měiguó le!

(upcoming event, something that is to happen very soon)

2) 我爸爸媽媽很快就要來了。
Wǒ bàba māma hěn kuài jiù yào lái le.

(immediacy)

3) 我的錢快没有了！
Wǒ de qián kuài méiyǒu le!

(*is about to . . .*)

Future actions: definite vs. likelihood

1) 回美國以前，爸爸媽媽要來看我。
Huí Měiguó yǐqián,　bàba māma yào lái kàn wǒ.

(volition, confirmed schedule)

2) 我可能會出去旅遊。
Wǒ kěnéng huì chūqu lǚyóu.

(likelihood, tendency, being planned)

Planning

1) 我打算出去玩。
Wǒ dǎsuàn chūqu wán.

(打算 V: *plan/intend to do . . .*)

2) 今年寒假我不打算回家。
Jīnnián hánjià wǒ bù dǎsuàn huíjiā.

(不打算: do not plan/intend to. This is softer than 打算不V.)

3) 現在很多同學已經開始做寒假計劃了。
Xiànzài hěn duō tóngxué yǐjīng kāishǐ zuò hánjià jìhuà le.

(已經 V 了: *has/have already started to . . .*)

4) 有的同學打算回家過春節，
Yǒu de tóngxué dǎsuàn huíjiā guò Chūn Jié,

有的想出去旅遊。
yǒu de xiǎng chūqu lǚyóu.

(*Some plan to . . . , and others want to . . .*)

5) 我還不知道我要做什麼。
Wǒ hái bù zhīdào wǒ yào zuò shénme.

(還不知道 + embedded question)
(*still unsure . . .*)

Interrogative and negative forms 　　　　快要 V 了，要 V，會 V，打算 V

Ask and answer the questions following the cues.

Negative answer:

Imminent change 快要 V 了　　　　　　　　還不 V 呢

1) 你<u>快要去</u>中國了嗎?　　　　　　　→ _____

2) 他的生日是不是<u>快到了</u>?　　　　　→ _____

Definite action/plan 要 V　　　　　　　不 V ; 不知道

3) 他假期裡<u>要</u>回家嗎? (不V)　　　　→ _____

4) 他們下周<u>要</u>開新年晚會嗎? (不知道V不V)　→ _____

Probability/Likelihood 會 V　　　　　不會, (還) 不知道

5) 你假期裡<u>會</u>出去玩嗎? (不會V)　　→ _____

6) 你<u>會不會</u>參加新年晚會? (還不知道…)　→ _____

Intention/Planning 打算 V　　　　　　不打算 V ; 不知道

7) 他們假期<u>打算</u>回家嗎? (不打算V)　→ _____

8) 他們<u>打算不打算</u>開新年晚會? (不知道…) → _____

Intensified form with QW　　　　　　QW 都/也不 V

9) 你春節會去<u>哪兒</u>? (哪兒都…)　　　→ _____

10) 你春節要做<u>什麼</u>? (什麼也…)　　→ _____

1 **Pair work**

Ask and answer questions based on the pictures using appropriate expressions and forms:

a) Event/Action will take place soon: 快V了，要V了，快要V了

b) Definite/scheduled plans: 要V

c) Likelihood and intention: 會，可能會，想，打算

星期五

1) 李小林為什麼這麼高興？
   Lǐ Xiǎolín wèishénme zhème gāoxìng?

下個星期二

2) 回家以後她打算做什麼？
   Huíjiā yǐhòu tā dǎsuàn zuò shénme?

2月1日

3) 寒假裡她會去哪裡旅遊？去幾天？
   Hánjià li tā huì qù nǎlǐ lǚyóu? Qù jǐ tiān?

春節以前

4) 她會不會在家過春節？
   Tā huì bú huì zài jiā guò Chūn Jié?

春節以後

5) 她什麼時候會回來？
   Tā shénme shíhou huì huílai?

   回來以後還去哪兒？
   Huílai yǐhòu hái qù nǎr?

2月16日以後

6) 她打算哪天回學校？
   Tā dǎsuàn nǎ tiān huí xuéxiào?

Illustration © Cengage Learning 2015

2 **Interview and report**

1) **Interview:** Move around the classroom and speak to at least two classmates. Ask and answer questions about holiday or vacation plans: when, what, where, with whom, and for how long.

2) **Report:** Share with the class what you learned from interviewing your classmates.

3) **Quiz:** Your teacher may choose to quiz the class on the information that is shared. Be prepared to say if statements he/she makes about the reports are true or false.

A 7.6 語法鞏固 *yǔfǎ gǒnggù* **REINFORCE THE GRAMMAR**

These exercises are also available online with automatic feedback.

1 **Give the Chinese equivalents for the following expressions**

A) Time Expressions: X以前/以後，V的時候

1) before 2:00 p.m. → _____

2) before going to bed at night. → _____

3) before class / after class → _____

4) after lunch → _____

5) while taking the test / at the time of the test → _____

6) while [I was/am] in China → _____

B) Talking about imminent and future activities

A: The dance will start soon. Are you going? → _____

B: No, because I'm taking a friend to dinner at 7:00. → _____

A: Will you be back before 9:00? → _____

B: I don't know if I'll be back before 9. I'll give you a call. → _____

A: OK, but I probably won't be back until after 11:30. → _____

A 7.7 聽答對話 *tīngdá duìhuà* **LET'S CHAT**

In this listening-speaking activity you'll be asked to answer questions about the **video** segment as well as about **yourself.** You may be asked to record and submit your answers to the teacher.

B 第二課

我們打算出去旅遊
We plan to travel

 B 7.8 詞語預習 cíyǔ yùxí　　　　**PREVIEW THE VOCABULARY**

Use the **online audio flashcards** to familiarize yourself with the new vocabulary in this section.

Nouns (N)

Means of Transportation

車	chē	vehicle
汽車	qìchē	car, automobile
公交車	gōngjiāochē	public bus (also 公共汽車)
火車	huǒchē	train
地鐵	dìtiě	subway
高鐵	gāotiě	high speed rail
飛機	fēijī	airplane
自行車	zìxíngchē	bicycle
船	chuán	ship

Others

地方	dìfang	place
雪	xuě	snow
父母	fùmǔ	parents, father and mother
路	lù	road, path

Adjectives (Adj)/Stative Verbs (SV)

久	jiǔ	long time
冷	lěng	cold
熱	rè	hot
難	nán	hard, difficult
容易	róngyì	easy

Adverbs (Adv)

先	xiān	first
最後	zuìhòu	last
也許	yěxǔ	perhaps, maybe
正好	zhènghǎo	just in time; happen to

Auxiliary Verb (AV)

能	néng	can, able to

Verbs (V)

坐	zuò	ride on, travel by
坐(車)	zuò (chē)	travel by (car, bus or taxi)
開車	kāi//chē	drive (a vehicle)
騎車	qí chē	ride a bicycle or motorcycle
打車	dǎ//chē	take a cab
走路	zǒu//lù	walk, go on foot
想	xiǎng	miss (someone, home, etc.)
待	dāi	stay
滑雪	huá//xuě	snow-ski

Conjunctions (Conj)

然後	ránhòu	afterward, then
如果/要是	rúguǒ/yàoshi	if, suppose, in case
那	nà	then, in that case

Question Words (QW)

多久	duō jiǔ	how long
怎麼	zěnme	how

Idiomatic Expression (IE)

幹嘛呢?		What are you doing?
Gànmá ne?		

Structures

- 怎麼去
- 到 Place 去 (V)
- 坐 X 到 PW 去
- 在 X 待多久
- Sb 先…，然後…（最後）…
- 如果…，（那）就
- 要多長時間
- V 多長時間的 O

B | 7.9) 詞句聽說 cíjù tīngshuō　　　　**FOCUS ON GRAMMAR**

 Aural-Oral Exercises: Do the online exercises to further familiarize yourself with the new vocabulary and grammar when it is used in sentences.

> **Main Features:** In this lesson we'll introduce <u>travel-related expressions</u> and sentence forms, including means of transport and methods of coming and going (坐什麼去, 怎麼去). In addition to these travel-related topics, we'll learn about <u>verbs in a series</u> and <u>sequential expressions</u>. Be sure to pay special attention to the differences between how Chinese and your native language handle these verbs.

1 **Specifying departure and destination**　　　從 PW 去/來；到 PW 去/來

■ This form (preposition + place + verb) must be kept together as a unit and not separated. Note that the negative marker (不) appears before the preposition (從, 到) rather than before 去/來.

A) **Stating a departure point:** 從 PW 去/來
go/come from [place]

■ Note that in Chinese the sequence of elements follows the natural order (the Temporal Sequence), i.e., the departure point comes before the destination.

1) 從哪裡來/去?　　從學校來，從上海去，從這裡去
cóng nǎlǐ lái/qù?　　cóng xuéxiào lái, cóng Shànghǎi qù, cóng zhèlǐ qù

2) 你要從上海去(臺北)嗎?　→　不，我不從上海去，我從廣州去。
Nǐ yào cóng Shànghǎi qù (Táiběi) ma?　　Bù, wǒ bù cóng Shànghǎi qù, wǒ cóng Guǎngzhōu qù.

B) Stating a destination: 到 PW 去/來 (Interchangeable with 去/來 PW)
go/come to [place]

1) 到哪裡去？ 到香港去，到學校來，到她家去；去臺北， 來香港…
dào nǎlǐ qù?　　dào Xiānggǎng qù, dào xuéxiào lái, dào tā jiā qù;　　qù Táiběi,　　lái Xiānggǎng

2) 你假期要到香港去嗎？　➡　不，我不到香港去，我打算到臺北去。
Nǐ jiàqī yào dào Xiānggǎng qù ma?　　　Bù,　wǒ bú dào Xiānggǎng qù, wǒ dǎsuàn dào Táiběi qù.

1 — B) — 2)

---

2 **Describing means of transport**　　　坐X去/來；開車去/來

A) To go/come by riding on a means of transport 坐 X 去/來
to go/come by taking X

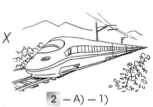

2 — A) — 1)

1) 坐什麼去/來？ 坐公交車去，坐火車去，坐飛機來， 坐地鐵來
zuò shénme qù/lái?　zuò gōngjiāochē qù, zuò huǒchē qù,　zuò fēijī lái,　　zuò dìtiě lái

2) 我們怎麼去他家？ 坐地鐵去還是坐公交車去？　➡　我們坐地鐵去吧。
Wǒmen zěnme qù tā jiā?　Zuò dìtiě qù háishi zuò gōngjiāochē qù?　　Wǒmen zuò dìtiě qù ba.

B) To go/come by other means　　(開車，騎車，走路) 去/來
to go/come by driving a car, riding a bicycle, or walking

■■■ Note that the word 騎 is the action of sitting on something and controlling its movements, and should be used for describing the actions of riding bicycles, motorcycles, horses, etc. To describe an action of traveling in a car, subway, ship, or airplane, use 坐.

1) 他打算怎麼來？ 會不會開車來？　➡　他不想開車來，可能會騎車來。
Tā dǎsuàn zěnme lái? Huì bú huì kāichē lái?　　Tā bù xiǎng kāichē lái, kěnéng huì qí chē lái.

A)   去多久；在那裡待多久
to be gone for a certain length of time; to stay for a certain length of time

1)   你要去中國了嗎？要去多久/多長時間？ → 我要去2個星期。
    Nǐ yào qù Zhōngguó le ma? Yào qù duō jiǔ/duō cháng shíjiān?   Wǒ yào qù liǎng gè xīngqī.

2)   你打算在北京待多久？   我可能會在那裡待3天。
    Nǐ dǎsuàn zài Běijīng dāi duō jiǔ?   Wǒ kěnéng huì zài nàlǐ dāi sān tiān.

3 — A) — 2)

B)   要V多久，要 V [多長時間] 的O；[doing Sth]要多長時間
How long will it take to get there by . . . ?

▬   要 here means "to need" or "to require."

1)   要坐3個多小時的飛機（坐飛機要3個多小時）
    yào zuò sān gè duō xiǎoshí de fēijī (zuò fēijī yào sān gè duō xiǎoshí)

2)   要開2天的車（開車要2天）
    yào kāi liǎng tiān de chē (kāichē yào liǎng tiān)

3 — B) — 1)

C)   [doing Sth]要 [多長時間]

1)   從這裡到北京要多長時間？ → 坐飛機要10多個小時（要坐10多
    Cóng zhèlǐ dào Běijīng yào duō cháng shíjiān?   Zuò fēijī yào shí duō gè xiǎoshí (yào zuò shí duō
                                    個小時的飛機）。
                                    gè xiǎoshí de fēijī).

2)   從上海到南京要多長時間？ → 很快，坐高鐵只要1個多小時就
    Cóng Shànghǎi dào Nánjīng yào duō cháng shíjiān?   Hěn kuài, zuò gāotiě zhǐ yào yí gè duō xiǎoshí jiù
                                    到了。
                                    dào le.

4 | Sequencing the information 什麼時候 – 跟誰 – 從哪裡 – 坐什麼 – 到哪裡去 – 做什麼

A) When several elements of information are present in a sentence, follow their natural order (The Temporal Sequence Principle): when—with whom—from where—by what means—to where—to do what.

1) 到臺北去，到臺北去玩，跟家人到臺北去玩，
dào Táiběi qù, dào Táiběi qù wán, gēn jiārén dào Táiběi qù wán,

跟家人從香港到臺北去，下個月跟家人從香港坐飛機到臺北去玩
gēn jiārén cóng Xiānggǎng dào Táiběi qù, xià gè yuè gēn jiārén cóng Xiānggǎng zuò fēijī dào Táiběi qù wán

4 – A) – 1)

B) Focusing on key information

▬ In a conversation, speakers focus on one point at a time rather than including all the information they have in one sentence.

1) 春節你有什麼計劃？　→　我打算跟家人到臺北去玩。
Chūn Jié nǐ yǒu shénme jìhuà?　　　Wǒ dǎsuàn gēn jiārén dào Táiběi qù wán.

2) 你們打算什麼時候去？　→　我們打算春節以前去。
Nǐmen dǎsuàn shénme shíhou qù?　　Wǒmen dǎsuàn Chūn Jié yǐqián qù.

3) 你們打算怎麼去？　→　我們打算從香港坐飛機去。
Nǐmen dǎsuàn zěnme qù?　　　　　Wǒmen dǎsuàn cóng Xiānggǎng zuò fēijī qù.

4) 你們打算在臺北待多久？　→　我們可能在那裡待一個星期。
Nǐmen dǎsuàn zài Táiběi dāi duōjiǔ?　Wǒmen kěnéng zài nàlǐ dāi yí gè xīngqī.

5 | Specifying the order of actions/events

先…，然後…，最後…
first . . . , then . . . , and finally . . .

▬ Note that 先 is an adverb and can only appear after personal pronouns and before the action verb.

1) 我們先去北京，然後去上海，最後去廣州。　　(先我們… ✗)
Wǒmen xiān qù Běijīng, ránhòu qù Shànghǎi, zuìhòu qù Guǎngzhōu.

2) 我們先坐飛機去北京，然後從北京坐高鐵去上海，
Wǒmen xiān zuò fēijī qù Běijīng, ránhòu cóng Běijīng zuò gāotiě qù Shànghǎi,

最後從上海坐火車去廣州。
zuìhòu cóng Shànghǎi zuò huǒchē qù Guǎngzhōu.

6 **Expressing conditional situations**   如果/要是…，（那）[Sb] 就…
If . . . , then . . .

▰ In this case, 就 is used in a statement. It always comes after a subject or other personal pronoun in a dependent clause.

1) 如果飛機票不貴，（那）我就跟你去。   (就我… ✗)
Rúguǒ fēijī piào bú guì,   (nà) wǒ jiù gēn nǐ qù.

2) 如果你開車去，那我可以坐你的車去嗎？ (就 is not used in questions.)
Rúguǒ nǐ kāichē qù,   nà wǒ kěyǐ zuò nǐ de chē qù ma?

▰ 要是 is commonly used in colloquial speech.

3) 要是你有3天的假期，那你打算去哪裡？
Yàoshi nǐ yǒu sān tiān de jiàqī, nà nǐ dǎsuàn qù nǎlǐ?

6 – 2)

7 **Using a verb or verb phrase as a noun modifier**   (Sb) V 的 N

▰ A verb or verb phrase can be used to modify a noun. In English, the modifying clause comes after the head noun (e.g., the place where we plan to go). In Chinese, however, the modifier with 的 always comes before the head noun, whether it is an adjective (e.g., 漂亮的衣服) or a verb phrase (e.g., 我們想去的地方).

1) 我們要去的那個地方很冷。   *(The place where we are going to go is cold.)*
Wǒmen yào qù de nàge dìfang hěn lěng.

2) 你知道不知道他說的那個地方？ *(Do you know the place he is talking about?)*
Nǐ zhīdào bù zhīdào tā shuō de nàge dìfang?

7 – 1)

7 – 2)

Before viewing . . .

1) Where would you prefer to go to spend your winter break: a warm or a cold place?

2) Would you prefer to travel with friends or by yourself? By airplane or train? Why?

While viewing . . .

1) During your first viewing, focus on meaning.

2) During your second viewing, pay special attention to speech forms and tones.

3) Finally, practice saying the sentences by answering the questions below.

▶ **U7-B1**

阿龍問劉英和曉雪在幹什麼？
Ā Lóng wèn Liú Yīng hé Xiǎoxuě zài gàn shénme?

劉英說：
Liú Yīng shuō:

"我們正在＿＿＿＿＿＿＿＿＿！"
Wǒmen zhèngzài……

曉雪有什麼計劃？
Xiǎoxuě yǒu shénme jìhuà?

"我父母＿＿＿＿＿＿，
Wǒ fùmǔ……

我也＿＿＿＿＿＿，
wǒ yě……

所以＿＿＿＿＿＿＿＿＿。
suǒyǐ……

可是＿＿＿＿＿＿＿＿＿＿，
Kěshì……

我還不知道＿＿＿＿＿＿。"
wǒ hái bù zhīdào……

劉英打算去室友家，她説：
Liú Yīng dǎsuàn qù shìyǒu jiā, tā shuō:

"我們可以先＿＿＿＿＿＿＿＿＿＿＿＿＿，
Wǒmen kěyǐ xiān……

＿＿＿＿＿＿＿＿＿＿＿＿＿＿，

然後還可以＿＿＿＿＿＿＿＿＿＿＿，
ránhòu hái kěyǐ……

最後＿＿＿＿＿＿＿＿＿＿＿＿＿＿＿。"
zuìhòu……

阿龍想看雪，他想去哪裡？
Ā Lóng xiǎng kàn xuě, tā xiǎng qù nǎlǐ?

"寒假裡我想去＿＿＿＿＿＿＿＿＿＿＿＿。
Hánjià li wǒ xiǎng qù……

正好＿＿＿＿＿＿＿＿＿＿＿＿＿，
Zhènghǎo……

我想＿＿＿＿＿＿！那會＿＿＿＿＿！"
wǒ xiǎng……　　　　Nà huì……

曉雪和劉英都不想去太冷的地方，
Xiǎoxuě hé Liú Yīng dōu bù xiǎng qù tài lěng de dìfang,

小東呢？
Xiǎodōng ne?

"我哪兒＿＿＿＿＿，就＿＿＿＿＿＿＿。"
Wǒ nǎr……　　　　jiù……

阿龍覺得怎麼樣？
Ā Lóng juéde zěnmeyàng?

"如果＿＿＿＿＿＿＿＿，
Rúguǒ……

＿＿＿＿＿＿＿＿＿＿＿＿＿？

對了，我老爸説，＿＿＿＿＿＿，＿＿＿＿
Duì le,　wǒ lǎo bà shuō,……

＿＿＿＿＿＿＿＿＿＿＿＿！"

1 **Forms and structures**
See 7.9 for more notes and examples.

■ Describing the purpose of a trip: 去 V / VO

1) 她請我去她家過春節。
Tā qǐng wǒ qù tā jià guò Chūn Jié.

(go to . . . to spend the Lunar New Year)

2) 我想去東北滑雪。
wǒ xiǎng qù Dōngběi huáxuě.

(go to . . . to ski)

■ Describing an itinerary: 先⋯，然後⋯，最後⋯

1) 我們可以先坐火車到南京玩幾天，在我室友家過春節，
Wǒmen kěyǐ xiān zuò huǒchē dào Nánjīng wán jǐ tiān, zài wǒ shìyǒu jiā guò Chūn Jié,

(先 appears after 我們.)

然後(我們)還可以去上海待兩三天，
ránhòu (wǒmen) hái kěyǐ qù Shànghǎi dāi liǎng sān tiān,

(然後 introduces a sequential action.)

最後(我們)從那裡坐高鐵回學校來。
zuìhòu (wǒmen) cóng nàlǐ zuò gāotiě huí xuéxiào lái.

(Use commas and omit repeated subject pronouns)

■ Expressing probabilities and uncertainties: 可能，會，不知道能不能，也許，可以，如果⋯

1) 我也很想回家，所以我可能會回家去。
Wǒ yě hěn xiǎng huíjiā, suǒyǐ wǒ kěnéng huì huíjiā qù.

(可能會 "probably will, will likely . . ." is weaker in tone than 會.)

2) 春節以前的票很難買，我還不知道能不能回去。
Chūn Jié yǐqián de piào hěn nán mǎi, wǒ hái bù zhīdào néng bù néng huíqu.

(不知道 + Question Form)
(不知道要是我能回去 ✘)

3) 她請我去她家過春節，也許我們可以一起去?
Tā qǐng wǒ qù tā jiā guò Chūn Jié, yěxǔ wǒmen kěyǐ yìqǐ qù?

(也許: maybe, perhaps)

4) 如果你們都不去，我一個人有什麼意思?
Rúguǒ nǐmen dōu bú qù, wǒ yí gè rén yǒu shénme yìsi?

(要是 can also be used, usually in colloquial speech.)

2 Interrogative and negative forms

Each question focuses on one aspect. Answer the questions with a negative form following the hints provided.

1) 你到哪裡去？到北京去嗎？　　（上海和南京）　→　我不到北京去，我到上海和南京去。

2) 你什麼時候去？春節以前嗎？（春節以後）　→　_____

3) 你怎麼去？坐飛機去嗎？　　　（高鐵）　→　_____

4) 你從哪兒去？從香港去嗎？　　（廣州）　→　_____

5) 你跟誰一起去？跟朋友嗎？　　（一個人）　→　_____

6) 你去多久？去1個月嗎？　　　（7、8天）　→　_____

7) 你在上海待多久？待一周嗎？（3天）　→　_____

3 Story narration

Pay special attention to the verb forms and the use of punctuation marks.

寒假快到了，大家都在做計劃。曉雪説她很想家，所以她可能會回家
Hánjià kuài dào le, dàjiā dōu zài zuò jìhuà. Xiǎoxuě shuō tā hěn xiǎng jiā, suǒyǐ kěnéng huì huíjiā

去看父母。可是春節以前火車票很難買，她不知道能不能回家。劉英
qù kàn fùmǔ. Kěshì Chūn Jié yǐqián huǒchē piào hěn nán mǎi, tā bù zhīdào néng bù néng huíjiā. Liú Yīng

説她的室友的家在南京，她打算去室友家過春節，也許大家可以一起去。
shuō tā de shìyǒu de jiā zài Nánjīng, tā dǎsuàn qù shìyǒu jiā guò Chūn Jié, yěxǔ dàjiā kěyǐ yìqǐ qù.

阿龍想去一個有雪的地方過生日，他打算到東北去學滑雪。可是他想去的
Ā Lóng xiǎng qù yī gè yǒu xuě de dìfang guò shēngrì, tā dǎsuàn dào Dōngběi qù xué huáxuě. Kěshì tā xiǎng qù

地方太冷了，曉雪和劉英都不想去。小東説他哪兒也不去，只在家裡看看
de dìfang tài lěng le, Xiǎoxuě hé Liú Yīng dōu bù xiǎng qù. Xiǎodōng shuō tā nǎr yě bú qù, zhǐ zài jiā li kànkan

小説。阿龍説，如果大家都不跟他去，那他一個人去東北也沒意思。不過，
xiǎoshuō. Ā Lóng shuō, rúguǒ dàjiā dōu bù gēn tā qù, nà tā yí gè rén qù Dōngběi yě méi yìsi. Búguò,

阿龍很高興他爸爸要給他一個很大的生日禮物。
Ā Lóng hěn gāoxìng tā bàba yào gěi tā yí gè hěn dà de shēngrì lǐwù.

1 Pair work

Ask and answer questions based on the following information, using appropriate forms and structures. Be prepared to describe one of Lin Ying's trips to the class.

林英 is an international student at an American college. Her boyfriend, 小李, is coming to join her soon, since they are planning to travel together during her spring break! Describe their planned trip, including the following information: when, with whom, to where, from where, by what, and for how long.

他/她要去哪裡？去做什麼？什麼時候去？跟誰去？從哪裡去？怎麼去？
Tā/tā yào qù nǎlǐ? Qù zuò shénme? Shénme shíhou qù? Gēn shéi qù? Cóng nǎlǐ qù? Zěnme qù?

在X待多久？先……，然後……，最後……
Zài dāi duō jiǔ? Xiān……,   ránhòu……,   zuìhòu……

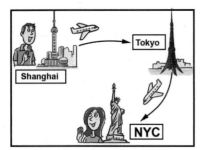

Trip 1: 小李

Departure point:	Shanghai
Stopover:	Tokyo (東京 Dōngjīng)
Destination:	New York City (紐約 Niǔyuē)
Purpose of trip:	to visit his girlfriend
Trip duration:	18 hours by plane
Days in NYC:	3 (March 10—12)

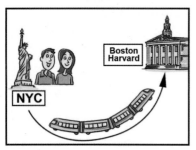

Trip 2: 林英和小李

Departure-Destination:	New York City to Boston (波士頓, Bōshìdùn)
Transportation:	5 hours by train
Purpose:	to visit Harvard University (哈佛, Hāfó)
Days in Boston:	2 (March 13—14)

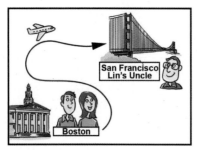

Trip 3: 林英和小李

Departure–Destination:	Boston to San Francisco (舊金山, Jiùjīnshān)
Transportation:	6 hours by plane
Purpose:	to visit Lin's uncle
Days in SF:	2 days (March 15—16)

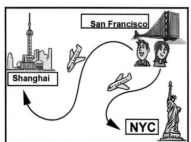

Trip 4: 林英/ 小李

Date:	March 17
Departure point:	San Fransico
Destination 1:	(林英) Return to New York City
Destination 2:	(小李) Return to Shanghai

These exercises are also available online with automatic feedback.

1 Fill in the blanks with the appropriate words

先，然後，最後，要，打算，過，從，到，看看，出去，回，坐，待，玩

1) 小李_____到紐約 (NYC)去看女朋友林英，和林英一起_____春假。

2) 他要先_____上海坐飛機到日本東京(Tokyo)，_____從東京到紐約去。

3) 他要_____18個小時的飛機。他打算在紐約_____3天。

4) 然後，小李和女朋友要_____旅遊。

5) 他們打算____坐火車到波士頓(Boston)去_____哈佛大學(Harvard)，

6) 在波士頓_____2天，然後從那裡坐飛機_____舊金山 (SF)去玩2天。

7) _____，小李會從舊金山坐飛機回上海，林英也會從那裡坐飛機

   _____紐約 (NYC).

2 Give the Chinese equivalent for each sentence
Be sure to use the correct word order.

1) I plan to go to Nanjing.   → _____

2) I plan to go to Nanjing by train.   → _____

3) I plan to go to Nanjing by train tomorrow.   → _____

4) I plan to go from Shanghai to Nanjing by train tomorrow.   → _____

5) I plan to go to Nanjing and take a train to Shanghai tomorrow.   → _____

6) I plan to go with my mom to Nanjing tomorrow and take a train to Shanghai.   → _____

7) I plan to go with my mom to Nanjing tomorrow and take a train to Shanghai to visit my dad.   → _____

In this listening-speaking activity you'll be asked to answer questions about the **video** segment as well as about **yourself.** You may be asked to record and submit your answers to the teacher.

"Super Girl Voice" Concert

NEW YEAR'S GALA

Chinese New Year—"Spring Festival" or **Chūn Jié** (春節)—is an important event on both the national and local levels in China. University students across the nation engage in various activities to celebrate the holidays. Among the most popular is the ritual of an annual gala performance.

Closely following the format of the New Year's Gala by China Central Television (CCTV), students, often joined by faculty and staff, use their talents and organizational skills to put on a great show of music, dance, poetry reading, and small theatrical performances. Among the performances are "cover songs" (new performances or recordings of previously recorded songs, usually by someone other than the original artist), but original works are also common, especially in the form of skits, or **xiǎopǐn** (小品), and stand-up comedy routines, known as **xiàngsheng** (相聲). Many of these skits or stand-up

Dashan

S.H.E., CCTV 2013 Spring Festival Gala

"Voice of China"

comedy performances are about academic studies and campus lives.

International students are often invited to participate in the Gala and to show off their talents. Some of them later even become celebrities because of their outstanding language skills in Chinese. One prominent example is Mark Henry Rowswell, an international student turned TV personality. A Canadian student who studied at Beijing University, he developed superb Mandarin skills. His study of Chinese stand-up comedy, xiàngsheng, and involvement with stage performance has helped him become a Chinese media darling. Dubbed Dàshān (大山, "Big Mountain"), his 1999 CCTV New Year's Gala premier made him an instant celebrity.

In recent years, a type of student singing contest has become increasingly popular on college campuses. Influenced by popular music competition shows on TV, such as Chāojí Nǚshēng (超級女聲, Super Girl Voice) and the Zhōngguó Hǎo Shēngyīn (中國好聲音, Voice of China), these student singing contests draw huge crowds of enthusiasts, undergraduates and postgraduates alike

from all majors. After several rounds of competition, the final round of the competition usually takes place in mid-December, when winners of the best singer competitions, along with other categories (including best original music and best performance), are determined by juries and popular votes. One positive outcome from such a singing contest is that it gives students who participate a boost in confidence, and as a result, some young talents have had breakthroughs and subsequently become recording artists.

One such example is a pop band called Shuǐ Mù Niánhuá (水木年華, literally, Water Wood Times), whose founding members all come from Tsinghua University and who received accolades for their musical works while still in college.

Most Chinese universities have a month-long winter break, which usually takes place during January and February, the dates always revolving around the Chinese lunar calendar. During the break, students return home to reunite with their families and celebrate Chinese New Year or Spring Festival. This is also the time for them to recuperate from their busy schedule of studies and finals.

QUIZ

1. Who is Mark Henry Rowswell? Search for information about him on the Internet and find out where he studied before he went to China.

2. The CCTV New Year's Gala is perhaps the most viewed TV entertainment show in China. In recently years, the show has become increasingly internationalized. Search online for the 2013 Gala and find out who performed a duet with Chinese soprano Song Zuying.

3. Why are Chinese universities' winter breaks always in January and/or February, not in December and/or January?

ACTIVITIES

1. Li Yuchun is the winner of the 2005 Super Girl (or Super Voice Girl) Contest. Do an Internet search to learn more about her and find out where she studied when she won the contest. What is her name in Chinese?

2. Search online for "Super Boy" (or Happy Boy) or "Super Girl" episodes and watch one or two. Discuss the similarities and differences between a Western version ("Pop Idol" or "American Idol") and the Chinese spin-offs.

單元復習
Review and Integration

 **7.16** 主課復習 zhǔkè fùxí   **REVIEW THE STORY**

 Read the following passages as fast as you can. Follow these steps:

1) Do not stop to check the meaning of words you don't recognize. Mark them and keep reading.
2) Read the passage again and guess the meaning of the marked words on a separate piece of paper.
3) Finally, look up the words in a dictionary or the vocabulary index and verify their meanings.

 Katie快要回美國了。回美國以前，她的爸爸媽媽要到中國來，所以他們會一起去旅遊。Katie很高興，她爸爸媽媽很快就要來了！

 曉雪很想家，父母也很想她，所以她覺得寒假的時候她應該回家去。可是因為春節的時候很多人都回家、旅行，所以火車票很難買，曉雪還不知道能不能回家。

 劉英寒假不打算回家，她的室友請她去她家過春節。她說如果大家也想去，那也許可以跟她一起去。她想先坐火車到南京玩幾天，在室友家過春節，然後還可以去上海待兩三天，最後從那裡坐高鐵回學校來。

 阿龍說正好他的生日快到了，他打算到一個有雪的地方去學滑雪。可是他想去的地方太冷了，曉雪和劉英都不想去。小東說他可能哪兒也不去，只在家裡看看小說。

 阿龍說，如果大家都不跟他去他想去的地方，那他一個人去那裡也沒意思。最後他說，他爸爸要給他一個很大的生日禮物，大家都想知道是什麼禮物。

Quickly provide the Chinese equivalents for the following phrases and sentences. Do not translate them word for word.

1 Time expressions

In Chinese you say . . .

1) before New Year's Day

2) a week ago

3) after 9:00 p.m.

4) from 9:00 a.m. to 5:00 p.m.

5) to arrive in two weeks

6) after finishing my dinner

7) to take a four-hour train ride

2 Telling what will be happening soon

1) Spring break is just around the corner!

2) I'm going to go home soon.

3) I'm so excited that I'll be traveling in a week!

4) We'll be taking our Chinese exam this Friday!

3 Talking about plans for a break

1) Winter break is coming soon.

2) I'm going to go home in two weeks.

3) I'm going to fly home from here.

4) I'm going to be at home for a week.

5) I plan to come back to school before school starts (開學).

6) I plan to go to a dance during spring break.

7) I'm not sure whether I'm going to travel during the break.

8) I may go to my friend's house for a couple of days.

4 Dialogue: Talking about travel plans

A: Where will you go for spring break?

B: I'm not going anywhere. How about you?

A: I'll go to Beijing for a week.

B: Really? Are you going to go by yourself?

A: I will probably go with two friends. _____

B: That's nice! When do you plan to leave? _____

A: In two weeks. _____

B: How long will it take you to get to Beijing from here? _____

A: I hear it will take 14 hours by plane. _____

B: That long? Maybe you can sleep for a few hours. _____

A: Yes, I can also watch the movie for a few hours. _____

B: When will you come back to school? _____

A: Maybe not until the last day of spring break. _____

7.18 語法小測驗 yǔfǎ xiǎo cèyàn **CHECK FOR ACCURACY**

1 **Correct the sentences**

Identify the error in each sentence and then rewrite the sentence correctly.

1) 我要去北京從上海。 ✘

　　_____
　　(. . . go to Beijing from Shanghai)

2) 先我去上海，然後去北京。 ✘

　　_____
　　(First I'll go to . . .)

3) 我春假不要回家。 ✘

　　_____
　　(I'm not going to go home . . .)

4) 以後新年我要出去旅遊。 ✘

　　_____
　　(After New Year's Day . . .)

5) 我要去上海坐飛機。 ✘

　　_____
　　(I'll go to Shanghai by plane.)

6) 要是你去旅遊，就我跟你去。 ✘

　　_____
　　(If . . . , then I'll . . .)

7) 我不知道要是他會來。 ✘

　　_____
　　(. . . if he will come.)

8) 我不去那個晚會。 ✘

　　_____
　　(I won't go to that party.)

9) 多長時間你要去那裡? ✘

　　_____
　　(How long are you going to . . . ?)

2 Choose the correct word

1) 要是你下午出去，你＿＿＿＿在10點以前回來嗎？
   a. 會   b. 要

2) 那個地方没意思，我可能不＿＿＿＿去。
   a. 會   b. 要

3) 坐公交車去只要10分鐘，所以你＿＿＿＿坐公交車去。
   a. 可以   b. 可能

4) 我不知道他在哪兒，＿＿＿＿在學校。
   a. 可以   b. 可能/也許

The following activities allow you to further practice your interpretive, interpersonal, and presentational communication skills in a meaningful, communicative context.

Interpretive

1 **Listening**

(U7.19_1_1: 阿龍的生日禮物)

As you listen to the clip, take notes based on the guided questions below, then answer the questions.

1) 阿龍為什麼給爸爸打電話? _____

2) 阿龍想去哪裡過生日? 為什麼? _____

3) 爸爸有什麼計劃? _____

4) 爸爸打算在哪兒過春節? _____

5) 阿龍喜歡爸爸給他的生日禮物嗎? _____

Based on the conversation, complete each statement with the most approriate choice.

1) This conversation is about _____.
   a. Ah Long's birthday   b. Ah Long's winter break   c. both

2) Ah Long calls his dad because he wants to _____.
   a. ask for money   b. ask about his birthday   c. ask about his dad's plans

3) Ah Long originally planned to spend his winter break and birthday _____.
   a. at home in Guangzhou   b. at a very cold place   c. at a warm place

4) His dad plans to take Ah Long to _____.
   a. Guangzhou and Hong Kong   b. Hong Kong and Taiwan   c. Taiwan

5) As far as Ah Long is concerned, his dad's plans are _____.
   a. exciting   b. very attractive   c. not so exciting

6) According to his dad's plans, they will likely spend Chinese New Year in _____.
   a. Taiwan   b. Guangzhou   c. Hong Kong

7) Ah Long's attempt to get money from his dad is _____.
   a. unsuccessful   b. successful   c. partially achieved

Listen to the dialogue and indicate if the following statements are true (T) or false (F).

1) ☐ The man wants to buy a ticket to Beijing from Guangzhou.

2) ☐ He wants to fly there before Chinese New Year.

3) ☐ He can get 20 percent off on an air ticket after Chinese New Year.

4) ☐ He thinks the discounted price is reasonable, although the date is not desirable.

5) ☐ The man wants to switch to a train departing before 8:00 a.m. or after 6:00 p.m.

6) ☐ All train tickets before Chinese New Year are sold out.

7) ☐ The man finally buys an air ticket.

2 Reading

Read the passage indicate if the following statements are true (T) or false (F).

Katie 的計劃

Katie 來中國已經快四個月了，她也快回美國了。今天是星期六，Katie在給爸爸媽媽打電話。打電話以後她很高興，因為爸爸媽媽説他們就要到中國來看她了，而且他們打算回美國以前一起去旅遊。他們會先坐飛機去杭州(Hangzhou)玩幾天，然後從杭州去蘇州(Suzhou)，最後去上海。小南的爸爸告訴Katie，從杭州到上海很快，坐汽車、火車、高鐵都可以。坐汽車只要兩個小時，可是如果坐高鐵，只要一半時間就到了。Katie和父母還打算去香港(Hong Kong)看看，最後從香港飛回美國。因為他們一共只有10天時間，所以每個地方只能待一兩天。

True or False?

1) ☐ Katie is excited because she is going to go home soon.

2) ☐ Her parents will come visit her and travel with her before she goes back to America.

3) ☐ They are going to visit two cities and stay for a few days at each city.

4) ☐ It takes only half an hour to reach Shanghai from Hangzhou by the bullet train.

5) ☐ Katie's family will stay in Hong Kong for up to two days before flying back home.

Interpersonal

3 Speaking

While studying abroad, you want to go sightseeing in some other cities. Talk to a travel agent about your travel plans and get ticket information. Ask how you will be able to get a discounted price (打折) by adjusting your travel dates, by taking an early or a late flight, by taking the train, etc.

4 Reading and writing

Your Chinese pen pal sends an email. Read the email and respond. Provide as many details as you can.

發件人: 李學新

主　題: 假期計劃

Hi筆友:

你好！最近怎麼樣？忙不忙？我的寒假已經開始了，所以我不忙了。

在中國，我們寒假有1個月，我有很多時間，所以我打算出去旅遊。可是現在我的錢還不夠，所以我想先打兩個星期的工，然後和幾個朋友一起去旅遊。我們打算去南方，可能會去廣州和海南，因為那邊不太冷，也很好玩。我們可能會在春節以後坐火車去，先在廣州待3天，然後去海南玩10天，那裡有很多好玩的地方。

聽說你們美國大學的寒假不太長，不過，你們還有一個春假，是嗎？那你的春假是什麼時候？你打算做什麼？會回家還是會出去旅遊呢？很想知道你的計劃。

祝好！

學新

A group of Chinese college students from Shanghai is coming to visit your university for a week-long winter program. The program activities include English lessons, campus tours (of your school and others), local tours, parties with American students who study Chinese, and welcome and farewell parties (歡迎會 huānyíng huì, 歡送會 huānsòng huì).

5 Writing

You and your partner work for your university's international office as assistants. Prepare the following for the Chinese student group:

1) A week-long program with itineraries in Chinese that list only key information and that follow this format: 2月1日, 晚上7:30, Smith樓101室, 歡迎會

2) Three to four images for a slide presentation using part of the information from the program itineraries you have prepared. Give information about local tours, including departure times, durations, means of transport, meals, and images of where you will be visiting. This will be used for your orientation presentation (see task below).

6 Speaking

Imagine the Chinese student group has arrived. You are to give an orientation for the winter program using a slide presentation. You and your partner should take turns giving the presentation.

City Highlights

Shanghai 上海

Shanghai Bund

Pudong

Appendices

Combination of initials and finals

Finals →	1 a	2 o	3 e	4 ai	5 ei	6 ao	7 ou	8 er	9 an	10 en	11 ang	12 eng	13 ong	14 i (yi)	15 ia (ya)	16 iao (yao)	17 ie (ye)	18 iou* (you)
1 b	ba	bo		bai	bei	bao			ban	ben	bang	beng		bi		biao	bie	
2 p	pa	po		pai	pei	pao	pou		pan	pen	pang	peng		pi		piao	pie	
3 m	ma	mo	me	mai	mei	mao	mou		man	men	mang	meng		mi		miao	mie	miu
4 f	fa	fo			fei		fou		fan	fen	fang	feng						
5 d	da		de	dai	dei	dao	dou		dan		dang	deng	dong	di		diao	die	diu
6 t	ta		te	tai		tao	tou		tan		tang	teng	tong	ti		tiao	tie	
7 n	na		ne	nai	nei	nao	nou		nan	nen	nang	neng	nong	ni		niao	nie	niu
8 l	la		le	lai	lei	lao	lou		lan		lang	leng	long	li	lia	liao	lie	liu
9 g	ga		ge	gai	gei	gao	gou		gan	gen	gang	geng	gong					
10 k	ka		ke	kai	kei	kao	kou		kan	ken	kang	keng	kong					
11 h	ha		he	hai	hei	hao	hou		han	hen	hang	heng	hong					
12 j														ji	jia	jiao	jie	jiu
13 q														qi	qia	qiao	qie	qiu
14 x														xi	xia	xiao	xie	xiu
15 zh	zha		zhe	zhai	zhei	zhao	zhou		zhan	zhen	zhang	zheng	zhong	zhi				
16 ch	cha		che	chai		chao	chou		chan	chen	chang	cheng	chong	chi				
17 sh	sha		she	shai	shei	shao	shou		shan	shen	shang	sheng		shi				
18 r			re			rao	rou		ran	ren	rang	reng	rong	ri				
19 z	za		ze	zai		zao	zou		zan	zen	zang	zeng	zong	zi				
20 c	ca		ce	cai		cao	cou		can	cen	cang	ceng	cong	ci				
21 s	sa		se	sai		sao	sou		san	sen	sang	seng	song	si				

19	20	21	22	23	24	25	26	27	28	29	30	31	32	33	34	35	36
ian	in	iang	ing	iong	u	ua	uo*	uai	uei*	uan	uen*	uang	ueng	ü	üe	üan	ün
yan	yin	yang	ying	yong	wu	wa	wo	wai	wei	wan	wen	wang	weng	yu	yue	yuan	yun
bian	bin		bing		bu												
pian	pin		ping		pu												
mian	min		ming		mu												
					fu												
dian			ding		du		duo		dui	duan	dun						
tian			ting		tu		tuo		tui	tuan	tun						
nian	nin	niang	ning		nu		nuo			nuan				nü	nüe		
lian	lin	liang	ling		lu		luo			luan	lun			lü	lüe		
					gu	gua	guo	guai	gui	guan	gun	guang					
					ku	kua	kuo	kuai	kui	kuan	kun	kuang					
					hu	hua	huo	huai	hui	huan	hun	huang					
jian	jin	jiang	jing	jiong										ju	jue	juan	jun
qian	qin	qiang	qing	qiong										qu	que	quan	qun
xian	xin	xiang	xing	xiong										xu	xue	xuan	xun
					zhu	zhua	zhuo	zhuai	zhui	zhuan	zhun	zhuang					
					chu	chua	chuo	chuai	chui	chuan	chun	chuang					
					shu	shua	shuo	shuai	shui	shuan	shun	shuang					
					ru	rua	ruo		rui	ruan	run						
					zu		zuo		zui	zuan	zun						
					cu		cuo		cui	cuan	cun						
					su		suo		sui	suan	sun						

Abbreviations	Grammatical Terms	Abbreviations	Grammatical Terms
Adj	Adjective	PW	Place Word
Adv	Adverb	PE	Polite Expression
AV	Auxiliary Verb	Pref	Prefix
Conj	Conjunction	Prep	Preposition
CV	Coverb	Pron	Pronoun
DV	Directional Verb	QF	Question Form
Exp	Expression	QW	Question Word
IE	Idiomatic Expression	RV	Resultative Verb
Interj	Interjection	RVE	Resultative Verb Ending
Loc	Localizer	Sp	Specifier
M	Measure Word	SV	Stative Verb
N	Noun	Suf	Suffix
Nu	Number	TE	Time Expression
Nu	Numeral	TW	Time Word
P	Particle	V	Verb
Pron	Personal Pronoun	VP	Verb Phrase
Phr	Phrase	VO	Verb-Object

APPENDIX 3: UNDERSTANDING GRAMMAR AND STRUCTURES

1 **General Sequencing Principles in Mandarin Chinese**

Word order in Chinese sentences is quite different from that in English, despite some seeming similarities. This course introduces the following four general word order principles to help you conceptualize Chinese grammar and structure.

1. Modifier-before-the-Modified Principle (Modifier 的 N)

A noun can be modified by various words or phrases, e.g., possessive adjectives, adjectives, time expressions, prepositional phrases, or verb phrases. The noun being modified is called "the head noun." In English, the modifier (the word or phrase that modifies the head noun) can be placed before the head noun (*premodification*), e.g., *my* **teachers**, *very good* **teachers**, or after it (*postmodification*), e.g., **teachers** *in China*, the **teachers** *who can speak English*.

In Chinese, however, noun modifiers are always placed before the head noun (*premodifiers*). Normally Chinese noun modifiers are marked by the particle 的 placed between the modifier and the head noun. The noun modifier can be very long. No matter how long a noun modifier is, when spoken, 的 is tied to the premodifier rather than to the head noun (e.g., 很好的|老師, not 很好|的老師). In principle, the head noun appears at the end of the noun phrase using this formula: **Modifier 的 + Noun**. Compare the English and Chinese:

English (Pre- and postmodifiers)	**Chinese** (Premodifiers only)
(Possessive adjective) <u>my</u> teacher	我的老師 (wǒ de lǎoshī)
(Adjective Phrase) <u>a very good</u> teacher	很好的老師 (hěn hǎo de lǎoshī)
(Prepositional Phrase) teachers <u>in China</u>	中國的老師 (Zhōngguó de lǎoshī)
(Verb Phrase) teachers <u>who speak English</u>	説英文的老師 (shuō Yīngwén de lǎoshī)

2. The Temporal Sequence Principle (TSP)

One of the main features of Chinese syntax is that sentence elements are sequenced according to the order in which they occur in real experience. For example, an element associated with the initiation of an action (when, where, with whom, etc.) would precede the action verb (*pre-verbal*), because they naturally occur before the action is carried out. By contrast, an element indicating a result of an action would follow the action verb (*post-verbal*), since the result only comes <u>after</u> the action begins. Because of this tendency to mirror the sequence of people's conceptual experience, Chinese word order has been referred to as following the *temporal sequence principle* (*TSP*) (Tai, 1985) or *natural sequence* (Liu, 1986). However, TSP is only a general default structure. Variations in word order do exist motivated by other principles and pragmatics. Examples of TSP are given throughout this course, and here are some simple examples:

English	Chinese Equivalent
I <u>eat</u> in a restaurant.	I in a restaurant <u>eat</u>.
I <u>eat</u> at 2:00.	I at 2:00 <u>eat</u>.
I <u>eat</u> with a friend in a restaurant at 2:00.	I with a friend at 2:00 in a restaurant <u>eat</u>.

3. The Whole-before-the-Part Principle (Whole-Part)

This principle simply states that the bigger unit comes before the smaller unit in sequencing. In other words, the bigger unit is the "framework" that "owns" the smaller (or sub-) units. This concept is consistent with the TSP explained above because a bigger unit comes on the scene before a smaller unit. It also supports the modifier-before-the-modified principle, as the framework, in a way, functions as a modifier. Compare the following examples with their counterparts in English).

Time: year-month-day (2015年9月1日)， day-section-hour (今天上午9點)

Location/address: country-city-district-street-building-room (中國北京X區X街X樓X室)

Number: whole–fraction (1/3: 三分之一；5%: 百分之五)

4. The Communication Topic and Focus Principle (Topic and Focus)

The Topic-Comment Structure

It is widely recognized that Mandarin Chinese is a topic-prominent language. A sentence is divisible into two major parts, *Topic and Comment* (which may or may not align with the subject + predicate exactly). The Topic, normally taking the sentence initial position, indicates what the sentence is about. The Comment, the rest of the sentence, carries a message or new information about the Topic (something said about the Topic).

Topic-Comment vs. Subject-Predicate: How does the topic-comment (T-C) structure differ from a subject-predicate (S-P) one? Simply put, the T-C focuses on pragmatic functions (what the speaker chooses to highlight in the message), while the S-P addresses the basic formal structure of a sentence, i.e., a sentence contains a subject (S) followed by a predicate (P) containing a main *verb.*

Making an Object the Topic: In Chinese, often an object is fronted (topicalized), and the grammatical subject and verb together would then be shifted rightward to serve as the *comment* of that fronted object, now the topic (Example 1). Also, inanimate items (such as food or homework) are commonly used as the topic/subject of the sentence and followed by an action verb as the comment (Example 2).

Subject-Predicate Sentence	Topic-Comment Sentence
1) 我不認識這個人。 I don't know this person.	這個人(T)我不認識(C)。 This person (T), I don't know [her/him](C).
2) 你怎麼寫這個字？("You" vs. others) How do you write this character?	這個字(T)怎麼寫(C)? This character (T), how is it written (C)?
Incorrect: 我都要大的和小的。	大的小的我都要。 The big one and the small one, I want both.

Here is one more typical example: Statements, short or long, are frequently used as the topic of a sentence, which are then followed by a comment. Such a comment can be as short as one syllable or two (好/很好,行/不行), as shown in Example 3, and cannot be reversed as can be done in English.

3) 周末跟朋友去商店買東西 (T)很好(C)。　　　　Incorrect: 很好周末跟朋友去……
Going to stores to shop with friends on weekends (T) is good (C). (It's good to . . .)

The End-focus feature

Normally the second part of a sentence carries new information and often the sentence-end marks the focal point of the message, especially for sentences using extended verbal phrases such as resultative, directional, and positional verbs. Compare the following pairs in terms of the focus (F):

1a) 這個周末我要看完那本書(F)。   This weekend I'll finish reading <u>that book</u> (F).

1b) 那本書這個周末我要看完(F)。   As for that book, this weekend I'll <u>finish reading (it)</u> (F).

2a) 她坐在屋子裡(F)。   She sat/was sitting <u>in the room</u>. (i.e., not outside)

2b) 她在屋子裡坐著(F)。   She is <u>sitting</u> in the room. (i.e., instead of standing or doing something else)

2   Place Words (PW)   [U2-A]

Place words in Chinese include the following general types:

1. Proper names of places, e.g., China (中國), Beijing (北京), Washington (華盛頓)
2. Nouns that denote places, e.g., school (學校), dorm (宿舍), home (家)
3. General locative words, e.g., here (這裡/這兒), there (那裡/那兒), front (前面)
4. Nouns with localizers, e.g., inside of the room (屋子裡), on the table (桌子上)

<u>General Rules:</u>

- PWs can be used in front of the sentence as the subject.
  這裡是我們的學校. This place (over here) is our school.

- When a PW is used elsewhere in the sentence to denote a <u>location</u>, it is typically introduced by 在.
  我家在北京。 My home is in Beijing.
  我住在這裡。 I live here.

To use or not to use 裡:

裡(inside) is a localizer that is often attached to a noun to form a PW indicating an <u>enclosed</u> or a <u>confined</u> space such as *at home* (家裡), *in a room* (屋子裡), or *in the school* (學校裡).

If the statement refers to common places or general locations such as 學校 (school) or 商店 (store), 裡 can be omitted.

NEVER use 裡 for proper names such as country and city names.
在中國裡，在北京裡

(For more examples of place words and localizers, see Units 2, 11 and 13.)

3 Adjectives/Stative Verbs (SV) [U3-A, B]

The main functions of Chinese adjectives (also referred to as stative verbs) are described below.

1. Predicative/Stative

Predicative adjectives are adjectives or adjective phrases that describe the subject of a sentence. Note that a Chinese predicative adjective follows the subject immediately without the verb to be (i.e., no 是) as if it were functioning as a verb, e.g., 她很好 (She very good). This Subj-Adj (or S-SV) sentence type is consistent with the Topic-Comment structure.

1) Attach 很 or another modifier to a Predicative Adjective

很，不太，有點兒，不夠

這本書很貴。This book is expensive. (很 is unstressed and acts as a dummy.)
這本書<u>很</u>貴。This book is <u>very</u> expensive. (很 is stressed to mean "very" or "really.")
這本書<u>不太</u>貴。This book is not very expensive. (不太 is more common than 不很.)

2) Use adjectives without adverbs

This usage typically occurs in direct response to a question focusing on the adjective. Avoid using this form in regular statements and self-initiated comments as it often carries a contrastive tone.

哪本書貴？ ——這本書貴。 Which book is expensive? —This one is. (by contrast)

3) Adjective + 了 to indicate a changed/new status

Predicative adjectives can attach 了 to indicate a new/changed state.

他高了。He has grown taller. (The focus is on the change and new state.)
以前她很漂亮，可是現在她老了。She was pretty before, but now she is aging.

不……了 not ... any more, no longer ...
現在手機不貴了。Cell phones are no longer expensive (as they used to be).

2. Attributive

1) Adj/AP-的+N: Adjectives are commonly used to premodify nouns with the particle 的.
(很)貴的東西，很好的書，便宜的衣服，很漂亮的書包，不太大的桌子

2) Monosyllabic Adj + Noun: Some adjectives premodify nouns without 的, typically those that fall into common conceptual categories, e.g., good/bad, big/small, new/old, etc.
好書，壞人，小孩子，大桌子，新朋友，舊書

3. Adj-的 as a noun phrase

Often a generic noun (東西, 人) or an understood one (書, 衣服…) following an adjective can be omitted once introduced to avoid repetition.

新的 the new, the new one; 我的書是新的。 My book is new/a new one.
你想要哪個本子：大的還是小的？ Which book do you want, the big one or the small one?

Note: As a noun phrase, Adj-的 cannot follow a subject directly (as in S-SV sentences, discussed above). 是 should be used (我的書是新的). The difference between 我的書是新的 and 我的書很新 is that the former(是) identifies the topic while the latter (SV) describes it.

(See more examples in U3-A, B.)

Prepositions (Prep), also referred to as *coverbs* (CV) or *first position verbs* in some Chinese textbooks, are words that introduce a noun or noun phrase, e.g., study Chinese *in* China, go to a store *with* my friend, buy something *for* my mom.

However, a preposition in Chinese may not act in the same way as its English counterpart. Here are some examples of their major differences.

1. The word order

English prepositions are normally placed after the verb, e.g., study *in* China, go *with* a friend, sit *on* the chair. In Chinese, the position of the preposition again follows the natural order of occurrence, either before or after the action verb.

He is studying Chinese *in China*.
他在中國學中文。 Lit. "He in China study Chinese." (He is already in China before the action occurs.)

I go to the bookstore *with my friend*.
我跟朋友去書店。 Lit. "I with my friend go to the bookstore." (I'm with my friend before going.)

She sat on the chair.
她坐在椅子上。 Lit. "She sat on the chair top ". (The "sitting down" occurs before being on the chair.)

2. The verb form

Most Chinese prepositions were originally verbs (e.g., 在, 跟, 給). When a prepositional phrase appears before the main action verb, it becomes tied to the main action verb to form one unit. The preposition (coverb), if not preceded by an auxiliary verb (要, 想, 會, etc.), acts like a verb and can be used in negative (不V) as well as interrogative (V不V) forms of the sentence.

(See more examples in U4-A)

5   V 得 + Comment on quality/degree: How well or to what degree   [U5-A]

In English we can make comments on a person's skill or performance in various ways. For example, when we are impressed by someone's language ability and performance, we may say *he is a good learner*, *he learns fast* or *he is a fast learner*. We may also tell the person directly with expressions such as *Good job! Well done!*

In Chinese, however, all those expressions are best conveyed with the **V得 + Comment** structure, often referred to as the *verb complement* structure. The comment part introduced by 得 adds information on how well a person performs, to what extent a job is done, or what results the action brings. In other words, this structure is about action- or performance-related comment rather than the action process itself. As such, the verb does not carry with it any "tense" marker. For example, V得很好 can refer to a past or a current situation depending on the context or time word used.

Three Basic Forms:
Topic-Comment: Often a verb-object (VO) phrase can be added in front of V得 to clarify the activity (topic) being commented upon. V得 is typically followed by a short adjective phrase (AP), e.g., 很好, 不錯, 不太好, 不多, 很少 . . .

1) **VO V 得 + AP:**

VO clarifies the topic on which the comment is being made. VO can be omitted only when the activity is understood, e.g., 看電影, 看書, 看電視 and 看球賽.

> 她看書看得很多。 (For reading books) She reads a lot.
>
> 她看書得很多。 ✗ (得 <u>follows the verb, rather than the VO.</u>)

2) **V 得 + AP:** VO fronting is unnecessary if VO or O is pre-stated or clear in the context.

> [她很喜歡看書……] 她看得很多。 [She likes reading books.] She reads a lot.

3) **O V 得 + AP:** The O is fronted for emphasis or contrast.

> 她書看得多, 電視看得少。 She reads books a lot and doesn't watch a lot of TV.

Rules:

1) 得 immediately follows <u>the verb</u> rather than the VO or O, as shown in the three forms above.

2) The interrogative and negative forms are reflected in the comment part <u>after</u> 得.

> 她看書看得多不多? Does she read a lot? 她看不看書…… ✗
>
> 他唱得不好。 He doesn't sing very well. 他不唱得好。 ✗

3) V 得-sentences cover both past and present times depending on the context, as far as quality and degree are concerned. Do not use 了 or 過 for a past event in this structure.

(See more examples in U5-A)

6 Question Forms [U1-U7]

Unlike many languages, Chinese interrogative sentences normally do not require changes in word order or intonation. To understand a Chinese question, you must be alert to the sentence particle or the embedded question word (QW) in the sentence. Normally a question particle appears at the end of the sentence. That means, the sentence looks like a statement until you reach the very end. As for QWs such as *who, what, which, where, when, how,* they may appear at the exact spot where the answer is called for: You are *who*?, You are *whose* student?, You live *where*?, etc. (instead of *Who* are you?, *Whose* student are you?, and *Where* do you live?).

Question Types:

1. Questions marked by a sentence final particle

1) Yes/No 嗎- questions: Statement + 嗎(ma) [U1-A]

他是一個大學生。➜ 他是大學生嗎? Is he a college student?

2) Supposition 吧- questions: Statement + 吧(ba) [U4-A]

他是一個大學生。➜ 他是大學生吧? He is a college student, isn't he?

3) Abbreviated 呢- questions: Subject + 呢(ne) [U2-B]

他是一個大學生。你呢? He is a college student. How about you?

2. Alternative Question Forms: (是) A 還是 B; V不V

1) 是A還是B? (Is it A or is it B?) [U2-A]

她是老師還是學生? Is she a teacher or a student?

The initial 是 can be dropped if the main verb is anything but 是. For example:

他(是)説中文還是説英文? Does he speak Chinese or English?
他學什麼? 中文還是日文? What language does he learn? Chinese or Japanese?

2) V不V...? [U2-B]

This is a yes-no question form, also known as the "choice-type" question. This form is often favored over the 嗎-type as it can be easily detected as a question early on in the sentence.

她是不是學生? Is she a student?
她會不會説中文? Can she speak Chinese?

For有, use 有沒有......? (Do NOT use 不.)
你有沒有室友? Do you have a roommate or roommates?

Note: The generic 是不是 form (*Is it the case that/Is it true that . . . ?*) should be used if there is another element attached to the main verb, e.g., an adverb before the verb (也V, 都V).

Incorrect: 他也會不會説中文?   Can he also speak Chinese?
Correct: 他是不是也會説中文?   Is it the case that he can also speak Chinese?

3. Question-Word questions ("Wh-questions"):

Note that the QW occurs exactly where the answer should be in the sentence.

1) QWs: 什麼, 誰, 誰的, 幾 [U1-A, B]

他叫王一名。 →	他叫什麼(名字)?	What's his name?
他是一個大學生。 →	他是誰? (誰是他? ✗)	Who is he?
她有三個孩子。 →	她有幾個孩子?	How many children does she have?
他是老師。 →	誰是老師?	Who is a/the teacher?
他是我的老師 →	他是誰的老師?	Whose teacher is he?

2) Positioning of QW 誰 in a 是- Sentence: 王一名是誰? vs.誰是王一名? [U1-B]

In English, these two questions share a single form: "Who is WANG Yiming?" In Chinese, however, two different sequences are used to call for different information, as shown below.

王一名是誰? (Sample answer: 他是一個大學生。)
(The speaker is interested in knowing <u>about</u> this person, e.g., personal information and status.)

誰是王一名? (Sample answer: 他是王一名。)
(The speaker is trying to <u>identify</u> the person among other people. The focus is on which one.)

3) QWs: 哪, 哪裡/哪兒, 哪國 [U2-A, B]

哪 (which) corresponds to specifiers 這 (this, these), 那 (that,those) or calls for specific information.

他是北京人。 →	他是哪裡/哪兒人?	Where is he from?
她是美國人。 →	她是哪國人?	Which country is she from?
他住在這棟樓。 →	他住在哪裡/哪棟樓?	Where / In which building does he live?

261

4) QW for comments: 怎麼樣   **[U3-A]**

怎麼樣 can be attached to a simple phrase or a sentence or can be used as an added question. It always appears at the end of the sentence.

(你覺得)這個書包怎麼樣？	<u>How do you like</u> this schoolbag?
我們現在去商店買東西，怎麼樣？	<u>How about</u> we go shopping now?

5) QWs for quantity and numbers: 幾個，多少   **[U4-A, B]**

幾 is treated as a number (normally under 10) and can be used either in a statement to indicate a vague quantity ("a few") or in a question specifying a number or quantity (how many/much . . . ?). Like a number, a measure word is usually attached to 幾. 多少 can be used for any number/quantity and the measure word is normally omitted.

他有<u>三個</u>室友。	➜	他有<u>幾個</u>室友？	<u>How many</u> roommates does he have?
這個書包要<u>100塊</u>錢。	➜	這個書包要<u>多少</u>錢？	<u>How much</u> is this schoolbag?

6) QW: 怎麼

  a) 怎麼V？ (How does one [do] . . . ?)

    怎麼 (how) is used before a verb. The subject or topic can be a person or an inanimate object.

    這個字怎麼寫？   How do you write this character?

  b) 怎麼⋯⋯？ (How come . . . ? Why . . . ?)

    This is said when asking how or why something is the case. It may serve as a "why" question like 為什麼, although it is more rhetorical than a real question. 怎麼 can be placed before or after the subject.

    你<u>怎麼</u>不學中文？ / <u>怎麼</u>你不⋯⋯？ Why aren't you studying Chinese?

  c) 怎麼這麼/那麼⋯⋯？ (How can it be that . . . ? How come . . . ?)

    This is used to show an emotion such as surprise, disappointment, etc, and it is basically rhetorical.

中文<u>怎麼這麼</u>難？	How come Chinese is so hard?
他的英文<u>怎麼那麼</u>好！	How can his English be so good?!

7) QWs for time expressions: 什麼時候，多久，多長時間

  a) 什麼時候 (When)：(哪年/哪天，幾月幾號，星期幾，幾點)   [U6-A, B]

    This QW appears <u>before</u> the main verb, either before or after the subject.

    他什麼時候去？(哪年/天，幾點)   When is he going? (what year/day, at what time)

  b) 多長時間/多久(How long)：(幾年/天，幾個月/星期，多少天/小時)   [U6-U9]

    These QWs refer to length of time (duration / time spent or time elapsed).

    For duration of an action, they appear <u>after</u> the main verb.

    For time elapsed they appear <u>before</u> the main verb.

Duration: 他要學<u>多長時間</u>的中文？	How long is he going to study Chinese?	[U6-B, U7]
Time spent: 他學了<u>多久</u>的中文？	How long did he study Chinese?	[U8-B]
Time elapsed: 他<u>多久</u>沒學中文了？	How long have he stopped studying Chinese?	[U9-B]

APPENDIX 4: GRAMMAR INDEX

To find the grammar notes and examples, please refer to the part number and the item number. For example, U1-A stands for Unit 1, Part A. The item number refers to the grammar item number in the Focusing on Grammar (詞句聽説) section which immediately follows the vocabulary lists in Part A and Part B, respectively.

Note the items included here are selective. This index does not include all grammar points or word usage covered in this book.

	Part #	Item #	Page #
Use of 的			
Modifier + 的 N 她的爸爸，他的名字	U1-A	1	5
Adj phrase 的 N: 很好的書 *very good book(s)*	U3-B	1	85
Adj + 的: 新的 *the new (one)*	U3-B	2	86
Color word + 的 N: 紅色的書包，紅書包，紅的 *red school bag, the red one*	U4-B	1	119
V 的 N: 唱歌的那個人，那個人唱的歌 *the person who is singing, the song that the person sings*	U5-B	6	159
V 的 N: 你想去的地方 *the place you want to go to*	U7-B	7	231
Adverbs			
Usage of 也 *also, too*	U1-B	6	20
也(不)V *also . . . / not . . . either*	U2-A	6	43
[Plural item] 都 VP *both/all . . . :* 我們都是新生 *We are all freshmen.*	U2-A	7	43
A 和 B, Sb + 都 V *I like both . . . and . . . :* 紅的和黃的，我都喜歡 *I like both the red one and the yellow one.*	U4-B	5	122
夠，不夠，不夠[大] *enough, not enough, not [big] enough*	U3-B	8	89
Different tone of voice: 很，太，不夠，有點兒，. . . *very, too, not . . . enough, a little bit . . .*	U3-A	2	75
Frequency of an action: 經常 V 不常，很少，有時候 *do Sth often, rarely, sometimes*	U5-A	5	147
Auxiliary / Modal Verbs			
會 V: 會說 + language *can speak [language]:* 會說英語 *He can speak English.* 會說 + region + 話 *can speak [regional] speech:* 會說廣東話 *She can speak Cantonese.*	U2-B	2--3	52-53

Location, Distance, and Directions

在 PW, 住在 PW *at [place], live in/at [place]*	U2-A	4	41
Location 有 ... *There is/are . . . [at location]*: 這裡有很多東西 *There are many things here.*	U4-A	3	109

Verb Forms and Sentence Structures

General

Subj + Adj phrase: 他高，他很高 ... *He is tall.*	U3-A	3	76
Accepting 吧: 好吧 *All right. / OK then.*	U4-A	8	111
吧 for suggestions: 我們打籃球吧 *Let's do . . . / Why don't we do . . .*	U5-B	4	158
給 Sb + Obj *give [Sb] Sth*: 他給我一本書 *He gives me a book.*	U4-B	3	120
給 Sb + Action V *do . . . for Sb*: 給他買一件衣服 *Buy a shirt for him.*	U4-B	4	121
喜歡 VO, V 不 VO *like doing/to do . . .*: 她喜歡唱歌 *She likes singing.*	U5-A	1	143–144
V + Mod + O: 看英文書 *read English books* V + specific O: 說中文 *speak Chinese*	U5-A	2	144
Sb (VO) V 得 + comment *Sb is [good] at doing . . . ; Sb does . . . [well]*: 他打球打得很好 *He is good at playing ball games. /He plays . . . well.*	U5-A	3	145
一起 V, 跟 Sb 一起 V *do Sth together with Sb*: 我跟他一起學中文 *I'm studying Chinese together with him.*	U5-A	4	146
跟 Sb V *receive Sth from Sb*: 我跟他學中文 *I'm learning Chinese from him.*	U5-A	4	146
Sb 在 / 正在 V *Sb is doing Sth right now*: 我正在看書 *I'm reading right now.* TW 在 / 正在 PW + V *Sb is doing Sth at [place] at [time]*: 我現在(正)在北京學中文 *I'm currently studying Chinese in Beijing.*	U5-B	1	155–156
別 V, 不要 V *Don't . . .*: 別/不要跟我說話 *Don't talk to me.*	U5-B	5	158
去 Place *go to [place]*: 去商店 *go to a store*	U4-A	4	110
去 Place + Action VP *go to [place] to do . . .*: 我去商店買東西 *I'm going to the store to shop.*	U4-A	5	110
在 Place + Action VP *do . . . at [place]*: 我在商店買東西 *I'm shopping in the store.*	U4-A	6	110
跟 Sb + Action VP *do . . . with Sb*: 我跟室友去商店 *I'm going to the store with my roommate.*	U4-A	7	111
Downtoner V-下，VV *do . . . briefly*: 看一下/看看 ... *take a look at . . .*	U4-B	6	123
Clock time + Action *do . . . at [time]*: 我 12 點睡覺 *I go to bed at 12:00.*	U6-B	2	192

V+多長時間的O; VOV 多長時間 do . . . for [duration]: 學2年的中文;學中文學2年 *has/have studied Chinese for 2 years*	U6-B	5	194

Verbs: 姓，叫，是

Equative verbs 姓, 叫 *be surnamed, be called:* 我(不)姓王，我(不)叫王林 *My last name is (not) Wang. My [full] name is (not) Lin Wang.*	U1-A	3	7
誰:王小名是誰 vs. 誰是王小名 *(lit.) Wang is who vs. Who is Wang*	U1-B	2–3	18–19
是:他是大學生，他不是我哥哥 *He is a college student. He is not my brother.*	U1-B	2–4	18–19
是 Place 人，是 Place 來的 *to be from [place], to come from [place]:* 我是北京人，他是廣州來的 *I'm from Beijing; he came from Guangzhou.*	U2-A	5	42
是 Adj 的:是新的 *is a new one / is new*	U3-B	2	86

Sentence 了 for Changed State or Update:

Used for changed status: 我高了;我是大學生了 *I've grown taller; I'm a college student now.*	U3-A	4	77
該 V 了 *It's time to do . . . :* 衣服小了，該買新的了。 *My clothes have all gotten too small! It's time to buy new ones.*	U3-B	6	89

Future Action/Planning

Upcoming and imminent events: 快要V了，就要V了 *Sb is going to do . . . soon / Sth is upcoming soon:* 新年快到了，我就要回家了 *New Year is around the corner; I'll be going home soon.*	U7-A	2	216
Sb 會+ Action Verb *would, could, likely to, tend to:* 會去旅遊 *would go traveling*	U7-A	4	218
要 V *need to do, will do, be going to do:* 我要買新的 *I'm going to buy a new one; I need to buy . . .*	U3-B	5	88
想 V *want to / would like to:* 我想買一個手機 *I want to buy a cell phone.*	U3-B	5	88
TW+PW+有 Event *There is [event] [where and when]:* 明天在學生中心有活動 *There is an event in the Student Center.*	U5-B	2	156
請 Sb V *treat Sb to . . . , ask Sb to do . . . together:* 我請你看電影，請你跟我去 *I'll treat you to a movie; I'm inviting you to go with me.*	U6-B	7	195
到 Place 去/來 *come/go to [place]:* 到美國來 *come to America*	U7-B	1	228
從 Place 來/去 *come/go from [place]:* 從上海來 *come from Shanghai*	U7-B	1	227
坐(飛機、車)來/去 *come/go by [airplane, bus . . .]*	U7-B	2	228

APPENDIX 5: VOCABULARY INDEX 1 (CHINESE TO ENGLISH)

A

阿姨	āyí	N	aunt; a term of address for a woman of one's mother's generation	51
矮	ǎi	Adj/SV	(of height) short	72
爱好	àihào	N	hobby	142

B

把	bǎ	M	(used for chairs,umbrellas, etc.)	38
爸爸	bàba	N	father, dad	4
吧	ba	P	(used at the end of a question)	107
白	Bái	N	a Chinese surname (also means white)	50
白色	báisè	N	white	118
百	bǎi	Nu	hundred	84
半	bàn	TE	half	190
棒球	bàngqiú	N	baseball	142
北/北方	běi/běifāng	N	north	16
北京	Běijīng	PW	Beijing	38
北京话	Běijīnghuà	N	Beijing dialect	50
本	běn	M	(used for books)	72
本地	běndì	PW	local, this locality	38
本来	běnlái	Adv	originally	106
本子	běnzi	N	notebook, exercise book	72
筆	bǐ	N	writing instrument (pen, pencil, etc.)	72
比赛	bǐsài	N	competition	154
筆試	bǐshì	N	written test	190
表	biǎo	N	watch	190
别	bié	Adv	don't	154
别的	biéde	Sp	other, else	118
不错	búcuò	Adj/SV	impressive	72
不够	búgòu	Adv	not enough	73
不過	búguò	Conj	but	118
不	bù	Adv	not	4
不常	bù cháng	Adv	seldom	142
不同	bù tóng	Adj/SV	different	143

C

才	cái	Adv	only, only then	190
餐馆	cānguǎn	N	restaurant	190
参加	cānjiā	V	join, participate in	190
差	chà	TE	short of	190
長	cháng	Adj/SV	long	72
唱	chàng	V	sing	142
唱歌	chàng//gē	VO	sing (a song)	143
車	chē	N	vehicle	226
陳	Chén	N	a Chinese surname	50
吃飯	chī//fàn	VO	have a meal	190
出去	chūqu	V	go out	215
除了⋯⋯以外	chúle...yǐwài	Conj	in addition to; apart from	179
穿	chuān	V	wear	118
船	chuán	N	ship	226
床	chuáng	N	bed	38
春假	chūnjià	N	spring break	214
春節	Chūn Jié	N	Spring Festival, Lunar New Year	214
從	cóng	Prep/CV	from	191

D

打	dǎ	V	hit, play	142
打八折	dǎ bā zhé	Exp	give 20% off	119
打車	dǎ//chē	V	take a cab	226
打電話	dǎ diànhuà	VO	make a phone call	143
打電話	dǎ diànhuà	VO	make a phone call	179
打工	dǎ//gōng	V	do a temporary job	214
打球	dǎ//qiú	VO	play a ball game	143
打拳	dǎ//quán	VO	do/practice martial arts	143
打算	dǎsuàn	N	plan (spoken)	214
打算	dǎsuàn	V	plan, intend	214

們	men	Pron	(a suffix used to make plural forms of personal pronouns and nouns)	4
—迷	—mí	N	fan of...	142
秒鐘	miǎozhōng	TE	second	190
明年	míngnián	N	next year	178
明天	míngtiān	TW/Exp	tomorrow	154
明天見。	míngtiān jiàn	IE	See you tomorrow.	155
名字	míngzi	N	name	4
母語	mǔyǔ	N	mother tongue	50

N

哪	nǎ, něi	QW	which	39
哪裡/哪兒	nǎlǐ/nǎr	QW	where, which place	39
哪年/哪天	nǎ nián/nǎ tiān	QF/Exp	which year / which day	179
那我走了。	Nà wǒ zǒu le.	IE	I'll leave then.	155
那	nà/nèi	Pron/Sp	that	38
那	nà	Conj	then, in that case	227
那好吧！/好吧！	Nà hǎo ba!/Hǎo ba!	Exp	Okay then!	85
那裡/那兒	nàlǐ/nàr	PW	there	38
難	nán	Adj/SV	hard, difficult	226
南/南方	nán/nánfāng	N	south	16
男孩	nánhái	N	boy	16
南京	Nánjīng	PW	Nanjing	38
呢	ne	P	(a marker for abbreviated questions or a tone softener)	51
能	néng	AV	can, able to	226
你	nǐ	Pron	you	4
你的意思是……	nǐ de yìsi shì……	IE	You are saying that . . . / You mean . . .	155
你好！	Nǐ hǎo!	Exp	(A common greeting) Hello! Hi!	5
你是哪裡/哪兒來的？	Nǐ shì nǎlǐ/nǎr lái de?	Exp	Where do you come from?	39
你是哪裡人/哪兒人？	Nǐ shì nǎlǐ rén/nǎr rén?	Exp	Where are you from?	39
年	nián	N	year	178

年級	niánjí	N	grade, year	16
您	nín	Pron	you	4
您貴姓？	Nín guìxìng?	Exp	What's your (family) name, please?	5
牛仔褲	niúzǎikù	N	jeans	118
女兒	nǚ'ér	N	daughter	4
女孩	nǚhái	N	girl	16

P

朋友	péngyou	N	friend	38
便宜	piányi	Adj/SV	cheap, inexpensive	72
票	piào	N	ticket	190
漂亮	piàoliang	Adj/SV	pretty, good-looking	72
乒乓球	pīngpāngqiú	N	table tennis, ping-pong	142
平常	píngcháng	Adv	normally, usually	190
普通話	Pǔtōnghuà	N	common speech (a term used in mainland China)	50

Q

騎車	qí chē	V	ride a bicycle or motor-cycle	226
其他	qítā	Sp	other, else	118
起床	qǐ//chuáng	VO	get up, get out of bed	190
汽車	qìchē	N	car, automobile	226
千	qiān	Nu	thousand	84
錢	qián	N	money	84
請	qǐng	V	ask, invite, treat	190
請問……	Qǐngwèn……	Exp	May I ask . . .; Excuse me . . .	5
請稍等。	Qǐng shāo děng.	Exp	Just a moment, please.	119
球	qiú	N	ball	142
球賽	qiúsài	N	ball game, match	154
去年	qùnián	N	last year	178
拳	quán	N	fist, punch	142

R

然後	ránhòu	Conj	afterward, then	227
熱	rè	Adj/SV	hot	226
人	rén	N	person	16
認識	rènshi	V	know, meet (new people)	51
日	rì	N	day (formal)	178

274

外語/文	wàiyǔ/wén	N	foreign language	50
外語學院	Wàiyǔ xuéyuàn	Phr	School of Foreign Languages	51
玩	wán	V	play (game), have fun	142
晚	wǎn	Adj/SV	late	190
晚會	wǎnhuì	N	evening party, soirée	154
晚上	wǎnshang	N	evening, night	178
萬	wàn	Nu	ten thousand	106
王	Wáng	N	Wang (a Chinese surname)	4
網球	wǎngqiú	N	tennis	142
為什麼	wèishénme	QW	why	73
文學院	Wénxuéyuàn	Phr	School of Liberal Arts	51
文字	wénzì	N	written language; script	50
問	wèn	V	ask	84
問題	wèntí	N	problem, question	154
我	wǒ	Pron	I, me	4
舞	wǔ	N	dance	142
舞會	wǔhuì	N	dance party, ball	154
武術	wǔshù	N	martial arts	142

X

西/西方	xī/xīfāng	N	west/Occident	4
喜歡	xǐhuan	V	like	118
下課	xià//kè	VO	finish/leave class	179
下午	xiàwǔ	N	afternoon	178
先	xiān	Adv	first	226
先生	xiānsheng	N	Mr., Sir	4
先生	xiānsheng	N	a polite form used for male adults in general; husband	51
現在	xiànzài	TW	now, currently	73
想	xiǎng	V	miss (someone, home, etc.)	226
想要	xiǎng yào	V	want to, intend to, desire	84
小	xiǎo	Adj	small	4
小姐	xiǎojiě	N	Miss, young lady	4
小時	xiǎoshí	TE	hour	190
小説	xiǎoshuō	N	novel	142
小學	xiǎoxué	N	elementary school	16
小學生	xiǎoxuéshēng	N	elementary school student	16

些	xiē	M	some, a few (used to indicate an indefinite amount or a very small amount)	72
鞋子	xiézi	N	shoes	106
寫	xiě	V	write	142
寫字	xiě//zì	VO	write (a character)	190
謝謝！—不謝！	Xièxie! Búxiè!	Exp	Thank you! -- You are welcome!	51
新年	xīnnián	N	New Year	214
新生	xīnshēng	N	new student, freshman	16
星期/周	xīngqī/zhōu	N	week	178
星期二	xīngqī'èr	N	Tuesday	178
星期幾	xīngqī jǐ	QF/Exp	which day (of the week)	179
星期天/日	xīngqītiān/rì	N	Sunday	178
星期一	xīngqīyī	N	Monday	178
姓	xìng	V	be surnamed	4
兄弟姐妹	xiōngdì jiěmèi	N	siblings	16
學	xué	V	learn	51
學生	xuésheng	N	student	16
學習	xuéxí	V	study, learn	190
學校	xuéxiào	N	school	16
學院	xuéyuàn	N	college or school in a university	51
雪	xuě	N	snow (used as a given name)	51
雪	xuě	N	snow	226

Y

顏色	yánsè	N	color	118
要	yào	V	want, need, to be going to	84
也	yě	Adv	also	16
也許	yěxǔ	Adv	perhaps, maybe	226
衣服	yīfu	N	clothes	72
一月	yīyuè	N	January	178
一共	yígòng	Adv	altogether, in all	118
以後	yǐhòu	TW	after, later	214
已經	yǐjīng	Adv	already	214
以前	yǐqián	TW	before, previously	73
以前	yǐqián	TW	before, ago	214
椅子	yǐzi	N	chair	38
一起	yìqǐ	Adv	together	142

A

English	Chinese	Pinyin	Type	Page
a bit, a little	有(一)點兒	yǒu (yì) diǎnr	Adv	73
a Chinese surname	陳	Chén	N	50
a Chinese surname	劉	Liú	N	50
a Chinese surname (also means white)	白	Bái	N	50
a few	幾個	jǐ gè	Nu	72
a lot, many, much	很多	hěn duō	Nu	72
a number of, some	一些	yìxiē	Nu	72
a place other than where one is	外地	wàidì	PW	38
a polite form of address for a married woman; wife	太太	tàitai	N	51
a polite form used for male adults in general; husband	先生	xiānsheng	N	51
activity	活動	huódòng	N	154
after, later	以後	yǐhòu	TW	214
afternoon	下午	xiàwǔ	N	178
afterward, then	然後	ránhòu	Conj	227
airplane	飛機	fēijī	N	226
all, both	都	dōu	Adv	39
already	已經	yǐjīng	Adv	214
already, as early as	就	jiù	Adv	190
also	也	yě	Adv	16
also, still	還	hái	Adv	39
altogether, in all	一共	yígòng	Adv	118
American	美國人	Měiguórén	N	50
and	和	hé	Conj	17
and also, moreover	而且	érqiě	Conj	84
arrive	到	dào	V	214
ask	問	wèn	V	84
ask, invite, treat	請	qǐng	V	190
at	在	zài	Prep/CV	107
aunt; a term of address for a woman of one's mother's generation	阿姨	āyí	N	51

B

English	Chinese	Pinyin	Type	Page
bad, broken	壞	huài	Adj/SV	72
ball	球	qiú	N	142
ball game, match	球賽	qiúsài	N	154
bargain, haggle over the price	講價	jiǎng//jià	V	106
baseball	棒球	bàngqiú	N	142
basketball	籃球	lánqiú	N	142
be (at a place)	在	zài	V	38
be surnamed	姓	xìng	V	4
because	因為	yīnwèi	Conj	51
bed	床	chuáng	N	38
before, ago	以前	yǐqián	TW	214
before, previously	以前	yǐqián	TW	73
Beijing	北京	Běijīng	PW	38
Beijing dialect	北京話	Běijīnghuà	N	50
bicycle	自行車	zìxíngchē	N	226
big	大	dà	Adj	4
bilingual	雙語	shuāngyǔ	N	50
birthday	生日	shēngrì	N	178
black	黑色	hēisè	N	118
blue	藍色	lánsè	N	118
book	書	shū	N	72
bookcase	書架	shūjià	N	38
bookstore	書店	shūdiàn	N	106
boy	男孩	nánhái	N	16
breakfast	早點	zǎodiǎn	N	190
British	英國人	Yīngguórén	N	50
busy	忙	máng	Adj/SV	179
but	不過	búguò	Conj	118
but	可是	kěshì	Conj	17
buy	買	mǎi	V	84

C

English	Chinese	Pinyin	Type	Page
California	加州	Jiāzhōu	PW	38
call, be called	叫	jiào	V	4

can, able to	能	néng	AV	226
can, be allowed to	可以	kěyǐ	AV	106
Cantonese, Guangdong dialect	廣東話	Guǎngdōng huà	N	50
cap, hat	帽子	màozi	N	106
car, automobile	汽車	qìchē	N	226
celebrate (the New Year/ a festival)	過(年/節)	guò(nián/jié)	V	215
cent, fractional unit of the Chinese currency, equals to 1/100 of a yuan	分	fēn	M	106
center	中心	zhōngxīn	N	154
chair	椅子	yǐzi	N	38
cheap, inexpensive	便宜	piányi	Adj/SV	72
child	孩子	háizi	N	4
China	中國	Zhōngguó	N	50
Chinese	中國人	Zhōngguórén	N	50
Chinese (referring to spoken Chinese, used in mainland China)	漢語	Hànyǔ	N	50
Chinese language, Chinese	中文	Zhōngwén	N	50
class, lesson	課	kè	N	178
classroom/room	教室/室	jiàoshì/shì	N	178
clock	鐘	zhōng	TE	190
clothes	衣服	yīfu	N	72
club, organization	社團	shètuán	N	190
coat, jacket, outerwear	外衣	wàiyī	N	106
cold	冷	lěng	Adj/SV	226
college or school in a university	學院	xuéyuàn	N	51
college student	大學生	dàxuéshēng	N	16
college, university	大學	dàxué	N	16
color	顏色	yánsè	N	118
come back / go back	回來/去	huílai/qu	V	215
come/go	來/去	lái/qù	V	106
come/go home	回家	huíjiā	V	215
common speech (a term used in mainland China)	普通話	Pǔtōnghuà	N	50
competition	比賽	bǐsài	N	154
computer	電腦	diànnǎo	N	84
concert	音樂會	yīnyuèhuì	N	154
country	國家	guójiā	N	50

D

dance	跳舞	tiào//wǔ	VO	143
dance	舞	wǔ	N	142
dance party, ball	舞會	wǔhuì	N	154
date	日期	rìqī	N	178
daughter	女兒	nǚ'ér	N	4
day	天	tiān	N	178
day (formal)	日	rì	N	178
different	不同	bù tóng	Adj/SV	143
do a temporary job	打工	dǎ//gōng	V	214
do homework	做作業	zuò zuòyè	VO	179
do, engaged in	做	zuò	V	106
do/practice martial arts	打拳	dǎ//quán	VO	143
dollar, yuan	元	yuán	M	84
dollar, yuan	塊	kuài	M	84
don't	別	bié	Adv	154
dormitory	宿舍	sùshè	N	38
dragon (used as a given name, usu. for males)	龍	lóng	N	51
drive (a vehicle)	開車	kāi//chē	V	226

E

each, every, per	每	měi	Sp	179
early	早	zǎo	Adj/SV	190
east/Orient	東/東方	dōng/dōngfāng	N	4
easy	容易	róngyì	Adj/SV	226
elementary school	小學	xiǎoxué	N	16
elementary school student	小學生	xiǎoxuéshēng	N	16
English language	英語/文	Yīngyǔ/wén	N	50
evening party, soirée	晚會	wǎnhuì	N	154
evening, night	晚上	wǎnshang	N	178
everybody	大家	dàjiā	Pron	214
examination	考試	kǎoshì	N	178
exercise	運動	yùndòng	V	154
extracurricular, outside class, after school	課外	kèwài	N	178

F

family	家	jiā	N	16
fan of…	—迷	- mí	N	142
fast	快	kuài	Adj/SV	190
father, dad	爸爸	bàba	N	4
February	二月	èryuè	N	178
feel, think	覺得	juéde	V	84
festival, holiday	節日	jiérì	N	214
few, little, scarce	少	shǎo	Adj/SV	72
fine, good	好	hǎo	Adj	4
finish/leave class	下課	xià//kè	VO	179
first	先	xiān	Adv	226
fist, punch	拳	quán	N	142
flower, talent (used as a given name)	英	yīng	N	51
foreign country	外國	wàiguó	N	50
foreign language	外語/文	wàiyǔ/wén	N	50
foreigner	外國人	wàiguórén	N	50
fractional unit of the Chinese currency, equals to 1/10 of a yuan	角	jiǎo	M	106
friend	朋友	péngyou	N	38
from	從	cóng	Prep/CV	191
fun, interesting	好玩	hǎowán	Adj/SV	143

G

game	遊戲	yóuxì	N	142
get up, get out of bed	起床	qǐ//chuáng	VO	190
girl	女孩	n)hái	N	16
give	給	gěi	V	118
give a discount	打折	dǎzhé	V	118
give change	找錢	zhǎo//qián	V	118
go online	上網	shàng//wǎng	VO	143
go out	出去	chūqu	V	215
go to class	上課	shàng//kè	VO	178
go to college (high school/elementary school)	上大學(中學/小學)	shàng dàxué (zhōngxué/ xiǎoxué)	VO	178
go to school	上學	shàng//xué	VO	178
good	好	hǎo	Adj/SV	72
good-looking	好看	hǎokàn	Adj	106
grade, year	年級	niánjí	N	16
green	綠色	lǜsè	N	118
Guangdong (Canton)	廣東	Guǎngdōng	PW	38
Guangzhou	廣州	Guǎngzhōu	PW	38

H

half	半	bàn	TE	190
happy, glad	高興	gāoxìng	Adj/SV	72
hard, difficult	難	nán	Adj/SV	226
have a meal	吃飯	chī//fàn	VO	190
have free time	有空	yǒu kòng	VO	179
have, possess	有	yǒu	V	16
he/she, him/her	他/她	tā	Pron	4
here	這裡/這兒	zhèlǐ/zhèr	PW	38
here, this side / there, that side	這邊/那邊	zhè biān/nà biān	PW	107
high school	高中	gāozhōng	N	16
high school student	高中生	gāozhōng shēng	N	16
high speed rail	高鐵	gāotiě	N	226
hit, play	打	dǎ	V	142
hobby	愛好	àihào	N	142
hot	熱	rè	Adj/SV	226
hour	小時	xiǎoshí	TE	190
hour (spoken)	鐘頭	zhōngtóu	TE	190
how	怎麼	zěnme	QW	227
how is/about	怎麼樣	zěnmeyàng	QW	73
how long	多久	duō jiǔ	QW	227
how long (i.e.,length of time)	多長時間	duōcháng shíjiān	QW	191
how many, which (grade, etc)	幾	jǐ	QW	17
how much/many	多少	duōshao	QW	84
how old	多大	duō dà	QF/Exp	179
hundred	百	bǎi	Nu	84

I

I, me	我	wǒ	Pron	4
if, suppose, in case	如果/要是	rúguǒ/yàoshi	Conj	227

English	Chinese	Pinyin	Type	Page
impressive	不錯	búcuò	Adj/SV	72
in addition to; apart from	除了……以外	chúle……yǐwài	Conj	179
interesting, fun	有意思	yǒu yìsi	Adj	106
interesting, intriguing; (person, thing) good-looking	好看	hǎokàn	Adj/SV	143
is, am, are	是	shì	V	16

J

English	Chinese	Pinyin	Type	Page
January	一月	yīyuè	N	178
jeans	牛仔褲	niúzǎikù	N	118
join, participate in	參加	cānjiā	V	190
jump, leap, dance	跳	tiào	V	142
just in time; happen to	正好	zhènghǎo	Adv	226
just, only	只	zhǐ	Adv	154

K

English	Chinese	Pinyin	Type	Page
karaoke	卡拉OK	kǎlā-OK	N	154
know how to, can	會	huì	AV	51
know, meet (new people)	認識	rènshi	V	51
know, realize, understand	知道	zhīdào	V	215
kung fu	功夫	gōngfu	N	142

L

English	Chinese	Pinyin	Type	Page
language	語言	yǔyán	N	50
last	最後	zuìhòu	Adv	226
last year	去年	qùnián	N	178
last/next month	上/下個月	shàng/xià gèyuè	N	178
last/next week	上/下個星期	shàng/xià gè xīngqī	N	178
late	晚	wǎn	Adj/SV	190
learn	學	xué	V	51
learn (from Sb)	跟(Sb學)	gēn (...xué)	Prep/CV	154
Li (a Chinese surname)	李	Lǐ	N	4
Lin (a Chinese surname)	林	Lín	N	4
listen to music	聽音樂	tīng yīnyuè	VO	143
listen, hear	聽	tīng	V	142
local, this locality	本地	běndì	PW	38
long	長	cháng	Adj/SV	72

English	Chinese	Pinyin	Type	Page
long time	久	jiǔ	Adj/SV	226

M

English	Chinese	Pinyin	Type	Page
make a phone call	打電話	dǎ diànhuà	VO	143
make a phone call	打電話	dǎ diànhuà	VO	179
make a plan	做計劃	zuò jìhuà	V	214
mall, department store	商場	shāngchǎng	N	106
many, much, more	多	duō	Adj/SV	72
martial arts	武術	wǔshù	N	142
matter	事(情)	shì(qing)	N	154
meal (breakfast, lunch, dinner)	飯(早飯，午飯，晚飯)	fàn (zǎofàn, wǔfàn, wǎnfàn)	N	190
medium-sized	中號	zhōng hào	N	118
meeting, gathering, party	會	huì	N	154
minute	分鐘	fēnzhōng	TE	190
miss (someone, home, etc.)	想	xiǎng	V	226
Miss, young lady	小姐	xiǎojiě	N	4
mobile phone	手機	shǒujī	N	84
Monday	星期一	xīngqīyī	N	178
money	錢	qián	N	84
month	月	yuè	N	178
morning	上午	shàngwǔ	N	178
morning	早上	zǎoshang	N	178
most	最	zuì	Adv	142
mother tongue	母語	mǔyǔ	N	50
mother, mom	媽媽	māma	N	4
movie	電影	diànyǐng	N	142
Mr., Sir	先生	xiānsheng	N	4
music	音樂	yīnyuè	N	142

N

English	Chinese	Pinyin	Type	Page
name	名字	míngzi	N	4
Nanjing	南京	Nánjīng	PW	38
national language/standard Chinese (a term used in Taiwan)	國語	guóyǔ	N	50
need, have to, must	得	děi	AV	106
new student, freshman	新生	xīnshēng	N	16
New Year	新年	xīnnián	N	214

English	Chinese	Pinyin	Type	Page
next year	明年	míngnián	N	178
No problem.	没問題。	méi wèntí	IE	154
noon, midday	中午	zhōngwǔ	N	178
normally, usually	平常	píngcháng	Adv	190
north	北/北方	běi/běifāng	N	16
not	不	bù	Adv	4
not enough	不夠	búgòu	Adv	73
not having, be without	没	méi	Adv	16
notebook, exercise book	本子	běnzi	N	72
novel	小説	xiǎoshuō	N	142
now, currently	現在	xiànzài	TW	73
number (for rooms, phones, etc.)	號	hào	N	38
number, code	號碼	hàomǎ	N	118

O

English	Chinese	Pinyin	Type	Page
o'clock	點鐘	diǎn zhōng	TE	190
often, frequently	經常	jīngcháng	Adv	142
old, aged	老	lǎo	Adv/SV	72
older brother	哥哥	gēge	N	16
older sister	姐姐	jiějie	N	16
only	只	zhǐ	Adv	118
only, only then	才	cái	Adv	190
or	還是	háishi	Conj	39
oral test	口試	kǒushì	N	190
originally	本來	běnlái	Adv	106
other, else	別的	biéde	Sp	118
other, else	其他	qítā	NU	118
over a specified amount; and more	多	duō	M	106

P

English	Chinese	Pinyin	Type	Page
pair (used for shoes)	雙	shuāng	N	106
paper	紙	zhǐ	N	72
parents, father and mother	父母	fùmǔ	V	226
pay	付錢/款	fù//qián fù//kuǎn	Adv	118
perhaps, maybe	也許	yěxǔ	Adv	226
perhaps, maybe, possibly	可能	kěnéng	N	214
person	人	rén	N	16
phone	電話	diànhuà	M	118

English	Chinese	Pinyin	Type	Page
piece (used for luggage, clothes, furniture, matters, etc.)	件	jiàn	M	72
pink	粉色	fěnsè	N	118
place	地方	dìfang	N	226
plan	計劃	jìhuà	N	214
plan	計劃	jìhuà	V	214
plan (spoken)	打算	dǎsuàn	N	214
plan, intend	打算	dǎsuàn	V	214
play (game), have fun	玩	wán	V	142
play a ball game	打球	dǎ//qiú	VO	143
pleasant to listen to	好聽	hǎotīng	Adj/SV	143
present, gift	禮物	lǐwù	N	118
pretty, good-looking	漂亮	piàoliang	Adj/SV	72
price	價格	jiàgé	N	106
problem, question	問題	wèntí	N	154
public bus (also 公共汽車)	公交車	gōngjiāochē	N	226

Q, R

English	Chinese	Pinyin	Type	Page
quarter (of an hour)	刻	kè	TE	190
rarely	很少	hěn shǎo	Adv	142
read books	看書	kàn//shū	VO	38
red	紅色	hóngsè	N	190
reside, live (at)	住(在)	zhù(zài)	V	226
restaurant	餐館	cānguǎn	N	190
ride a bicycle or motorcycle	騎車	qí chē	V	226
ride on, travel by	坐	zuò	V	226
road, path	路	lù	N	226
room	房間	fángjiān	N	72
roommate	室友	shìyǒu	N	38

S

English	Chinese	Pinyin	Type	Page
school	學校	xuéxiào	N	16
school bag	書包	shūbāo	N	72
School of Business	商學院	Shāngxué éyuàn	Phr	51
School of Foreign Languages	外語學院	Wàiyǔxué éyuàn	Phr	51
School of Liberal Arts	文學院	Wénxuéyuàn	Phr	51
schoolmate, classmate	同學	tóngxué	N	16

second	秒鐘	miǎozhōng	TE	190
secondary school	中學	zhōngxué	N	16
secondary school student	中學生	zhōngxué shēng	N	16
see, look at	看	kàn	V	106
see, watch, look at	看	kàn	V	72
seldom	不常	bù cháng	Adv	142
sell	賣	mài	V	84, 106
set	套	tào	M	84
Shanghai	上海	Shànghǎi	PW	38
Shanghainese, Shanghai dialect	上海話	Shànghǎihuà	N	50
shoes	鞋子	xiézi	N	106
shop assistant, salesperson	售貨員	shòuhuòyuán	N	118
shop, store	商店	shāngdiàn	N	106
short	矮	ǎi	Adj/ SV	72
short of	差	chà	TE	190
short, low	短	duǎn	Adj/ SV	72
should, ought to	應該	yīnggāi	V	84
siblings	兄弟姐妹	xiōngdì jiěmèi	N	16
sing	唱	chàng	V	142
sing (a song)	唱歌	chàng//gē	VO	143
sleep	睡覺	shuì//jiào	VO	190
slow	慢	màn	Adj/ SV	190
small	小	xiǎo	Adj	4
snow	雪	xuě	N	226
snow (used as a given name)	雪	xuě	N	51
snow-ski	滑雪	huá//xuě	V	226
so, indeed	真	zhēn	Adv	214
so, such, in this way, like this	這麼	zhème	Sp	84
some	有的	yǒude	Pron	214
some, a few (used to indicate an indefinite amount or a very small amount)	些	xiē	M	72
sometimes	有時候	yǒu shíhou	Adv	142
son	兒子	érzi	N	4
song	歌	gē	N	142

south	南/南方	nán/nánfāng	N	16
speak	說	shuō	V	51
speech, spoken words	話	huà	N	50
spoken form for 角	毛	máo	M	106
sports, exercise	運動	yùndòng	N	142
spring break	春假	chūnjià	N	214
Spring Festival, Lunar New Year	春節	Chūn Jié	N	214
stay	待	dāi	V	226
still	還	hái	Adv	214
storied building	樓	lóu	N	38
student	學生	xuésheng	N	16
study, learn	學習	xuéxí	V	190
subway	地鐵	dìtiě	N	226
suitable, fit	合適	héshì	Adj/ SV	118
summer break	暑假	shǔjià	N	214
Sunday	星期天/日	xīngqītiān/rì	N	178
sweater	毛衣	máoyī	N	106
sweatsuit, tracksuit	運動服	yùndòngfú	N	84

T

table	桌子	zhuōzi	N	38
table tennis, ping-pong	乒乓球	pīngpāngqiú	N	142
Taipei	臺北	Táiběi	PW	38
take a cab	打車	dǎ//chē	V	226
take an examination	考試	kǎo//shì	VO	179
tall, high	高	gāo	Adj/ SV	72
teacher	老師	lǎoshī	N	4
television	電視	diànshì	N	142
ten	十	shí	Nu	84
ten thousand	萬	wàn	Nu	106
tennis	網球	wǎngqiú	N	142
that	那	nà/nèi	Pron/ Sp	38
then, in that case	那	nà	Conj	227
there	那裡/那兒	nàlǐ/nàr	PW	38
therefore	所以	suǒyǐ	Conj	51
thing, object	東西	dōngxi	N	72
this	這	zhè/zhèi	Pron/ Sp	38
this year	今年	jīnnián	N	178

English	Chinese	Pinyin	Type	Page
thousand	千	qiān	Nu	84
ticket	票	piào	N	190
time	時間	shíjiān	N	178
timetable	時間表	shíjiānbiǎo	N	178
tired	累	lèi	Adj/SV	179
to, until	到	dào	Prep/CV	191
today	今天	jīntiān	TW/Exp	154
together	一起	yìqǐ	Adv	142
together with, with	跟	gēn	Prep/CV	107
tomorrow	明天	míngtiān	TW/Exp	154
too, extremely	太	tài	Adv	73
train	火車	huǒchē	N	226
travel	旅行	lǚxíng	V	214
travel by (car, bus or taxi)	坐(車)	zuò (chē)	V	226
travel, tour (for pleasure)	旅遊	lǚyǒu	V	214
trousers, pants	褲子	kùzi	N	72
try	試	shì	V	118
T-shirt	T恤衫	T-xùshān	N	106
Tuesday	星期二	xīngqī'èr	N	178

U

English	Chinese	Pinyin	Type	Page
uncle; a term of address for a man of one's father's generation	叔叔	shūshu	N	51
United Kingdom	英國	Yīngguó	N	50
United States	美國	Měiguó	N	50
used, worn	舊	jiù	Adj/SV	72

V

English	Chinese	Pinyin	Type	Page
vacation, break	假期	jiàqī	N	214
vehicle	車	chē	N	226
very, extremely	非常	fēicháng	Adv	142
very, quite	很	hěn	Adv	73

W

English	Chinese	Pinyin	Type	Page
walk, go on foot	走路	zǒu//lù	V	226
walk, go, leave	走	zǒu	V	154
Wang (a Chinese surname)	王	Wáng	N	4
want to, intend to, desire	想要	xiǎng yào	V	84

English	Chinese	Pinyin	Type	Page
want, need, to be going to	要	yào	V	84
watch	表	biǎo	N	190
watch, see	看	kàn	V	142
wear	穿	chuān	V	118
week	星期/周	xīngqí/zhōu	N	178
weekend	周末	zhōumò	TW/Exp	154
west/Occident	西/西方	xī/xīfāng	N	4
what	什麼	shénme	QW	5
what time (i.e., time of the day)	什麼時間	shénme shíjiān	QW	191
when	什麼時候	shénme shíhou	QW	154
when	的時候	de shíhou	TW/Exp	154
where, which place	哪裡/哪兒	nǎlǐ/nǎr	QW	39
which	哪	nǎ, něi	QW	39
white	白色	báisè	N	118
who, whom	誰	shéi/shuí	QW	5
whose	誰的	shéi de	QW	5
why	為什麼	wèishénme	QW	73
winter break	寒假	hánjià	N	214
with, from	跟	gēn	Prep/CV	142
would, will	會	huì	AV	214
write	寫	xiě	V	142
write (a character)	寫字	xiě//zì	VO	190
writing instrument (pen, pencil, etc.)	筆	bǐ	N	72
written language; script	文字	wénzì	N	50
written test	筆試	bǐshì	N	190

Y

English	Chinese	Pinyin	Type	Page
year	年	nián	N	178
year (referring to age)	歲	suì	N	178
yellow	黃色	huángsè	N	118
yes, right	對	duì	Adj	4
yesterday	昨天	zuótiān	N	178
you	你	nǐ	Pron	4
you	您	nín	Pron	4
younger brother	弟弟	dìdi	N	16
younger sister	妹妹	mèimei	N	16
Yu (a Chinese surname)	于	Yú	N	4

第一單元：我和家人	
U1-A	**第一課：我叫林小東**
U1-A1	【我姓林】
小東	你好！我姓林，叫林小東。"大小"的小，"東西"的東。嗯，不，"東方"的東。對，"東方"的東！
小東	你好！我姓林，叫林小東。"大小"的小，"東方"的東。
U1-A2	【請問你叫什麼名字？】
小東	你好！我叫林小東。請問，你叫什麼名字？
小東	老師好！我叫林小東。請問您貴姓？
小南	"我叫林小東。請問您貴姓？請問你叫什麼名字？"
U1-B	**第二課 我的家人**
U1-B1	【我家有四口人】
小東	我是大學新生。我們家有四口人。誰是我爸爸？他是我爸爸，他叫林子新。她是我媽媽，她不姓林，她姓于。她是誰？我姐姐？不，她不是我姐姐，她是我妹妹。她叫小南。
U1-B2	【我是高二的學生】
小南	你好！我姓林，叫林小南。小是"大小"的小，南是"南方"的南。我是高二的學生。我有一個哥哥，名字叫林小東。他也是學生，可是他不是高中生，是大學生。我沒有姐姐，也沒有弟弟和妹妹。
第二單元：認識新朋友	
U2-A	**第一課：這是我的宿舍**
U2-A1	【這是我們大學】
小東	我是北京人。我家在北京，我們大學也在北京。這是我們大學，我住在這棟樓。

U2-A2	【我的宿舍】
小東	這是我的宿舍。我有一張床、一張桌子、一把椅子和一個書架。我還有三個室友，我們都是新生。嗯，他們是哪兒人？是本地人還是外地人？
U2-B	**第二課 你是哪裡人？**
U2-B1	【我是你的室友】
室友	你好！
小東	你好。你是——？
室友	哦，來，認識一下。我是你的室友，我姓陳，叫陳一龍。
小東	成龍？
室友	噢，不是成龍，是陳一龍。"一二三"的一，"成龍"的龍。朋友們都叫我阿龍。
小東	陳一龍——阿龍？你好你好！我叫林小東，"大小"的小，"東方"的東。很高興認識你！
室友	我也很高興認識你。
U2-B2	【你是哪裡人？】
阿龍	哎，你是哪裡人？是北京人嗎？
小東	對，我是本地人。你呢？
阿龍	哦，我是廣東人，是廣州來的。
小東	噢，因為你是廣東人，所以叫阿龍！
U2-B3	【我們是外語學院的】
曉雪	謝謝！
阿龍	不謝。哦，認識一下吧，我叫陳一龍，是商學院的。他叫——
小東	我叫林小東，是文學院的。我們都是新生，很高興認識你們！
劉英	我們也很高興認識你們！我叫劉英，是外語學院大二的學生。
曉雪	我叫白曉雪，也是外語學院的，我是新生。

劉英	再見！
東/龍	再見！
U2-B4	【她是哪國人？】
鄰居	那個女孩是誰啊？是哪國人？
小南	她叫Katie，是美國人，是美國華盛頓來的。
鄰居	美國人？她是大學生還是高中生？
小南	她是高中生，她住在我們家。
鄰居	是嗎？她會不會說中國話？
小南	她會說。

第三單元：我的東西

U3-A	第一課：我的書包太小了
U3-A1	【我高了】
小南	我高了，所以我的衣服小了，我的褲子也不夠長了！看，這是我的書包。我的書和本子都很多。這個書包太小了！這兒也壞了。
U3-A2	【這個書包怎麼樣？】
	這個書包怎麼樣？嗯——很漂亮，這個也不錯，可是兩個書包都有點兒貴。衣服呢？嗯，衣服也不便宜。媽——我的書包壞了，衣服也小了……
U3-B	第二課：買一個新的
U3-B1	【我要一個新書包】
媽媽	什麼事？
小南	媽，我要一個新書包。
媽媽	新書包？你的書包不是很好嗎？為什麼要買新的？
小南	因為我的書和本子太多了，這個書包太小了！而且這兒也壞了，你看。所以該買一個新的了。
媽媽	嗯，是有點兒小了。那好吧，買新的、大的！
小南	太好了！
U3-B2	【這個書包很漂亮】
小南	媽，你看，你覺得這個書包漂亮嗎？
媽媽	很漂亮！什麼？兩百塊！太貴了！

小南	貴嗎？我覺得一點兒也不貴。看，還有三、四百塊的呢！
媽媽	400塊？這麼貴？
U3-B3	【我還想要新運動服】
小南	哎，媽，我還想要一套新運動服。
媽媽	你的運動服不是還很好嗎？為什麼也要買新的？
小南	因為現在我高了！ 看，衣服小了，褲子也不夠長了！
媽媽	嗯，是高了！好吧好吧，買新的！
小南	一個新書包和一套新運動服，太好了！

第四單元：買東西

U4-A	第一課：這個多少錢？
U4-A1	【在商店買東西】
Katie	現在我和小南在商店買東西。這裡有很多東西，便宜的、貴的都有，而且可以講價。跟賣東西的人講價很有意思。看，這頂帽子多少錢？本來賣帽子的人說要50塊，我說，50塊太貴，我不買，10塊賣不賣？賣帽子的人說，10塊不賣，要15塊。我說，好吧，15塊！有意思吧？
U4-A2	【去那邊看看】
Katie	現在我（要）跟小南去那邊看（一）看。小南要買一套運動服，我得買一雙鞋，所以我也要去鞋店看一看。
U4-B	第二課：你要什麼號的？
U4-B1	【給我看一下中號的】
售貨員	歡迎光臨！請問你想買什麼衣服？
小南	嗯，我想看看這套紅色的運動服。
售貨員	你要什麼號的？大號中號都有，沒有小號。
小南	嗯，麻煩你給我看一下中號的。
售貨員	這是中號的，你可以試試。

小南	嗯，我覺得中號的很合適。
U4-B2	【請問有其他顏色嗎？】
小南	請問有其他顏色嗎？
售貨員	還有黃色和粉色。
Katie	這幾個顏色都很好看！小南，你喜歡哪一個？
小南	這套紅的和這套黃的我都喜歡！
U4-B3	【可以打折嗎？】
Katie	255元。
小南	可以打折嗎？
售貨員	嗯，要兩套我可以給你打8折，一共是408元。
小南	嗯，打8折，太好了！我現在正好有400多塊，夠了！我要這套紅的和這套黃的。這是420塊。
售貨員	好的。找你12塊。還要什麼嗎？
Katie	我還想買鞋。
售貨員	鞋在那邊。
第五單元：我的愛好	
U5-A	第一課 你喜歡做什麼？
U5-A1	【我有三個室友】
阿龍	你們都認識我吧？對，我的名字叫陳一龍，朋友們都叫我"阿龍"。 我有三個室友：林小東，張大明，和朱宇。我們的愛好不同。 小東喜歡看書，也喜歡打乒乓球。 大明是個籃球迷，籃球打得不錯。 朱宇呢，他覺得在網上玩遊戲最有意思，所以經常上網。
U5-A2	【我喜歡什麼？】
阿龍	我喜歡什麼呢？對，我最喜歡功夫、武術！ 我也非常喜歡看電影。這個電影很好看！ 我想學武術，可是誰跟我一起學呢？
U5-B	第二課 明天有晚會
U5-B1	【我正在……】

阿龍	朱宇，你在玩什麼？想不想跟我一起學武術？
朱宇	哎呀，別跟我說話，我正在打遊戲呢！
阿龍	小東，你呢？你在做什麼呀？
小東	我在看英文小說。你想看嗎？我還有一本。
U5-B2	【我什麼球都不想打】
阿龍	我不想看書，我想運動運動。
小東	嗯，你想不想打乒乓球？
阿龍	乒乓球我會打，可是我打得不好。
小東	那沒問題，我可以教。
大明	阿龍，別打乒乓球，跟我打籃球吧。打籃球最好玩！
阿龍	我什麼球都不想打，我只想打拳。你們跟我一起學吧！
小東	嗯，不想學。
大明	你們不打球啊？那我走了！
U5-B3	【跟我學跳舞】
阿龍	喂，曉雪嗎？哎，你好你好！有事嗎？ 啊，周末有活動？明天有新生晚會？ 哦，跳舞、唱卡拉OK？在哪兒啊？ 哦，學生中心。 好的好的，沒問題沒問題。 明天見！
阿龍	哎，白曉雪說，明天在學生中心有一個新生晚會，跳舞、唱卡拉OK。咱們一起去吧，很好玩！
小東	好玩？我覺得沒意思。唱歌我唱得不好，跳舞我也不會！
阿龍	你不會跳舞？我可以教你！
大明	對，你可以跟他學跳舞。
小東	我跟你學跳舞？
阿龍	怎麼樣？
朱宇	啊，你的意思是，小東跟一個男生跳舞？
小東	你去跳你的舞吧，我看我的書！

第六單元：時間和活動	
U6-A	第一課：這個星期做些什麼
U6-A1	【今天我有文學課】
劉英	你好，我叫劉英，是外語學院的學生，現在上大二。 這個是我們的教室，今天上英國文學課。 星期三是我每周最忙的一天，上午、下午、晚上都有課！ 星期五的課最少，只上兩節課，可是有時候有考試。星期六星期天都不上課。
U6-A2	【我還有課外活動】
劉英	除了上課以外，我還有很多課外活動，所以每天都很忙。 這個星期五是我的生日，今年我20歲了！ 啊，是曉雪的電話。 哎，曉雪——對，星期五下午有活動，在學生中心。晚上是我的生日晚會。 哎，好的，星期五下午見！
U6-B	第二課：你周末有空嗎？
U6-B1	【我去參加社團活動】
阿龍	哎，曉雪！哎，曉雪，你好！
曉雪	阿龍，這兩天怎麼樣？
阿龍	還不錯！你去上課嗎？
曉雪	嗯，不是，我去圖書館。你呢？
阿龍	哦，我去參加社團活動，4點半到6點。
曉雪	4點半就有活動了？是哪個社團？
阿龍	我有兩個社團，一個是武術學社，一個是電影學社，每天都有1個半小時的活動。 武術學社是4點半到6點，電影學社是7點半到9點。 你呢？
曉雪	哦，我在外語學社，我們星期一、三、五晚上8點才有活動。 我有時候去參加。
U6-B2	【明天晚上有空嗎？】

阿龍	對了，我們電影學社明天晚上7點半有電影。想不想跟我一起去？
曉雪	嗯，我星期五上午有考試，要考15分鐘的口試，1個小時的筆試。所以我明天晚上得學習，12點才睡覺。
阿龍	你每天都睡得這麼晚嗎？
曉雪	是啊，除了周末以外，我每天都有課，還有很多別的事！
U6-B3	【我周末也沒空】
阿龍	哎，周六下午有空嗎？我想請你(去)看電影。
曉雪	你請我？為什麼？
阿龍	因為——我有兩張票，我覺得一個人去太沒意思了，(所以)想請你跟我一起去。
曉雪	謝謝你！可是我周末兩天都有事。再見啊！
阿龍	哎，下個周末怎麼樣？我給你打電話！
第七單元：旅行計劃	
U7-A	第一課：寒假快到了
U7-A1	【打算做什麼(1)】
Katie	寒假快到了，我也快要回美國了！回美國以前，爸爸媽媽要來看我，所以我們可以一起去旅行。我真高興！
阿龍	寒假快到了，我打算出去玩。可是，我的錢快沒有了！
U7-A2	【打算做什麼(2)】
劉英	今年寒假我不打算回家，我可能會出去旅遊。
小東	現在很多同學已經開始做寒假計劃了：有的同學打算回家過春節，有的想出去旅遊。 可是我還不知道我要做什麼。
U7-B	第二課：我們打算出去旅遊
	【我還不知道能不能……】
阿龍	幹嘛呢？

劉英	我們正在做寒假計劃呢!
小東	哎,你們有什麼計劃嗎?
曉雪	嗯,我父母很想我,我也很想回家,所以我可能會回家去。 可是春節以前的票很難買,我還不知道能不能回去。
劉英	那就別回家了。我想去旅遊。 我室友的家在南京,正好她請我去她家過春節。 也許我們可以一起去?
小東	那你打算怎麼去? 去多久呢?
U7-B2	【你打算怎麼去?】
劉英	我們可以先坐火車到南京玩幾天, 在我室友家過春節, 然後還可以去上海待兩三天, 最後從那裡坐高鐵回學校來。 你們覺得呢?
阿龍	嗯,南京沒有雪,可是寒假裡我想去一個有很多雪的地方。 正好我的生日快到了,我想去東北滑雪! 刷—— 那會很好玩的!
U7-B3	【想不想跟我一起去?】
阿龍	怎麼樣?你們想不想跟我一起去?
曉雪	嗯,太冷了,我不去。
劉英	我也不去。
阿龍	那小東呢?
小東	我哪兒也不去,就在家看看小説。 你自己去吧!
阿龍	如果你們都不去,我一個人有什麼意思? 對了,我老爸説,我過生日,他要給我一個很大的生日禮物!
三人	什麼禮物?